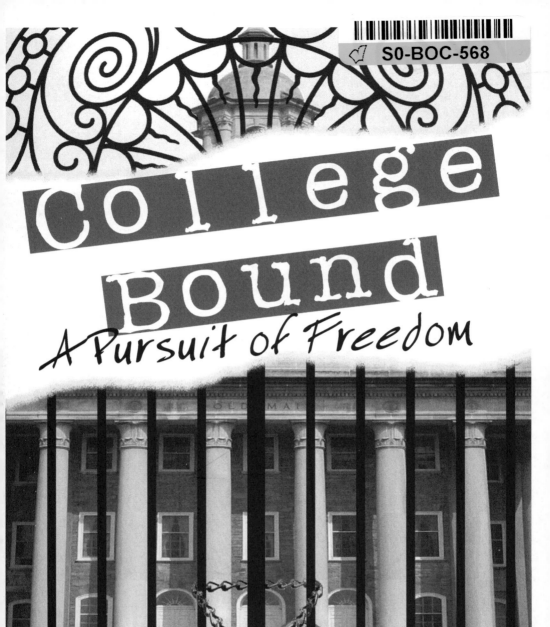

College

Bound

A Pursuit of Freedom

Emily Tomko

College Bound: *A Pursuit of Freedom*
By Emily Tomko

Published by
Evangel Publishing House
2000 Evangel Way
P.O. Box 189
Nappanee, IN 46550

Toll-Free Orders: (800) 253-9315
Website: www.evangelpublishing.com

ISBN-13: 978-1-934233-20-7

Library of Congress Control Number: 2012934882

Printed in the United States of America
11 12 13 14 15 /EPH/ 5 4 3 2 1

Endorsements for
College Bound: A Pursuit of Freedom

"I found that as a college student, *College Bound: A Pursuit of Freedom* truly expresses the feelings I experienced my first semester. Leaving home and having such a new sense of freedom, many veer off the path. We find ourselves entangled in the grips of peer pressure, alcohol, drugs, and sex. *College Bound* helped me remember who I truly am, and who God intended me to be. I couldn't put the book down, even when I knew I probably should have been reading my Chemistry textbook instead."
-Kaitlyn Benson, Penn State University

"*College Bound: A Pursuit of Freedom* is a great reminder of our need for God's direction in our lives, and demonstrates that ignoring Him will only lead to trouble. It also illustrates God's faithfulness to us even in the midst of our sin."
-Alex Redcay, Geneva College

"My son, who does not like to read, was spending most of his free time on our vacation reading this book, *College Bound: A Pursuit of Freedom*. Every time he had a chance he was reading. Curious as to what had his interest, I asked him to let me read it. This book is a great testimony. I feel young people can understand and relate very well to what she went through in those early college years. Her story shows how easy it can be to make compromises. I enjoyed reading the book. I even recommended to the daughter of a friend that she read the book before heading off to college."
-Sheila Eckert, parent of teen

"This book impacted the teens in our youth ministry by the teens coming away with a stronger desire to get into the word of God and to seek Him more in daily devotions."
-Youth & Young Adult Pastor Dwight Gehman, HD Youth Ministries

"Everybody makes mistakes, and to Christ, the criminal's sins are as equal to the devout Pastor's sins. *College Bound: A Pursuit of Freedom* allowed me to see the most beautiful thing about God...the fact that He doesn't hold anything against us. It's a story that readers can completely relate to, no matter what their age. This book is such a good read. Once I picked it up, I couldn't put it down!"
-Courtney DiStasio, RIT

"I loved how real this story was. It felt like it could be a testimony of an actual college student."
-Ben Fouse, 2010 high school grad

Table of Contents

About the Author

Emily Tomko lives with her husband and two daughters near Lancaster, Pennsylvania. She teaches and mentors youth and young adults, and has a passion for the scriptures. Emily attended Dickinson College in Carlisle, Pennsylvania and spent a year studying abroad in Germany. A former prodigal, she writes with a deep desire to see people freed from the miry clay of this world and walking in the truth.

To schedule Emily to speak at your youth group or gathering, please contact her at

Emily.Tomko@gmail.com

Or find her on Facebook at

http://www.facebook.com/CollegeBoundAPursuitOfFreedom

Dedicated to:
The members of the Cross Roads
Brethren in Christ Youth Group
3 John 1:4

With special thanks to
my loving husband, Craig

Chapter 1 – Strange New World

"Molly?" I turned around to face the owner of the voice. Aqua-green eyes stared back at me from the kind of a face that could star in a music video. My heart sank a little within me as I nodded. She smiled and I noticed she had a tiny dimple above the left corner of her mouth. "I'm Caitlyn, your new roommate."

And from here on out I'm the ugly sidekick, I thought to myself a little morosely, taking in her sleek, professionally-cut-and-highlighted hair and understated make-up. She was cute alright.

We had already spoken once on the phone back in July, and now she kind of did a half-squeal as we hugged like old friends. My mom snapped a picture of the two of us to commemorate our first day at college – me in my mesh shorts and t-shirt, and Caitlyn in her fashionable cropped pants and scoop-necked top.

My dad brought our motley array of decrepit 1970's poop-green and puke-orange suitcases into the dorm room and Caitlyn helped me carry the boxes bearing my photos, paper supplies, and my favorite novels in from the car. After we made the last trek from the August heat back into the dorm room, my sister Anne helped me hang my *Gone with the Wind* poster, featuring Rhett carrying a fainting Scarlett, on a spot of bare wall above my bed while my dad set up my desk lamp. The hallway outside our room was noisy with the voices of parents and younger brothers and sisters and the other freshmen girls whom I'd soon know by name – hopefully among them some potential new friends. *None, of course, whom could ever compare to Kendra,* I thought wistfully.

It was hard to believe that it was less than twenty-four hours since I had bid a tearful good-bye to my dear friend and cohort. We had exchanged a lingering hug on the front porch of her big old farmhouse, me studying its worn, bluish-gray boards fondly and with more than a tinge of sadness as I thought of how often we'd sat there on breezy summer days and twilit evenings, discussing high school melodrama and classmates and God and the universe. I was quite sure that Kendra was irreplaceable as a best friend, and even more certain that it would be difficult to find another companion at college who would pour so much gentle wisdom into me. Kendra was more than just a pal – she was someone whom I had come to look up to spiritually and whose outlook I relied on more than I realized, until swiftly and suddenly the prospect of living without it was upon me.

After my boxes had all been hauled in and it was time to say good-bye to my parents and my sister, I forced back the wetness that threatened to seep out from under my eyelids. The longest I'd ever been away from them was a week at summer camp, and even though home was within driving distance, it was small comfort knowing that I wouldn't be there at the dinner table with them tonight, or at Anne's soccer game that weekend. Glancing at my mom, I could see she looked more traumatized by the pending separation than anyone, so I forced on my face a smile of inner strength that I didn't feel, and with false cheer reminded her that my room at home would be cleaner than ever, and that "there would be one less suspect if a completely empty milk jug was found stashed in the back of the fridge. The three of them exchanged emotional hugs with me, all of us choking back tears as though I were being deported, rather than simply going to college.

Watching them pull away from the curb moments later, I wanted to bawl like a toddler. I could see Anne's face staring back at me through the window of the car, and we waved until my parents' silver sedan turned the corner a block away. *Eighteen going on three-and-a-half,* I thought to myself reprovingly. *You're in college now, Molly. Turn off the waterworks!* I jabbed my knuckles at the corners of my eyes, angry at myself for being so gutless.

My roommate, Caitlyn, was from a little town in New Jersey, right smack in the middle of the state, as she described it, and her parents had dropped her off the day before. She explained that going away to college wasn't a huge deal because she'd spent all four of her high school years in boarding school. That meant she was only home certain weekends anyway, and she had already experienced dorm life. The hardest part, she informed me, was saying good-bye to her boyfriend, Dave, who had left the same day to attend school in Virginia. "I miss him already," she sighed, looking down at her manicured toes.

Silently, I sympathized with her, and for a moment, even considered telling her about Hank Bobek. I quickly ruled this out, however, figuring that relaying my secret feelings revolving around a guy whom I had merely "loved from a distance" for the last three years would only widen the gap between her South Jersey sophistication and my primitive, Pennsylvanian perception.

Quickly, I set about the task of unpacking my suitcases and boxes, setting up picture frames on the cheap wooden bureau and looking longingly into the faces of the friends and family captured in them. I taped the little black and white print of Mae West on my mirror, thinking how *she* wouldn't have been afraid of going away to a college where she knew no one. Lovingly, I placed my stuffed mouse, Leopold, whom I'd had since I was a baby, onto my pillow. *Good old Leopold.*

"It's four o'clock," Caitlyn said presently, glancing at her trendy, lavender-faced watch. "Ready for orientation?"

I was not. My stomach did a half-somersault as we walked down the steps of Watson dorm to the basement floor and into a room filled with the giggles of girls and the deep exchanges of several meaty-looking guys, whom I'd later find out were on the football team and had already been living on campus the previous week. Durst had co-ed dorms which meant that the guys' rooms were on the first floor and the girls' were on the second. Neither of my parents had been thrilled about this prospect, but Durst had the best language arts program around, and I guess the real reason they relented was the unsavory prospect of me going out-of-state to my second choice school.

"Besides," I had pointed out previously in making my argument for Durst-, "It's not as though the bathrooms or showers are co-ed." I knew that this *had* been the case at my cousin's college in California, but even I drew the line at the thought of sharing a restroom with a bunch of males. Never mind the privacy factor – I could only imagine that the cleanliness had to rival that of a gas station.

Caitlyn drew several admiring stares and sideways glances from some of the guys as she took a seat on one of the overstuffed sofas in the room, and I quickly slid in next to her, thinking how much easier my life would be if I were drop-dead gorgeous as well. Immediately in my mind I could hear a gentle reproach: *"Charm is deceitful, and beauty is vain, but a woman who fears the Lord is to be praised."* I smiled to myself, thanking God for that Spirit-driven reminder. *No,* I thought silently, as the verse from Proverbs resonated its truth. *I have something much better to share with the people in this room. I won't let go of who I am, nor forget the Truth in the midst of a secular campus.*

"Listen up, everybody!" called a petite, Asian girl who wore a nametag that said "Dolyn" and had next to it a loopy smiley face. She left her post where she'd been chatting with another girl whom I'd seen moving her things into our dorm earlier, and walked into the center of the room. "My name is Gwendolyn but you guys can call me "Dolyn" because I hate 'Gwenn.' I'm your RA, along with Nathan, otherwise known as 'Jonathan,' except in this dorm." She pointed to a short, stocky guy with a shaggy red goatee and glasses, who signaled himself as the other RA by raising his left arm and pointing with his right hand to the nametag on his chest.

"Or, you can call me 'Yo-Nathan,'" he said, the play on his name meeting mostly stony stares. As I studied him, it occurred to me that if he had a conical hat placed on his head, he'd resemble one of those garden gnomes you see standing in people's yards.

Dolyn proceeded to read over a list in her hand of dormitory rules and guidelines, making mention of what to do and where to go in case of a fire and advising against trying to rob the washers and dryers of their contents in order to get some free laundry time at someone else's expense.

As she ran through a litany of regulations, I only half listened as I studied the faces of the strangers around me who were about to be my cohabitants. It felt like summer camp all over again, but we were simply older. Superficially, I couldn't help but notice that my roommate was the only one who looked to be a contender for homecoming queen, although our dorm had been blessed with a substantial population of good-looking guys. This, I thought, was fortunate.

"Something else, you guys," chimed in the orange-haired one dubbed 'Nathan,' bringing me out of my aimless thoughts. He looked smug. "Be careful about hook-ups here in the dorm. Remember, you have to live with each other for the rest of the year."

I looked around at the sly smiles on the faces of my new dorm mates, wondering to myself what exactly constituted a "hook-up." I bet that Caitlyn knew and wondered if she'd designate me a hayseed once and for all if I plied her for the definition.

"We're going to go around the room and everyone has to say where they're from and one thing about themselves that sets them apart," Dolyn announced.

As she began this "getting-to-know-you" game my mind scrambled over what to say. For a moment, I thought about boldly proclaiming my faith to this group of strangers whom I'd be housing with for the next year. But what to say? That I'm a Christian? What would that mean to them? Wouldn't half the room describe themselves the same way? Perhaps I could say it more pointedly. I played around with some sentences in my mind, trying to figure out a "cool" way to say that I knew and loved the Lord. Or would that proclamation instantly get me categorized as a "Puritan," like I'd once overheard whispered about me by my supposed friend Ceci on the high school trip to

Washington, when I caught her telling her boyfriend on a cell phone why she couldn't confide in me what they'd done? Would I be alienating myself before I even had a chance? I felt a different kind of nervousness tingle up my forearms and make my stomach flip again as I contemplated the most important thing about myself that I would want someone to know, and what it might mean to share that.

One by one, each of the three dozen or so guys and girls stated their names and some factoid about themselves. One girl freaked us out by displaying her double joints. Another had some father who was an ambassador to an Eastern Bloc country. A crescendo of uncertain laughter rose up in the room as a nasally guy named Mike shared that he was into making his own perfume and potions and that his favorite pastime was fencing.

Then all eyes turned to me. I hesitated. I looked around the room and cleared my throat. "My name's Molly. I went to high school about an hour away from here, and…I like sports, old movies, and English literature."

Lame!

Everyone took in this monumental information in silence, then quickly shifted rapturous attention to my roommate. I looked down at my hands. The nervous energy was replaced by that deflating feeling best described as wishy-washy cop-out. I felt unremarkable, and very cowardly.

***

That evening, lying in bed and listening to shrieking laughter and the rising and falling of voices outside the dorm, I thought longingly of my family. A great deal of my security and identity came from home and relatives, and to be suddenly detached from them left me out of sorts. I suddenly missed high school, too, which was absurd. I hadn't been among the popular elite, although high school hadn't been unbearable (as it often is if you're not a celebrity during those adolescent years). I had a group of close, salt-of-the-earth type friends – most of them "good girls" like me – of whom Kendra had been the closest. Graduation had felt bittersweet, and the fleeting summer which had since come and gone had been the shortest in my memory. The harder I had tried to hold onto those days, the more rapidly they flew.

I thought of Hank and how he must be settled into his first week of art school by now. He had opted for design school in Rhode Island and planned to pursue advertising or something else commercial when he finished. "Only sure way to avoid being a starving artist," he'd told me woefully. "I'll probably end up living in lukewarm suburbia after all." I thought of the evening we'd spent together one week ago, after running into one another the day before he left. We'd sat on the curb outside my house until the wee hours of the morning, and I ran through my mind all the elements of the conversation we'd had. His mind was like one of those gifts that you get that had been wrapped dozens of times – even after you peeled off layer after layer, the surprise inside remained. He probably already had a steady following of "Hank groupies" pursuing him by this point, charismatic and sensitive guy that he was. In high school, he certainly had had a devoted bunch of females always swarming him – I used to refer to them in my head as "Hank's Harem" and enviously resented them. Of course, these girls had posed as his friends, but I knew better. Could any female possibly *not* be attracted to Hank Bobek? No, the idea was as plausible as being indifferent to chocolate mousse or a Caribbean vacation. Oh, there might be a tiny minority who didn't care about such things, but clearly something was wrong with them. Hank was universally appealing. I sighed and rolled over, clutching poor bedraggled Leopold, who was growing mangy after all these years. As I thought about youth group and Kendra and high school and the fleeting fun of the summer, I wondered why time had to change everything so much, and why it moved on so mercilessly. A verse from Hebrews sprang into my mind. "Jesus Christ is the same yesterday, today, and forever." My eyelids grew heavy as I pondered the prospect of someone who never, ever changes and who time itself does not alter at all. I wondered what time would do to me one year from now, and four years from now what my life would look like as I graduated from Durst and walked down those limestone steps to take my diploma.

Chapter 2 –Make Way for Ryan

"Welcome to Durst, ladies!" The blond-haired guy seemingly materialized out of nowhere, as though he'd been beamed there by a supernatural force. He looked at Caitlyn with an air of formality and said, "I'm one of the upperclassmen guides designated to help new students learn their way around campus." Snorting laughter came from behind him, and I saw another guy watching us, finding the statement hilarious. The blond dude's handsome face broke into an infectious grin. "Well, not officially. Actually, I *would* like to make your acquaintance and show you around campus." He had a medium build and wore a crew shirt with blue jeans and flip flops. With his tan, height, and apparent lack of body fat, he looked like he might qualify as Barbie's boyfriend, Ken. He also had a perfect little cleft in his chin.

"I'm Ryan," he said, still smiling and taking in Caitlyn.

"I'm Caitlyn," my roommate giggled.

I'm invisible, I thought glumly.

"There's a party at Theta Chi tonight," continued the owner of the perfect chin.

"Where's Theta Chi?" Caitlyn giggled again.

"Corner of College and Spruce," he replied, making a vague sweeping gesture behind him. His eyes never left Caitlyn. "Where are you ladies from?"

"Near Princeton," Caitlyn giggled.

"I *love* Princeton!" the Ken doll said. "What dorm do you live in?"

"Watson," Caitlyn answered.

"I *love* Watson!" he echoed. "That's where I lived freshman year!" He slung an arm over Caitlyn's shoulders with a familiarity that I found repelling and began walking with her down the sidewalk. Not totally sure what to do, I followed behind the two of them, feeling much like a dutiful maidservant.

As we approached our dorm, Caitlyn sat down on the limestone wall outside and he stood beside her, completely engaged in a bantering conversation, in which their flirtatious body language signaled to me that Ken Doll was going to become a regular sight.

Back in our room, I read during the three hours it took for Caitlyn to return. During this time, her boyfriend Dave called twice, and I hardly knew what to tell him as to his dear girlfriend's whereabouts. The best I could do to remain truthful without tattling on Caitlyn was to say that we'd gone separate ways after dinner, and that I'd be sure to give her the message he'd called. The second time he called, I wondered absently what he'd think if I informed him, "Well, Dave, she's with some guy who looks like he could model surf gear and who seems to love everything about her. Don't worry, she's in good hands!"

When Caitlyn came back to the room a little after ten, she gave me the personal history of perfect-chinned Ryan. I learned that he was originally from California, was a Policy Studies major, and as a kid he had once held a bit part in a film and had touched Helen Hunt's leg.

As Caitlyn seemed to be his newest and most ardent biographer, I continued to hear about Ryan-the-Great throughout the next day. He called before we left the room Saturday morning to go buy our books, and he must have been very funny because Caitlyn giggled after everything he said on the phone. Standing in line, waiting to have our freshmen ID's made, Caitlyn continued her narration. After dinner and well into the evening, the Ryan news-feed and commentary continued.

"He's *really* cute," Caitlyn sighed as she tried on a different top that evening, this one a little more low-cut than the last. "He's really nice, too."

I wanted to ask her if Dave and she had broken up since yesterday evening when he'd called after dinner. If not, I wondered where Ryan fit into the picture, as Caitlyn seemed to have forgotten that she had a boyfriend.

We were getting ready in our room for the party Ryan had invited us to join (well, he had invited Caitlyn mainly– and me by default I supposed), and I was peering out the door to witness a game of "Redlight-Greenlight" some of the girls on our floor were engaged in out in the hallway.

"They're so mature," a voice droned sarcastically. It belonged to a girl named Taylar, who rolled her eyes as three girls thundered past her down the hall. Taylar, I remembered from our dorm meeting, was from Connecticut where she'd been some sort of track star up there. I'd already seen her racing around the streets that threaded through Durst a couple times in the last few days. I opened the door wider and she meandered into our room, perching herself on Caitlyn's bed with a sigh, watching Caitlyn pull clothing and jewelry from the drawers of the cheap stock dresser that furnished the room.

"Which party are you going to?" she inquired. She had a husky voice that made questions sound like accusations.

"Theta Chi's," Caitlyn responded with an undertone of pride.

"Oh, yeah...I got invited there, too. The soccer team is having something over at Pratt and I'm going there instead." Taylar glanced up at my poster of Scarlett and Rhett with an air of boredom. Adjacent to it was a poster of a man standing on a mountain with his arms stretched towards the heavens, and Philippians 4:13 etched across the bottom. I saw her squint at it and then scowl. "Do you need any condoms?"

Caitlyn looked up at her with faint surprise and I nearly dropped my hairbrush. "I'm good," Caitlyn said.

"Um, me too," I mumbled.

"Well, just remember," Taylar said sagely, "If you can't be good, be careful."

With this dubious advice, Taylar dragged herself to her feet and shuffled out of our room and past the Redlight-Greenlight amateurs.

"I'm still in the V-club, how about you?" Caitlyn asked, after Taylar had left and the two of us had started our journey over to the Theta Chi house. I nodded, reassured that we had at least *one* thing in common.

When Caitlyn mentioned going to the party at Ryan's fraternity, I had been reluctant to go. I didn't really know what to expect with a frat house, but I knew there would be alcohol and probably not a lot in the way of intelligent conversation, and the suggestion didn't have a huge appeal to me. Curiosity, combined with a genuine concern about Caitlyn's welfare, however, finally won the argument on whether or not to go.

Since our arrival at Durst, we had been assaulted with warnings about "The Red Zone." In our freshmen orientation ample time had been devoted to this subject, and throughout the campus bright red signs had been plastered on walls, doorways, and bathroom stall doors. In three days, I'd read it so many times I had it memorized, word for word:

The RED ZONE

The Red Zone is defined as the time period between Freshman Orientation and Homecoming, when a new student is most likely to be date raped. Excessive alcohol consumption is often a contributing factor to this pandemic.
Some tips to ensure your safety during this high-risk phase and any other time during your college tenure:

- *Use "the buddy system" when attending social events.*
- *Never leave a beverage unattended.*
- *Check in with your roommate before you leave as to your whereabouts and when you will return.*
- *Remember, No means NO!*

The Theta Chi fraternity house was a yellowish-brick Victorian that featured sloping eaves and stained glass and cozy-looking dormers peeping out of its roofline like two eyes. On its huge wrap-around porch sat a battle-weary couch that held two smirking girls. A curly-haired guy wearing a backwards baseball cap, jeans and flip-flops greeted us at the door and drew a red "x" on our hands after asking our ages. Glancing down, I could see the nail on his left big toe was broken half off and a momentary flicker of queasiness shot through my stomach. A kid with prolific acne stumbled out the door past us, giving Caitlyn a lopsided smile and a slurred "Hel-lo." A Green Day tune belted out of a speaker behind Mr. Flip-Flops, and we cautiously entered the front door.

If the outside was picture perfect, inside it looked as though the house had been gutted. A putrid smell overwhelmed me as we made our way inside; I'd later come to associate the odor – which I soon discovered and knew all too well as cheap beer that was permanently embedded in the floors and carpets – with *all* fraternity houses. Pockets of people stood in thick clusters throughout what must have been a stunning living room at one time in this house's history; now, all the furniture had been moved to one side and overlaid with bed sheets, and a couple of halogen lamps provided a sickly glow to the room.

"Caitlyn!" a deep voice assaulted us from overhead. There on the stairway was ol' Ryan, looking magnificently all-American in a rugby shirt and Tommy jeans as he ambled easily down the wooden staircase. Caitlyn gave him a smile that radiated the idea that she found him the most wonderful creature on earth at that given moment.

"Would you ladies like something to drink?" he shouted above the music.

Caitlyn looked at me, and I shook my head. "Not right now," she replied, giggling.

"I'm a little thirsty!" Ryan announced, smiling broadly at Caitlyn. "Come with me." He grabbed her by the hand and Caitlyn laughed and grabbed my hand as we slithered through the sticky throng of flesh in tank tops and T-shirts. The music was loud and the air thick with the smell of booze and smoke and perfume. I felt as though I'd been transported into somebody else's weird dream.

We forged our way into a dingy and equally packed kitchen that was completely bare, save for a card table pushed to the side of the room and a poster tacked on the refrigerator that instructed how much of which kinds of alcohol to include in order to make various cocktails.

"An educational poster," observed a voice next to me. I turned to see a guy with dark hair and silver-hoops in both his ears smile before swigging a sip from his cup. "I'm Graeme," he offered after he'd swallowed, holding out his right hand. He had a ring on his thumb.

"Molly," I returned, taking his fingers.

"Graeme, time to pull weeds," said a kid next to him, punching him lightly on the arm as he walked by us.

"Nice meeting you, Molly," Graeme said, kissing my hand with a sweeping gesture before he left to follow his friend. I turned to look at Caitlyn.

"Well, *that* was a little forward," she remarked. I glanced at Ryan, then back at her and raised my eyebrows.

A bony-thin girl with dark hair, wearing bright lipstick and huge chandelier earrings, gave Caitlyn and me a cold stare as we awkwardly stood there. There was a line of kids holding plastic cups, some talking to each other loudly and some just staring absently into space as they waited. They reminded me of the impoverished natives waiting patiently to get their share of water from a muddy creek in pictures of a mission trip I'd once seen when someone from our congregation had returned from Africa.

Ryan cut to the front of the line, joking with the guys who pumped the keg while they filled his plastic cup from the tap that was stashed under the sink. A girl wearing a tank top tight as plastic wrap, revealing kilometers of cleavage, drew stares from guys and girls alike as she stumbled past us with a hazy smile. A verse from Proverbs flashed through my mind suddenly: *"Like a gold ring in a pig's snout is a woman without discretion."* I loved the Bible's piercing imagery, in this instance the metaphor of outer beauty squandered because of a lack of inner subtlety, like jewelry set in a hog

A hip-hop song came on and a chorus of cheers erupted from the packed house. Glancing into the other room I could see the group of people converging into one body and gyrating in a slow, mindless mass. I was reminded of some primitive tribe that dances in a hypnotic trance for rain to come. The crowded kitchen felt suffocating, and my mind began to wander back to another place in the midst of my surreal environs.

****

Hank had been standing on my doorstep, hands stuffed in his jeans' pockets, wearing a plain white tee shirt, the muscles in his upper arms stretching the cotton sleeves. With his sideburns and slicked-back hair, he had made me think of a young Marlon Brando.

We had walked around the old neighborhood, talking about high school days as though they were already light years behind us. I was jittery and felt my stomach doing jumping jacks, just being close to him. I had wondered if he'd noticed when I quietly did some deep breathing techniques to calm myself.

"I think I'll have nightmares for the rest of my life about Mr. Kendig's hairy knuckles, jabbing my paper whenever he walked by my desk," Hank reminisced, referring to our math teacher, who *did* have ostensibly hairy hands. "That, and hearing the Beatles' "I Wanna Hold Your Hand" sung in German. German wasn't meant to be sung. It was a language created strictly for barking orders at people."

"I'm going to miss Mrs. Leventhal's English class" I said, clearing my throat as I found my voice. "I can still hear in my mind her explanation of all of Thomas Hardy's stuff: '*Phallic,* people, *phallic!*'"

"And Justin Koon's creative short stories, which were always loose copies of old *Twilight Zone* plots."

We had finished our stroll of the sleepy neighborhood and had sat down on the curb outside my house. The grass had been damp and dewy and the street silent. The stars had stood out clearly, and I had looked up and glimpsed the Pleiades – the Seven Sisters. I had almost pointed them out to Hank, but hesitated, and then the moment had passed.

"Go for the artistic ones," my grandfather had once advised, when he'd asked me if there were any interesting men in my life. "They're the sensitive ones." As I sat there, glancing sideways occasionally at Hank's quirky mouth and sturdy shoulders, I inwardly sighed. Nobody had to tell *me* twice.

"My faith has always been important to me," he had remarked suddenly, lighting up a cigarette and exhaling slowly as he leaned back. I had studied the shape of his lips as the smoke left them. "It's too bad about the arts, you know. A lot of the gifts we've been given have been taken and twisted and used for what wasn't intended." He had flicked the tip of his cigarette. "What annoys me about the church is that they've gone and thrown the baby out with the bathwater. Things like dancing and theater and even certain music, the church has simply tossed."

As we had discussed spirituality and the mind of God, I had gazed at Hank and secretly thought that God *must* love him more than any other being he'd created. How could He help it?

I had remembered Hank standing in the school gym, emceeing a donkey basketball game among the teachers, holding a microphone as the thousand or so of us who comprised the high school sat in the stands. Everyone had guffawed at his remarks intoned smoothly into the microphone, but only I had caught the subtlety of some of his quieter quips as the rest of the school had roared at the antics of the teachers.

A throb of nostalgia for days-gone-by rippled through me. "I'm feeling homesick already and I haven't even left."

"Homesick? You'll only be an hour away. Me, I'm leaving tomorrow for a place most Americans can't even locate on a map."

We had parted ways around three in the morning, the lingering warmth of his tobacco-and-aftershave hug leaving me feeling dizzy. I had stayed up until light cracked over the trees like an opening door on a dark room, and had watched the stars fade one by one into dawn.

****

The sudden cessation of music in the fraternity house, combined with the lights going out as some girl shrieked, brought me back to my present surroundings.

"SS is here, put your beers down!" a guy in front of me snarled at some boys whom I recognized from freshman orientation.

I felt a splash on my ankle as a girl next to me plopped her cup down right next to my foot and beer sloshed over the sides. The riotous house suddenly became eerily quiet and I heard older male voices coming from the front of the house.

"SS" stood for "Safety and Security" I would later discover, although I would forever have a vague image of uniformed soldiers in armbands because of the shared nomenclature with Hitler's National Socialists.

"Alright, party's over!" one of the security officers hollered gruffly. "Let's go...c'mon...*out!*"

"Some underage idiot must have ruined it for everyone," muttered a girl in front of me. "I *hate* freshmen."

All the lights were on I saw as we shuffled out the front room, and the house was blazing garishly from the wan light of the halogens. It was unbelievable how dirty the place really was, now that I could see. Subdued groans were audible as we were herded out the door.

"I don't see Ryan," Caitlyn fretted, glancing over her shoulder as we made our way towards the door.

"Don't worry. I'm sure he'll find *you*," I said dryly as I felt myself being sandwiched by sweaty skin on either side. Once free in the night air, I breathed a sigh of relief as we headed back to our dorm.

Chapter 3 – Campus Life

The pace of college suited me just fine, with its wide scheduling gaps and more focused courses. I was not a morning person, so my first class at eight-o-clock each day was always a rude awakening, especially since it was physics. Just the name "Physics" intimidated me, but I had to take three science courses during my time at Durst, and I decided it was best to get them out of the way as soon as possible.

My physics teacher, Professor Day, had made an impression on me the first day of class by peering over his rimmed glasses at all of us as though we were bizarre specimens which he'd seen before but couldn't quite identify. He had cleared his throat, turned to the white board behind him, and written the following statement on the board:

"WE ARE ALL STARDUST."

He had then proceeded to explain the Big Bang Theory in order to give us an understanding of the origins of our universe. Professor Day explained that the universe did in fact have a beginning. Prior to that moment there was nothing; during and after that moment there was something: our universe. The Big Bang Theory was, he said, an effort to explain what happened during and after that moment. I listened with interest to his explanation, only smiling when he started talking about "singularities."

"What is a 'singularity' and where does it come from? Well, to be honest, we don't know for sure. Singularities are zones which defy our current understanding of physics," Professor Day said, looking very much like a younger version of Wilford Brimley, his bushy eyebrows scrunched up just above his spectacles.

"Our universe is thought to have begun as an infinitely small, infinitely hot, infinitely dense, something -- a singularity. Where did it come from? We don't know. Why did it appear? We don't know."

"I know! I know!" I wanted to shout, waving my hand. Of course, I knew better than to speak up on this subject, especially as a brand new freshman, and be labeled a "fundamentalist Christian" derided from there on out with evil gazes and possibly injurious grades. Funny to think, though, that my knowledge on the origins of the universe – at least the "why" of it – was superior to my vastly schooled professor.

What came as more of a surprise my first day of actual classes at Durst was after introductions were made, and the syllabus and books passed out in my Calculus II class, the instructor – Professor Jankowski – had instructed us all to be silent as she played a song on her portable CD player:

On the corner there's this nice man
His name is Mark, he's always smiling
He's got this mom who comes on Wednesdays
In the evening with soup so steaming
He shares his house with his friend Martin
They're not brothers, they're not cousins
My little girl wonders all about these men
I take hold of her hand, and I begin

Home is where the heart is
No matter how the heart lives
Inside your heart where love is
That's where you've got to make yourself
At home

Across the yard live Deb and Tricia
With their tools and ladders
And their room addition
My kid yells over, are ya having a baby?
They wink and smile, they say, someday maybe.
But through their doors go kids and mommies
Funny how you don't see the daddies go in

My little girl wonders
'bout this house with no men,
I take hold of her hand
And I begin

Home is where the heart is
No matter how the heart lives
Inside your heart where love is
That's where you've got to make yourself
At home

We had sat there listening to the folksy lyrics and repeating chorus and looked around at each other a bit and I guess we were all waiting to hear the tie-in between this song and Calculus, which was too deep for me to recognize.

When the music finally came to an end, Professor Jankowski strode over to the CD player, pushed a button, and turned to face the class with an intense look in her eyes. "I think that this is just a really great reminder for all of us," she said gravely.

"It's the first time in my life I can remember hearing music played during a math class," I later recounted to Kendra over an e-mail. *"I didn't really mind the song so much, but I kept wondering what my parents would think if they could see where their tuition money was going."*

Durst certainly did a tidy job of making sure every race, religion, gender and transgender was represented in housing. There was the Friedman House (for those intent on Jewish studies), the Allies' Haven (for gay, bisexual, and transgender students), the multicultural house (which I later found out currently only housed black students), the al-Fayed House (for Muslims), and the list went on. They even had the Tree House for those whose greatest calling in life was saving the environment. It was rumored students who lived there only ever flushed the toilet after doing a number two, and they took a vow not to shower more than once a week. I never ventured inside the Tree House so I couldn't verify that report.

"It strikes me as funny that a college so focused on treating everyone equally and embracing differences makes such a point of offering housing designed to keep people living in groups of the same 'kind,'" I also mused to Kendra over the computer.

Then there was the whole thing about Tolerance. There were posters about it everywhere, urging us towards it and imploring us to become "educated." I learned quickly that the word "tolerance" didn't really mean *tolerance* at all. "Tolerance" actually meant "acceptance" and "acquiescence" and even "compliance." It meant embrace this particular socio-political agenda, or else Be Silent. If you choose anything else, expect to be ridiculed and given a label replete with "hate" somewhere in it. I took issue with Tolerance for another reason, besides its tyrannical approach to the First Amendment and rejection of true diversity of ideas and thoughts. As Christians, we were never called to tolerate one another. We were called to love.

Durst did have a Christian fellowship on campus. Although I wasn't much of a joiner, I did want to be around people who knew Christ. So I went to the meetings Friday nights and I became familiar with the kids who attended and I came to appreciate walking into the large, bare room where we met and sensing the instant brotherhood and sense of acceptance that marked it.

Durst's mascot, ironically, was a devil, and he held a pitchfork in one hand and wore a perpetual sly grin. I didn't particularly like it, and wondered whose idea it was to nominate a demon as one of the symbols of this institution of higher education.

After lunch, the computer room in the HUB was usually packed with students frantically typing out e-mails or surfing the net. Since I was not among Durst's wealthy, I didn't have a computer in the dorm room and was thereby forced to use the public ones like the other less fortunate kids.

Kendra told me about her Christian college in Indiana which had a rule about freshmen not dating for the first semester. I thought that that sounded rather totalitarian.

"What are you supposed to do if you meet 'Mr. Right' your first day there?" I typed incredulously. *"Smile and bat your eyes for a semester, or do you send notes through the mail?"*

"Both, I guess," Kendra replied unapologetically. *"If it's Mr. Right, I suppose he can wait."*

My mom sent me news from home every few days, though I knew that parents had been warned not to correspond too much the first couple months until their kids got adjusted. She kept me up-to-date on the neighbors and Anne's soccer and my dad's diet and my dog, Agnes, whom she claimed missed me fervently and looked at the door whenever my name was spoken.

The one person, however, whom it mattered most to connect with didn't use e-mail any more than necessary. Hank didn't have an online profile on any web site I knew of, and he avoided web networking in general.

"As egocentric as I am," he'd once remarked back in high school, "I'm not narcissist enough to set up a profile and *blog*."

So Hank had not connected himself to the flippant, speed-of-light networking communities where other kids marketed themselves like dry goods and where rampant, unfinished ideas flowed like a peculiar dream sequence. I could only wonder how college life was going for him.

Because I was not sponsored by affluent parents, I had a job working in the dining hall. Everyone wanted a job in the library or working for a professor, but the dining room paid the best, so I worked there. Besides, it was fun. Back in the dish room, my favorite of all the tasks assigned was being in the slop line, waiting for the trays to come back and empty their contents into the streaming trough of warm water which eventually churned the discarded food into a disposal. The plates and bowls and salad dishes were then stacked onto racks and run through the dish washer with its plastic fringes like a car wash. That dish room was like a sauna, with the hot steam coming out of the washer and the sounds of ceramic being stacked. I often blushed at the creativity that came through there, with obscene images often being formed with certain leftover food particles.

Depending on who was working, the other freshmen sang sit-com theme songs or talked about their courses or gossiped about professors or discussed trends in pop culture. Small talk generally made me anxious, and so I avoided it. Nevertheless, I was already forming a group of friends through regularly working with them, and for that I was grateful.

One of the workers there whom I'd befriended was Zach, or "Z" as they called him. He was a senior and he was always there, always working, always upbeat. He was recognizable by his Kool-Aid dyed hair and harlequin hat that he wore, reminiscent of a court jester. He had black earrings that reminded me of the "ear bobs" that the Victorian women wore, and his eyes were large and round and palest blue – like glass that you sometimes find at the seashore.

"The blue shirts don't like Zach," a wiry fellow freshman named Jason told me one day when Zach had run out to the loading dock to empty the trash.

"Why not?" I replied. I couldn't find any fault in Zach's work.

"He's a big-time stoner," Jason informed me, tossing a saucer onto one of the wash racks before it ambled by on the conveyor. "He always shows up for work, but they're never sure whether or not he'll be baked as a cake."

"Molly-wog!" I looked up upon hearing Zach's nickname for me. Jason ducked out of sight around the side of the conveyor. Zach was standing there in the doorway holding one of the large, plastic bags that held the milk. We had to stick the bags upside down in the huge coolers and poke the spouted end through the tap. I often saw the football players with six or seven of the little tumblers full of milk and chocolate milk lined up on their trays. "Would you give me a hand with this?" Zach asked me.

I studied the tattoos on his arm as I helped hold the fridge door open and Zach fit the beverage bag into position. He had a series of symbols on his forearm and I wanted to ask him what they meant.

"So how are you liking Durst so far?" Zach asked me as he took a dishrag over the front of the fridge, avoiding getting between the beverage tray and a burly, red-faced kid whom I recognized as one of the school's linebackers.

"I like it," I replied. "College is fun. I love having one class at ten and not having another till three. Sure beats high school."

"What are you going to major in?" Zach asked.

"No idea," I answered. "I really don't know."

"Well, you have plenty of time," Zach answered. "And believe me, have as much fun as you can and do whatever you feel like, because the time flies by. I'll be graduating this year and I have no clue what I'm going to do."

"Are you glad you came to Durst?" I asked him. "I mean, now that you're in your last year here."

"Durst is a great school, which is why I came here." Zach picked up a glass that someone had left sitting by the coolers. "But I hate how fake everyone is. Heaven forbid you don't pay over a hundred bucks for each shirt you wear or don't drive a German-manufactured car. They all have money and are used to 'mommy and daddy and breakfast in bed.' If you don't fit that carbon copy, you're nobody. It makes me sick. I can't stand fake people."

His face relaxed into a smile as he must have read my expression. "I don't mean to sound negative, you being a freshman and all and thinking this place is great. I don't mind the plastic people so much – the world is full of them. At the end of the day, the important thing is, you can always find a dime bag somewhere."

The muscles and veins in Zach's arms flexed as he hoisted some crates from beneath the beverage island and headed back towards the dish room. I thought of what Jason had told me and felt sad in knowing that the sickly sweet, forbidden weed Zach inhaled into his lungs each night was an empty and deceptive substitute for the Breath of Life.

Chapter 4 – A Defining Moment

Stedman Hall, like all the other buildings which pepper the lush, green campus of Durst, was fashioned in pristine limestone. When I think of the formation of the college structures, I always think back to a high school science field trip in which we visited a churchyard and did a geological "find" on the headstones there. Limestone did not fare well, and writing on these tombstones was nearly illegible. Only slate was worse, while granite and quartzite endured. It made me think of the campus one day washing away, melting into nothingness, long after humanity had left its walls, under the last torrents of a rainfall.

Entering through the double glass doors into the air conditioning, the stillness of the building engulfed me. It was eerie to go from the perpetual noise of the campus to this quietness. Someone had told me that there were pianos on the third floor that were available to be played by faculty, staff, or students at any time up until midnight. So I had hauled my motley assortment of piano books over to Stedman in the early September humidity and prepared to enjoy some moments alone in worship.

I had in my musical arsenal the greatest hits of Simon and Garfunkel, Elvis, and just about all the tunes the Beatles had ever composed or sung. Along with that, I had a compilation of American folk music and songs popular during the world wars. Songbooks containing half of what had been produced on Broadway I had in my possession as well, in addition to some wonderful German waltzes. I had seldom played any of these in the last six months, however. Not since a certain evening back in April when life as I knew and understood it changed irrevocably.

When Kendra had invited me to the Sunday evening service at Keller Mennonite last spring, I was a little dubious. I was a Christian and all, but her usage of the word "prophet" in conjunction with the guest speaker left me feeling somehow uneasy. Prophets existed 2,500 years ago of course, but not today. I didn't have any scriptural knowledge to back this up, but my gut feeling of how others – including my own parents – might perceive the very terminology was enough to convince me that this was possibly unorthodox by the standards of my own church denomination. However, I had known Kendra for years and she was in fact, "doctrinally sound." More than that, she was one of those rare people who was friends with just about everyone because she was so loving, and one of those exceptional individuals with whom you could hardly find any fault, but could find a great deal to admire. I figured I could hold my prejudices against the idea of a so-called prophet and go and find out for myself whether he wasn't just a little nutty, or Kendra wasn't just a bit overenthusiastic.

The evening had started out routinely enough, with the fifty or so of us standing in the pews, singing hymns like "I have decided to follow Jesus," and "Redeeming Love." The worship lasted longer than usual, and I thought of how often Kendra said that God loves to be in the praises of His people.

I was very curious that night to see how an alleged prophet looked. I don't know if I expected him to come out wearing a tunic or what. I did expect him to have a beard, and he didn't disappoint me there. His name was Alan, which I had found somewhat lackluster. I figured a prophet ought at least to have a Biblical-sounding name. He was middle-aged, slightly overweight, and dressed in khakis and a black button-down. He was from South Africa and had an accent.

He spoke of growing up with Apartheid and of what God was doing in South Africa to break down those terrible barriers, and what the Lord was doing everywhere around the world. He spoke of people he saw freed from bondage and of a tribe in a third world country so desperate for something spiritual that they holed themselves up in caves until demons possessed their bodies. This chilling outcome nevertheless shamed me as I contemplated the kind of passion for the spiritual I *didn't* have. For myself, I would have wished the Internet or a PlayStation in my cave, and that would have kept me pacified.

Then Alan addressed people in the room. "Who's Mandy?" he'd ask in his accent, face raised, looking around the room. "She's my best friend," a girl in front of me replied.

"Mandy is desperate and at a critical point right now in her life. God wants to reveal Himself to her," Alan stated in his accent. "Let's pray for Mandy."

So it went, with Alan addressing different people within the motley congregation who were virtual strangers. He even said something to Kendra, naming the very school she'd be attending up in New York, which instantly sent Kendra into tears. Somewhere in the back of my mind, I wondered if he could give me the scoop on Hank. It would certainly save me some time and trouble, I thought. Then it occurred to me that this was a purely selfish wish and probably not the point of getting a prophecy.

Alan had then asked if we would like to pray to receive a touch of the Holy Spirit right then and there, and leave this church changed. He said it could happen, and that if anyone was thirsty, to come to the altar and we would pray together. I lingered in my seat as I watched Kendra move forward. I was quite certain something like this wouldn't happen to me – *didn't* happen to people like me. I don't know why I thought that. Alan was alright…good guy, interesting stories. A touch of the Spirit? It sounded unsafe.

I was sitting in my seat watching half of the church go up, when suddenly I stood up where I was, ramrod straight, and ran up to the altar, compelled to go. *If nothing happened,* I thought, *nothing happened.* If, however, God would suddenly come near, I didn't want to miss out on getting a close-up of Him.

We stood up there at the little altar for what I figured was a matter of minutes, hands outstretched towards Heaven, silently praying while Alan led out. Had this been my home church, doubtless I would have stayed in my seat, too self-conscious to go up in front of so many people. With strangers, however, I felt a little less fearful.

Through my half-closed eyes I could see the pin stripes of the shirt on the bald man standing in front of me. I was suddenly aware that my hands were shaking. My breathing, likewise, was coming in long, ragged pants as though I had just sprinted the hundred-yard dash. More than that, I was becoming conscious of joy – billowing, all-encompassing, wondrous joy – that I had never experienced. It wasn't a feeling at all, really. It was something tangible and yet something invisible and it was all around me and in me. It was indescribable, and yet if I just had that one perfect word you'd know exactly what I meant. It was beyond words, and it was incredible and yet it was thoroughly believable. Yes, of course. This was *Him!* This is what it finally was like to *know* Him and to experience Him and to be *in – His – Presence!* Tears streamed down my face but I didn't want to move even to wipe them away for fear that if I stopped focusing on Him for even a moment, the nearness of Him would fade.

A vision began forming in my mind as I stood there of a great mass of people, immobilized, standing in an immense open hall – no, more like a stadium – turning speechlessly and awestruck to the person on either side, expressing with their eyes the wonder of being in such a perfect and holy Presence – overwhelmed, silent, breathless. Then suddenly, bursting into shouts of praise and adoration, they fell onto their faces.

There was no other place I wanted to be, and nothing better or greater on this earth. I knew at that moment at Keller Mennonite, that if I could fathom His mind and plunge right into it, it would be a great room all splendid and opulent, and beyond that another door leading to another room, and another and another and another! Each one going deeper into a place that I longed to be.

So I had stood there and I had worshipped Him, never wanting to leave that spot for the rest of my life.

Presently, I became aware of a man's voice. It was the minister of the church, and he was saying something that at first, I couldn't understand. Dimly I became aware of other people around me – a man lying facedown on the floor, a woman kneeling in the pew. Then it became clear that the minister was informing us that they had to lock up. That it was late. I didn't think he was being fair, so I didn't pay any attention at first. After all, it couldn't have been more than ten minutes or so since we'd gone up to the altar. Reluctantly, rebelliously, I glanced up at the round clock that hung like a sentry on the wall. It was nearly eleven o'clock. I'd been standing there in the same spot for three hours.

The days that followed that encounter with God were wonderful but difficult, like plowing through tasks that you know you have to do, or being somewhere you need to go, but with something else always on your mind and somewhere else permanently in your heart. It was like being in love and wanting to be with the object of your affection that made your heart throb, but instead having to go to a job. Daily life – the grind and the sundry bits of it – were a bore to me. Watching a lacrosse game after school, listening to a comedian the high school brought in as a special treat for the graduating seniors, television programming...it was all so horribly empty and dull. How could people stand it? The alternative rock music I'd occasionally listened to up until then suddenly irritated me. How could I have possibly found any meaning in those insipid lyrics? Instead and to my surprise, I found myself tuning in to Christian Rock, as well as the gospel radio my parents liked, of all things. Even the rocked out lyrics and old hymns didn't entirely do it, and I found myself ordering passionate and intimate worship music online – often with simple guitar accompaniment. To return to that realization at Keller's dominated my mind, and everything else just seemed a little flat.

Before that day, I used to worry a great deal about eternity. What if, after ten thousand years bright shining as the sun, I was simply so sick of myself I couldn't stand it? What if Heaven and perfection were flat out boring? What if a passing bad thought sprang into my mind and I got kicked out? Since that evening at Keller's, I feared the concept of "forever" no more. I believed that this is what Heaven would be like: forever and ever in the Lord's glorious presence, never desiring anything else than that, and with no concept of time.

Some people who have been "raised" Christians claim to have a specific instance of when their faith suddenly became very real and personal to them. For some I know, it was after they were baptized as believers. Others might have had an experience on a mission trip that cut them to the quick. For me, it was that night just a few months prior, at a tiny chapel with its ancient green carpet and cracking plastered walls, and the nagging white face of a superfluous clock on the wall.

As I sat for a moment on the piano bench in that ancient collegiate hall of Durst, I thought of all the party-goers and pot-smokers and impersonators and was glad I was not part of it. If I could have spoken a retort to the devil, I'd have conveyed that it was a waste of time to trip me up. I'd been a Christian since I was five, was stronger than ever, and my faith was solid as a rock. Better go bother someone else. I wouldn't stray from my First Love. Shivering with the fresh memory of my encounter with the Lord, I began to pray over the college campus, my home for the next four years.

Chapter 5 – An Unexpected Acquaintance

One of my mother's tidbits of wisdom that she'd imparted to me and Anne was the wish that we'd never marry a man who hadn't lived on his own for enough time to learn to do laundry.

"Make sure he's been away from his mother long enough to take care of himself," she'd implore us at random given moments, for seemingly no particular reason.

I thought of this advice with an even mix of horror and irony as I stood next to the washers in the basement of Watson, wishing I could go back in time for just two hours and *not do* what I had just done. I had a load of whites in one of the washers and didn't pay close enough attention to the line-up, misjudging mine, and had dumped the whitening liquid into a load of someone else's colors that were loaded in the machine right next to mine. It wasn't until I'd gone to take my clothes out and transfer them to the dryer that it dawned on me what I had done.

"Take your clothes back to the room and run," Caitlyn advised me, wide-eyed when I told her in utter dismay about the mix-up. "No one will know it was you who did it."

"As much as I'd like to, I can't do that," I replied miserably. "I have to figure out whose laundry that is and own up."

"Did anyone see you down there?" Caitlyn questioned me, making me feel indeed like a criminal in need of an alibi.

"No, I don't think so," I answered.

"Well, then don't worry about it," she had persisted. "What's the point in getting in trouble if you don't have to?"

"No, I've gotta take responsibility for it," I said again. "I can imagine how I'd feel if it were me, and someone did that to *my* clothes."

I went downstairs again and peered into the machine that *wasn't* mine and pulled out a couple of garments. It was definitely women's clothing, and since this wasn't transgender housing, that narrowed it down to the girls' floor.

As I wondered in real terror about how many days in the dining room I'd have to work just to compensate for the expense of refurbishing the owner's wardrobe, I began the frightening task of trying to pinpoint the owner.

Like a door-to-door salesman, I went around Watson Hall, asking if anyone had a load of clothes in the washer, waiting for the axe to fall. As I approached each door, it felt very much like volunteering to stand before a firing squad, knowing that someone would eventually take you up on it.

"No one said the clothes are theirs?" Caitlyn asked anxiously when I returned to the room minutes later.

"Apparently, whoever owns them is not in the building," I answered, going over to my desk and grabbing a piece of paper and a pen.

"So you're off the hook!" Caitlyn said brightly.

"I wouldn't say that," I responded, as I scribbled a note. I tore off a piece of tape, shuffled back downstairs, and taped the following to the washer which had so willingly swallowed the culprit bleach:

> To whomever is using this washing machine~
> I thought it was mine and accidentally bleached
> your clothes. I'm so sorry. I will pay to have
> whatever was damaged replaced.
> –Molly (Room 202)
> P.S. Please don't kill me

I returned to my dorm room and paced, waiting as one facing a judgment for the wrath to come. This was awful. What a dumb thing to do! Why hadn't I simply been more careful?

Caitlyn tried to make me feel better, assuring me it was an honest mistake and that perhaps only a few clothes ended up getting ruined.

"Whoever it is will probably be very nice and understanding," she assured me. I began to relax a little, hoping perhaps she was right.

About two hours later there was a knock at my door, and when I opened it, a slender, petite girl with dark hair stood before me. Even though they were scowling, her eyes were large and lovely, adorned with a shade of eye shadow that even in my catatonic state I wished mournfully that I too, could wear successfully. She had her arms crossed and a frown on her face, and was tapping her left foot impatiently.

"I'm gonna kill somebody named Molly," she said quietly.

I felt my insides shrink in remorse. College was going to be forever ruined because of this one mistake. Everyone would know me from then on out as "bleach girl" and would-be acquaintances and friends would now shun me. I figured I could wade out one more semester and then transfer to a community college near home. Of course, I'd probably have to take out a separate loan to pay for her clothing. I could tell by looking at her that she was someone who probably didn't own a single piece of clothing from any of the generic places *I* shopped.

"Are you Molly?" the girl demanded.

I nodded wordlessly, too terrified to trust myself to speak.

"Did you bleach my clothes?" It wasn't a question. It was an accusation.

"Yes," I squeaked.

"Well, I'm filing a lawsuit," she said with deadly calm.

My shoulders drooped as I began mentally calculating the cost of an attorney on *top* of court fees and clothing damages.

"Haha, gotcha!" the girl laughed loudly, slapping my arm that held open the door. "You *have* to be Molly because you look like you're going to puke. You're the one who figured my clothes could use some bleach?"

I was confused now and still in shock, but feeling some oxygen coming back into my bloodstream.

"My name's Anise," she told me, still grinning. She grew instantly serious. "I admit, I was pretty steamed when I found out what got ruined. But after I cursed a couple times, yelled at some stranger, and calmed down, I decided to look on the positive side. I figured, 'this is grounds for a shopping spree.' So, thanks to you, I'll have an excuse to break in my new credit card."

"I'll gladly pay for whatever was damaged," I told her, finding my voice.

"Don't worry about it," Anise shrugged off my offer. "About half of it was ruined, and it was mostly summer stuff anyhow. Now I don't have to worry about storing it for the winter. I'll replace them with some fall stuff instead." She flashed a wide smile, showing off a dazzling smile.

Still reeling from shock, I was even more surprised when Anise gave me a quick hug and then flittered past me into the room.

"I'm Anise," she repeated to Caitlyn, who had been hiding on the other side of the door, listening fearfully, but who now cautiously ventured out.

"Caitlyn," my roommate smiled, evidently relieved like me that the danger was over.

"Caitlyn and Molly...I wasn't at the freshman orientation meeting here in the dorm – I was still on my way back from Italy then – so I didn't meet anyone. Want to go to dinner together?"

I realized then that it was supper time, and now that the threat of impending death was fading, I found that my appetite was restored. It would not be my last meal after all.

Anise, as it turned out, lived just a couple doors down at the end of the hall, and her energy and humor I found invigorating, infectious. She reminded me of a hummingbird, tiny and lovely and in perpetual motion, even when she was in one place.

Anise was from northern Jersey, close to New York, and her family was Italian. She had a boyfriend who attended New York University, I found out. Her father was a plastic surgeon who split his time between his home office and his New York clientele. I was amazed when I walked into her dorm room for the first time and saw her open closet stocked with more shoes than I'd ever seen belong to one single owner. It made me think of that former prime minister's wife from the Philippines, Imelda Marcos, who had over two thousand pairs of shoes. The most extraordinary scarves and jackets and accessories climbed out the sides of her closet, and funky costume jewelry and colored pearls oozed over the tops of beautifully painted boxes and nick-knack chests, which were scattered haphazardly throughout her room.

Instead of those freakish Anne Geddes posters showing unfortunate babies in insect costumes or wearing produce on their heads, or pin-ups of hunks as the dorm décor, Anise had a three-layer deep border of tear-outs from fashion magazines. They featured intriguing shots of whippet-like females in outfits that I couldn't imagine anyone would purchase, some wearing elbow gloves and hats and knee-high boots and accessorizing with either small animals or wiry-thin, scruff-faced males with piercing eyes and sanguine gazes.

She had a huge stereo that was on whenever I came in the room, and it could be belting out anything from Pavarotti to ethnic progressive rock, depending on her apparent mood. Her music collection included artists I'd never heard of, and when I'd come in, if she wasn't studying or on her laptop, she'd often be dancing to whatever was playing.

In many ways, I thought Caitlyn better suited to be close friends with Anise than I. They both were worldly, cosmopolitan, and beautiful. I had the sneaking suspicion once again that I was the ugly, unsophisticated friend in the group, an opinion I voiced to Kendra in an e-mail.

"It's not that I think I'm a dog, per se" I had typed, anticipating her rebuke. *"It's just that they're roses and I'm a zinnia. The zinnia looks pretty until you place it next to the roses. Then you see how plain it is."*

Kendra had replied, *"Don't be deceived into seeing yourself so superficially. The world is desperate for authenticity. They're watching every move and every action and word from those who are following Christ, and when they're searching and they see somebody that's real they want to be around that."*

Anise's roommate, Jill, was seldom in her room, but I remembered her from the orientation.

"She's got a girlfriend over at Andersen Hall," Anise had told me matter-of-factly the first time I had come over to her room. "The two of them spend a lot of time together at the Allies' Haven, too." She was trying on a new pair of shoes that I figured cost more than my entire wardrobe combined.

"My mom sent them," she explained as she showed me the fiery-red heels. "Cute, no?"

"They're beautiful," I agreed.

"I personally don't get the Jill-lesbian angle," Anise said speculatively, slipping on one of the shoes. "Men have so much more to offer." She studied her reflection, turning her ankle and examining one shoe from the side. "But, whatever makes you happy, right?"

Anise's boyfriend was attending New York University. She had described in detail instances of getting caught in his room, and her subsequent punishments, which never included her parents finding out.

"I didn't even like him at first," Anise had said of her boyfriend. "I thought he was stuck on himself and wished he'd leave me alone. He kept writing me notes, sending me flowers, showing up…My friends kept telling me what a great guy he was, how hot he was, so I finally agreed to go out with him."

Staring at their picture, I secretly couldn't imagine needing that much persuasion to agree to date a guy that looked as good as Anise's boyfriend, Joe. He was dark and handsome and a head taller than her, and better dressed than any guy I'd ever seen in real life. He looked as though he were on his way to a fashion shoot in every photo he was in that hung in her room.

"We've been together almost a year-and-a-half," Anise said absently, kicking a knee-high boot out of her path as she went over to turn down the stereo.

She paused for a moment, examining one of her fingernails, and then turned around to face me. "Joe was my first," she announced, searching my expression as I took in the news.

I didn't know exactly how to respond, so I gave a little nod of acknowledgment, which was enough for her to continue.

"I always thought I'd wait till I was married before doing it," she confided. "I mean, I'm Catholic and all." She looked down at her hands, which gripped the back of her chair. "I really *wanted* to wait, too. It was just so hard. Joe kept talking about it, and I'd already had one guy in high school – a guy I was totally in love with, no less – cheat on me for giving him nothing at all. So, back in July, while my mom was out of town, Joe came over. My brother was at a friend's house, my dad was in New York, the house was empty, and…well, we did it."

She exhaled, cracking her knuckles against her chin. "Would you believe I *cried* afterwards?" she asked, smiling wryly.

"Before I left for school, my mom gave me this, which was a family heirloom," Anise pulled out of her top dresser drawer a small black box and opened it to expose a large, delicately hued pink pearl in an antique filigreed setting. "It's supposed to represent chastity and has been handed down from one generation of women to another in our family all the way back from before they first came over from Italy. I didn't have the heart to tell her I no longer deserved it."

"You still have the choice to remain pure," I told her, finding my voice. "You made a mistake and you can ask God's forgiveness. It will be as though it never happened."

"But it *did* happen," Anise responded, snapping the box shut, "and when Joe comes to visit me next weekend, I'm sure it will happen again. Once you've done it, it gets harder to say no. Besides, what's the point now in not going all the way? I already lost my virginity to him."

She shut the top drawer of her dresser firmly, jabbed the "Stop" button on her CD player, and yanked out the CD. "Let's change the subject," she said brightly, reaching for another disc. "You like Amy Winehouse?"

I shrugged my shoulders and smiled faintly.

****

40

I had tested out of German so it wasn't necessary for me to take a language at Durst, but I had a desire to continue to study it, mostly from family ancestry and also the broad Pennsylvania Dutch heritage that encompassed the region where I lived. I was placed in a 200-level course with a mix of other freshmen and sophomores.

My German teacher, Frau Bund, was an angular woman, narrow as a hockey stick, who wore paisley, kimono-like gowns that hung on her figure like some sort of 1970s-style camouflage tents. One of Ryan's Theta Chi brothers, Jon, also took the class, and gave me some advice if I were ever stumped on an essay question in her class.

"She's huge into women's issues," Jon told me in class, sliding his right foot in and out of his Birkenstock. His feet smelled terrible and I tried to avert my face slightly without being obvious. "Write anything you can think of about women and tie it into German history, German politics…hell, women and German *beer!* Whatever the topic is talk about women's issues somehow and you'll get extra points." He tapped his pen on my desk. "Are you coming to our 'Guys and Dolls' party next week?"

"I don't know," I replied, surprised. "I didn't know I was invited." I knew Caitlyn was going with Ryan. It was all I'd heard about for the past several days.

What was strange was how Caitlyn could switch it on and off when it came to flirting with and charming Ryan and instantly go into lovey-dovey devotion mode for her boyfriend David the moment he called. What was more, I'd often come back from class and find some new guy hanging inside our dorm room with her or listen to her pick up the phone and start chatting away with someone on the other end as though she'd known him forever. I'd overhear her tease and giggle and banter with Mr. New Guy as if the two of them had grown up together. Whoever the New Guy was, he was always instantly taken by her, and I'd watch Caitlyn chatter away, sometimes doing a task, and then perch back next to him while the guy just sat there with a simpleton grin on his face the entire time, clearly thoroughly amazed by this creature, but not at all amazed at the prospect that he was the first ever to command her attention this way. It was like watching a well-timed, carefully practiced vaudeville act, and I knew from observing her with other guys that had come a-calling around our dorm room that if you threw another man into the mix, she could alter the routine to juggle him just as easily. Once, two guys had shown up at the same time, and Caitlyn didn't blink an eye. She flirted and flattered them both in such a way that I think the two guys (who were both freshmen) left our dorm as tacit friends. It didn't matter how many of them there were or where they came from or what their height or personality or IQ happened to be, Caitlyn could juggle them effectively and make it look easy. It was, in a slightly troubling way, highly impressive.

"Of course you're invited to the party," Jon told me, jarring me back to German Literature, and leaning back in his seat till it creaked. He had a flabby belly that protruded like an unsightly overhang through his t-shirt. "Lucky for us SS didn't penalize us for the chick who got caught underage, so we'll have a full bar this time." He rubbed his heel along the side of his calf. "I have a date for you."

My stomach did a little flip flop at this news, but I played it off by responding with a casual, "Oh, really?"

"Yep," Jon said self-assuredly. "One of our associate members…great guy."

Frau Bund ambled into the room at that moment, paisley prints swirling around her sapling-width calves as she scrambled to unload all her books and write the lesson on the board, denying me any more details about Jon's schemes. As she wrote a series of umlaut-laden words on the white board, I studied the little cartoon devil gripping his pitchfork, stitched onto the back of the hat of the guy in front of me. He seemed to be looking me right in the eye and laughing.

Chapter 6 – The Pigbook

Without a doubt the most widely studied publication on Durst's campus is not a volume of scientific research, a history book, or the dictionary. It has to be what freshmen come to know as "the Pigbook."

The Pigbook was actually the colloquial name for the photograph directory of Durst's incoming freshmen class. Along with the person's picture, it listed his or her home town and high school. It was used primarily, I soon learned, as a means to classify which girls were invited to certain fraternity parties and other events. If the girl were deemed physically attractive by the standards of whoever was studying the Pigbook, she qualified. It was easy to figure out where it derived its name.

Anise and Caitlyn and I were all studying the Pigbook ourselves one afternoon, as we tried to piece together persons of interest with whom we had class or had perhaps seen in the cafeteria and were curious to check out their biographical stats.

"I know her," Anise said, tapping a manicured nail on a picture of a girl wearing a cheerleading shell and standing with her hands on her hips, clutching pom-poms. "She dated one of the guys at Whitley. She's as fake as half of Hollywood's hooters."

"Nikki Hutchison," I read off the caption, staring at her megawatt, just-for-the-camera smile and affected pose. "She looks like she could be an advertisement for a breath mint commercial."

"And I'll bet she dots the *i's* in her name with hearts," Anise added, flipping the page.

"Oh, there's Danny Huffman," Caitlyn exclaimed, pointing out a handsome kid with skater-like hair and dimples in both cheeks, who smiled back at us knowingly through his long bangs. "He's in my Policy Studies class and he's so funny!" She smiled back at Danny's picture. "I think he likes me."

"What man *doesn't* like you?" Anise answered matter-of-factly. "By the way, do you and your boyfriend have an agreement about seeing people at college? I mean, does he know about Ryan?"

"Well, we haven't really talked about it," Caitlyn said nonchalantly, with an edge of defensiveness in her voice.

"How long have you and David been together anyway?" Anise queried.

"He asked me out spring of my junior year," Caitlyn replied.

"Wait, so he's not the same year as you?" Anise was trying to piece the facts together about a story that I already knew well.

"No, he graduated a year ahead of me," Caitlyn explained. "He took a year off and worked in our home town while I was a senior, so we're both starting out as freshmen."

"So let me get this straight," Anise summarized in the tone of a fact-hunting detective. "Your boyfriend delayed college a year just to be with you?"

"Yes...*and* to work" Caitlyn explained, the note of defensiveness climbing up an octave.

"*Damn*, girl," Anise remarked, shaking her head.

"Well, I think it's immature to get too serious with one guy when you're young," Caitlyn explained, a pout in her voice.

I smiled to myself. It was the advice I had given her when she asked me what I thought about wanting to "play the field." However, Caitlyn had omitted the second part of that advice, which apparently wasn't as crucial to her. I'd told her "As long as the person you're with knows that you're seeing other people, I agree that it's good not to get too serious too fast," I had said.

David was completely unaware that she had taken a portion of this advice to heart, but had not bothered to pass along her decision to him so that he could do the same.

"Playing the field" indeed, I thought. *More like "man overboard."*

I quickly got to know the girls on my floor, although among them there didn't seem to be any who clicked with me as well as Anise and Caitlyn, nor did there appear to be any other Christians.

Taylar and I seemed destined to be instant enemies. She clearly had sized me up the first time we'd met and determined that I was a dork. Even though she may have been right, to dismiss me so positively and not even look at me when she wandered into the room to chat with Anise or Caitlyn I couldn't help but find somewhat offensive. Each time I passed her walking, and her gaze pointedly omitted me, I felt the resentment rise within me. *"If possible, as far as it lies with you, live in harmony with all men."* Paul's words to the Romans routinely popped up in my mind; I wondered wryly if the word "men" got me off the hook with Taylar? She *was* kind of masculine.

It seemed comical that Taylar would find me so distasteful for my apparent lack of sophistication (at least, I could only guess that's what it was) yet the rest of our floor was filled with pretty goofy girls. They stayed up at night giving each other makeovers or loaded up on caffeine and played foursquare out in the hallway until two in the morning or just squealed and shrieked and acted all hyper for no particular reason. Living on our floor seemed very much like an ongoing high school slumber party.

Among the mix was a girl named Marcy who had strawberry blond hair and freckles and was skinny as a pixie stick and spoke endlessly about home, about high school, and especially about "Gainer," a social studies teacher who seemed overly familiar with his students, and whom she clearly missed. I listened to her at first to be polite, and later out of kindness, but by the second week of school found myself avoiding her by darting into bathrooms in the dorm or in other buildings whenever I saw her coming. That worked at first, until she spotted me and followed me inside. If I hadn't shut the door, I seriously wondered whether she wouldn't have joined me in the stall, going on about some other "Gainer" tale or joke or mannerism that he had. By the third week, Marcy was gone, and I found out from her roommate that she had transferred to a school within minutes from her home back in Massachusetts.

There was one girl – Danielle – who lived on our floor, but by the second week we barely saw her. She apparently had moved down one level to the guys' floor and was sharing a bed with one of them. It was rumored that her newfound romance, Cal, had a girlfriend back at home. Cal was the son of some software tycoon and routinely pointed out the cost of different things that he owned or had bought Danielle. His way of dealing with the guilt of cheating on his girlfriend back home was to send her dozens and dozens of roses.

Danielle's roommate, Gigi, as she preferred to be called, got bored without Danielle there, and so she spent a great deal of time in our room. Since Caitlyn usually was out with some male when she wasn't studying at the library, I generally was left with Gigi. Gigi was alright, sweet actually, but she was perpetually talking and usually eating and often doing the two things at once. She wearied me at times, and she also routinely showered me with food particles if I was standing too close to her.

I knew that I should show love to all the girls on the floor, especially the ones to whom it was difficult, but I found myself more and more taking pride in my association with Anise and Caitlyn, and feeling apathy towards trying to reach out to the others.

My parents had told me all about the pranks that had been part of the standard fare of their college years: short-sheeting the beds, saran-wrapping doorframes, etc. The story of my mother's

46

college roommate was familiar – how the other girls had stolen all her clothes and towel while she was in the shower and how she had had to walk all the way back to her room at the end of the hallway wearing nothing but two slippers and holding a Kleenex box in front of her.

I was therefore prepared for all kinds of practical joke warfare, and was surprised to find that very little seemed to go on at Durst. Mostly, the kids here just drank, it seemed. Perhaps our generation was simply a lot less creative and devoid of imagination compared to our parents.

Of course, there were the occasional stories that filtered through snorts and guffaws when you were sitting around and happened to be listening. Most of them were intertwined with alcohol. Like the guy who had passed out facedown in the middle of the common area lounge in another dorm. His buddies had acquired a condom, which they then proceeded to stretch out and place strategically down the back of his pants while he slumbered on unconsciously. I probably shouldn't have laughed when one of the football players relayed the story, but I did.

*****

One afternoon, when Caitlyn, Anise, and I went down to the lower level of the HUB as was customary after lunch to check our mailboxes and e-mail, I found mixed in with some fliers a plain, white envelope post-marked "Providence." My heart skipped a beat as I studied my name addressed in the vaguely familiar male handwriting.

"Coming Moll?" Caitlyn was waiting to go in the bookstore and do some browsing as we had planned.

I tucked the envelope in between the fliers and followed my two friends into the bookstore. As they shuffled through sweatshirt racks and held up various items for my opinion, I don't think I saw a single thing that they showed me. My mind was galaxies away, and all desire for shopping was lost in the overwhelming, dire impetus to get somewhere alone so I could read Hank's letter.

Finally, an hour later in the solitude of my room, with shaky fingers, I tore open the letter. It was sparse in the way of news, but full of little drawings and caricatures in the margins, depicting people and places from home. He started out, as customary, with tongue-in-cheek formality:

"Miss Molly,

"How is academia treating you? Get into any hefty debates yet with the 1960's throwbacks teaching your classes? Art School is pretty interesting. My ceramics teacher made a pass at me the first week of class. Between stumbling upon my gay roommate's enlightening porn collection and the incessant practicing from a saxophone aficionado across the hall, it's a little different than home.

"Rhode Island is okay. Kind of claustrophobic. I'm still scouting but I haven't found anyone with your fiery brand of wit who can go a whole round with me and hurl affronts with the exact timing and expertise that you possess.

Peace Out,

Hank

I read the letter over four times, sifting every word. The last line of it was the closest Hank would allow himself to come to paying me a compliment...or saying he missed me.

****

It took me three days to formulate a reply to Hank's letter, even though it's all I thought about during that time. I didn't want to appear overeager, nor did I want my letter to be a sentence longer than his. I agonized over everything from semantics down to whether I should write neatly in cursive or make it look haphazard in sloppier print. In the end, my letter to him looked like a badly marked up essay which just need a large red "F" at the bottom to complete it.

My feelings for Hank had to be so obvious to him, I thought. Surely my concentrated attempt to hide such emotions with the rigidity of the letter relayed their very potency. Disgusted with myself, I threw my response away in the trash can.

Chapter 7 – Guys and Dolls

Theta Chi looked remarkably different this time as Caitlyn and I gave our names to one of the guys standing guard at the front door, who checked us off a list he was holding, leaving us with the feeling of being minor celebrities. We followed a throng of laughing girls and their cloud of perfume into the spacious front room. Poker and Blackjack stations were set up all over the room where previously the beer pong tables had stood, and several lamps with pastel shades gave off an aura of affected romance and mystery. Instead of hip hop, bluesy jazz now oozed out of the speakers. The place was charged with restless energy, and for reasons unknown I felt my stomach do a flip-flop.

We had spent a great deal of time getting ready for this party, although both of us for different reasons. Caitlyn had wanted to dazzle Ryan, and I was simply excited to have the chance to dress up in post-World War II garb.

Caitlyn shone as usual, this time opting for the sweater girl look and sporting a tight knit shell and cardigan, coupled with waist-high shorts and slingback heels that she'd found at a local thrift shop. We had fallen all over ourselves howling with laughter after she'd buttoned the shorts three inches above her bellybutton.

"Look, they're up to my ribcage!" she'd shrieked. "Do these scream 'mom jeans' or what?"

"The only way you could possibly improve on that look would be to wear one of those cone-shaped bras," I'd agreed. "You know, the Marilyn Monroe type that looks like two rockets about to launch." As outdated and outrageous as the outfit was, Caitlyn of course, easily made it look great.

I was wearing a knee-length skirt and a ruffled blouse, complete with white seamed kid gloves, chunky heels, and a flower-pot style hat. A cheap cameo clung to my throat on a choker.

Unlike Caitlyn, I hadn't spent any money on my ensemble. The kid gloves and cameo I'd gotten in high school when Kendra and I dressed up one time for a *Gone with the Wind* party in which we'd watched the film fully attired in hats and gloves (which now seemed hopelessly juvenile of us). The hat was a part of my collection from my short-lived *chapeau* phase, when I had nostalgically hoped to revive a trend that pretty much died in the 1950s.

There had been no end to the number of parties we'd seen hosted on campus since our arrival such a short time ago, either. We'd been to two other fraternity parties besides Theta Chi, and one that was just in the dorms. That bitter, stale smell of beer-saturated carpet was becoming familiar, and I was slowly gaining a first-hand education on the nuances of what constituted hard alcohol and when it was appropriate to drink that in concurrence with beer. Caitlyn and I, however, had steadfastly managed to avoid drinking anything, although at the last party she had nursed the same full beer for three hours without taking a sip, choosing instead to imbibe the attention of the adoring males around her, until we finally and mercifully left.

"We're practically the only girls dressed up here," Caitlyn whispered to me anxiously, as we caught the frosty stare of a tank-top clad, little brunette wearing skin-tight, below-the-hip jeans which were low enough to reveal a butterfly tattoo just where her back met her rear end.

"Well, we're the only ones that have a sense of fun, then," I replied, returning the gaze of Butterfly Butt levelly until she abruptly looked away. "Besides, Ryan told us people were dressing up."

"I hope *he's* dressed up," Caitlyn said.

"Where is Mr. Chiseled Chin anyway?" I muttered to myself, scanning the noisy room.

"Molly!" someone boomed my name. I turned to see Jon from my German class lumbering toward me with a beer in his hand. He was wearing pin-striped pants and a matching jacket, shirttail half untucked. I glanced down at his feet, but he had traded the smelly Birkenstocks for a pair of wingtips instead. "Nice threads," he told me, before giving me a long hug as if we were dear old friends who'd finally been reunited, and not two people who'd seen one another hours before in a German class.

"I think you've met Caitlyn," I said, gesturing towards her.

"Caitlyn!" he boomed, giving her an equally long hug, at which she giggled.

"Ryan asked me to take care of you two ladies and get you a drink," Jon said. "Follow me!" He gave a wobbly gesture that I took to mean we were to go towards the back of the room.

As we followed his zigzag path through a maze of flesh, I took in the architecture of the old house a second time. Crown molding edged the high ceilings, and the ceramic tile surrounding the hollowed fireplace was still intact. There was an adjoining space off the large front room that must have originally been designed for formal dining; it now was outfitted with a high bar and pretty much nothing else. On the cracked plaster walls, as through the rest of the house, hung lopsided portraits of the Theta Chi fraternities from days gone by. I studied the crazy hair styles and confident smirks on the officers from the 1982-1983 fraternity as I stood in line with Caitlyn and Jon, wondering in the back of my mind where these guys were now and what they had done with their lives since they had left the scene I was now experiencing.

"What do you want to drink?" Jon asked us, cutting into my thoughts. "Beer? Wine? A cocktail?"

Caitlyn looked at me as if I were better suited to handle this question.

"Just a soda," I said, eyeing the colorful mix of bottles at the bar.

"No rum in that?" the bartending frat brother asked me, eyebrows raised.

"Not right now," I replied.

"You gotta have something a little more exciting than that," Jon said derisively. "Bill, add a splash of Jack to that."

"No, thanks," I said lightly, taking my cup from the bar before the afore-named Bill could add anything else to it.

Jon turned to Caitlyn in a way that suggested he expected more sophisticated behavior out of her.

"I'll – I'll have a glass of wine," she said in response to the look he gave her.

"Now you're talking," Bill the bartender said, whisking a plastic goblet from a stack and uncorking a huge bottle with a label that read "Chardonnay." He filled the glass nearly to the brim and handed it to her.

"Love the outfit," a voice said next to me. I turned to face the guy with the silver hoop earrings that I'd seen the week before at Theta Chi's first party.

"Graeme!" Jon hollered, baptizing my shoe with beer as he leaned across me to grasp his hand. I took a step back and tried subtly to fling the beer droplets from my toe. "Graeme, this is Molly," he slurred, gesturing dramatically. "Molly...Graeme."

"Great threads," Graeme smiled admiringly, taking my hand as he gave my old-fashioned duds the once-over. "We met once before."

I nodded. Graeme was decked out from head to foot in a red-checked zoot suit, pants pulled high above his waist, complete with a fedora. The effect was strangely compelling. I could picture Hank in something like this, and he'd easily get away with it.

"Well, this is the friend I told you about that I wanted you to meet," Jon said enthusiastically, spit flying onto my knuckles as he spoke. I delicately placed my hand over my cup to avoid any renegade saliva making its way into my beverage. "Graeme's an associate member of Theta Chi....you two kids have fun." Jon patted Graeme on the back before emptying the last of his brew down his throat.

"I'm Molly's roommate," Caitlyn announced, holding high her glass of wine so that she could present him with her hand, along with the Miss America smile that she congenially bestowed on all men, which so easily lent them the impression that they were the only ones on earth.

"Caitlyn, nice to meet you. Ryan's talked about you quite a bit," Graeme said, taking her hand. Caitlyn giggled and kind of did a little shrug.

"Speaking of which, here he comes now," Jon said, wiping his mouth with his sleeve and letting out a long, low belch. "Gotta get some more liquid. Be back," he said, making a hasty exit.

Ryan was looking magnificent as usual in a single-breasted suit jacket, which was open to reveal a wide, eggplant-colored tie. He gave off the appearance as though he'd just finished up a modeling shoot for a documentary on mid-20th century America. There was an aura about him as well that indicated he *knew* he looked good. Striding through the crowd, he came over and kissed Caitlyn on the cheek. She, in turn, gave him a tiny, charming laugh combined with an award-winning smile.

"Well, would you like to play some blackjack?" Graeme asked me. The subtle upturn of his smile reminded me of Hank.

"Sure," I replied uncertainly.

Ryan and Caitlyn joined us at a table and the four of us began to play. Jon had explained to me when he gave me the initial invitation that the fraternities were not licensed to hold a real gambling party, but everyone was designated with a certain amount of chips and in lieu of money, these could be cashed in for various door prizes.

"I'm surprised Jon's not playing," Ryan said to Graeme. "He never misses a chance to gamble."

"He's half in the bag already," Graeme replied, not looking up from his hand. "Besides, he likes playing for the big bucks."

I watched Caitlyn frown and purse her lips together as she took a sip of her wine before setting it back down. I wondered if she'd ever tasted wine before.

We played several rounds of blackjack, with Graeme winning most of the time. Whoops and hollers were being heard around the room from other winners, and I had to admit I was having a good time. I had learned to play blackjack and other card games on a youth group retreat, ironically, so I knew what I was doing.

"Don't you like your wine?" Ryan asked, eyeing Caitlyn's full glass.

"It's okay," she said.

"Want me to get you something else?" he asked.

"No, this is good." She took another sip, longer this time.

We played another hand. Graeme won with two queens.

"I'm out," Ryan said, pushing himself away from the table and taking a long, last draught of his beer. "Want to walk around?" he asked Caitlyn. She nodded.

Caitlyn turned to me and asked in a whisper, "Is it okay to leave you two alone?"

"Sure," I said, with total uncertainty. I grabbed her hand and whispered low in her ear. "By the way, I'm not leaving this party without you. So when you're ready to go, let me know."

"Okay," Caitlyn agreed. I watched her walk off with Ryan, who put his arm around her shoulders in a way that denoted ownership.

"I need a refill," Graeme said, peering into his empty plastic cup. "How about you?"

"I'm okay," I said.

After making our way back to the bar, which was packed, we waded through the party-goers, who were growing increasingly louder, to the back door and out to the patio. Kids were sitting on top of a picnic table, some smoking, some drinking, and a guy and a girl were all over each other at one end of the table. Another group was off to the side playing a game of Quarters, in which the object was to bounce a quarter off the ground and into a cup of alcoholic beverage, then pass it to the next person. If successful, you drank the contents of the cup. Someone else was retching in the bushes that lined the backyard fence.

"Nice," Graeme commented in the general direction of the shrub-puker.

I was slightly mortified by the whole scene. It seemed surreal, like a weird dream that you are aware, even while you're dreaming it, must *only* be a dream.

"So, do you not drink or what?" Graeme asked, evidently not at all alarmed by the happenings surrounding us.

"No," I answered, flexing my fingers and examining one of my gloves.

"Why not?" he asked simply.

"I'm only eighteen, and it's against the law."

Graeme's face broke into a half grimace, half smile. "Is that the *only* reason?" he asked.

I thought about it. "That's the main reason," I concluded.

"So you never break the rules is what you're saying," he questioned slyly.

He already had me pegged as a goody two-shoes, I realized. I resented instantly my sense that he felt a little more secure knowing that he had categorized me. The tell-tale pounding of my heart suddenly started, the way it always slams when I know I'm going to have the opportunity to talk about my faith and yet might cop out on actually sharing.

"I wouldn't say *that,*" I responded evenly, determined not to let him ruffle me. "But I do believe in obeying the laws and authorities placed over us, even if I don't necessarily agree with them."

"So...let me get this straight," Graeme said, the mental re-evaluation of what made me tick that was going on in his head was now translating itself to his face. "You don't agree with the drinking age, but you're going to obey it because it's the law."

"Yep," I replied. "Actually, I totally *disagree* with the drinking age in this state being twenty-one. It's ridiculous. By age eighteen we're old enough to vote for candidates and vote legislation into being, and we're capable of enlisting in the military or being drafted and going off to fight and even die for our country. Worst of all," I smiled mischievously, "We're old enough to make the decision to get married. All these things have much more dangerous effects than drinking alcohol."

Graeme's features, which indicated he had been studying me intently, relaxed into a grin. "Good point," he said. "So why do you believe so strongly you should follow a law you actually think is bunk?"

"Because," I began slowly, pulling on the finger of my left glove. My voice was quiet. "I'm a Christian, and as Christians, we're commanded to obey those in authority over us, so long as what they say doesn't contradict any of God's ordinances. I don't personally see anything wrong with drinking alcohol – in moderation," I glanced over at the individual who was still holding his stomach, studying the grass up close over by the fence. "In fact, the first miracle Jesus performed was turning water into wine." I stopped for a moment, thinking that there were still Christians out there who I knew honestly thought he turned the water into not-from-concentrate grape juice. "However, since it's the law, I believe I should follow it out of devotion to God's will."

"Well," Graeme acquiesced. "I can see you really believe this stuff. Personally, I think you should relax and live a little."

I smiled and simply said, "I *am* living."

I could hear the party raging on inside and wondered whether I should check on Caitlyn. I soon got distracted from thoughts of Caitlyn as Graeme asked me about where I was from and how I ended up at Durst and so on. In talking with him I discovered that he was a junior and he came from a town in Connecticut near Hartford, and that he had an older sister. He was planning to go for his MBA after Durst.

"I thought at one time about going to culinary school," he admitted. "I love to cook. I was afraid, though, that if it turned into a job I had to do, sooner or later I'd start to hate it."

An artist of sorts, I thought. *Like Hank.*

We kept talking and I found out that among other tastes, he was a big fan of author Kurt Vonnegut and loved The Who.

Somewhere in the back of my mind I wondered what Hank thought of Kurt Vonnegut. I was sure he'd read at least some of his work. Hank was capable of classifying pop culture as either ultra-cool or unforgivably lame in a way that forever sealed something in my mind. For example, *South Park* was feeble because Hank deemed it so. *The Simpsons,* however, was higher entertainment. When Hank said it, you just didn't argue. It might as well be canonized.

I remembered the English class he and I had had together the last year. Our teacher, Mrs. Bard, had posed the question "Who are your modern heroes?" Alison Eppley, our senior homecoming-queen-turned-wannabe-hippie, raised a turquoise-bedecked hand and replied slowly, "I don't think there *is* such a thing as a hero any more. What's a hero to one person won't necessarily be a hero to another." She was too popular for the rest of us mere mortals in AP English to contradict, so Mrs. Bard kind of gave a nod and waited. Only Hank had spoken up.

"What about that guy who pulled the little girl out of the well?" he demanded. "He was a hero. I don't think anyone would have said, 'No, keep her down there.'" At this, the whole class had roared.

I felt a pang at the thought of Hank. I wondered what he was doing at that very moment, who he was with. "I'd better check on Caitlyn," I said, suddenly returning to the present and realizing that it was after midnight.

"Alright, if you want," he agreed.

Back inside the fraternity house, the noise had risen several decibels and the house was jam packed. Graeme had told me that after eleven the private party would end and the house would be open to the whole campus. Caitlyn was nowhere to be found, though we searched the entire downstairs. I began to get panicky when we came out to the porch and she still wasn't there.

"They probably went to Ryan's room for some quiet," Graeme said.

"Where's Ryan's room?" I wanted to know.

Graeme led me up the huge, wooden staircase to the second floor. I could smell the sickly sweet scent of marijuana as we ascended, and I felt a little woozy.

"This way," Graeme said. We turned down a short hall to a door that was decorated with a Jimi Hendrix poster. Graeme knocked.

There was no answer.

He knocked again, then pushed open the door.

My eyes adjusted to the dim light provided only by a lava lamp and a candle. Caitlyn was half sitting, half lying on the pillows on the bed next to Ryan. She looked up at me slowly through bleary eyes that weren't focusing.

"Hi, Molly!" she grinned sloppily. "Come in and party with us!"

I looked at the cup she raised unsteadily and saw that she must have switched over to sampling beer. If I had had to guess, it was not her first one, either.

"Caitlyn, it's late," I said. "Let's go home."

"Aw, c'mon," Ryan said. "You can't go yet. It's early"

I looked at Caitlyn imploringly.

Caitlyn giggled. "It's early," she parroted. "It's…What time is it?" her unsteady gaze searched the room for a clock. They came to rest on Ryan's alarm clock. "It's almost one in the morning. See how early it is!"

"Look," Ryan spoke up. "I'll see that she gets home. Don't worry about it."

"I'm not leaving without her," I insisted.

He was getting annoyed, I could tell. "Seriously, *don't worry about it*. I'll take care of her."

A hot flush stole over my neck as I felt a confrontation coming on between us. I dreaded and avoided altercations, but when pushed past a certain point I was powerless not to react. "I told Caitlyn I would not leave this party without her, and I'm not," I assured him boldly. "Now if you'll excuse me." I walked over to Caitlyn, plucked the beer cup from her hand, and held out a gloved palm to her. Grasping it, she rose shakily to her feet.

"Molly, it's Friday night, why do you *possibly* need to get home so soon?" Ryan demanded. "Can't you just relax? I told you I'd take care of her."

If there's one thing I consistently hate, it's being told to relax. I wanted to deepen that cleft in his chin with an elbow, but instead silently pushed past boorish Ryan with Caitlyn in tow.

"It was nice talking to you, Graeme," I mumbled hurriedly as I dragged my roommate through the doorway.

Caitlyn was having definite trouble maneuvering the steps to go downstairs. Graeme walked with us as far as the front porch, where Caitlyn began to flirt in exaggerated movements with the bouncer.

"Do you want me to walk you guys home?" Graeme asked.

"Nah, don't worry about it," I replied, eager to peel Caitlyn away before she attached herself to someone else.

"You sure? Well, good night then," Graeme said. I turned, escorting my sloppy sidekick down the porch stairs like one might help a toddler who is learning to walk.

"Wait! Molly?" Graeme called after me. "What's your cell phone number?"

"Don't have one," I answered over my shoulder. "But my extension's in the directory."

"I'll call you," he promised, waving.

I managed to get Caitlyn back to the dorm in record time. She fell only once, flat on her face in the grass. She lay there until I shook her shoulder and helped pull her up. Moments later, she asked me if she'd just fallen a few minutes ago.

"Yes," I assured her. "How many drinks did you have, by the way?"

"Two or three...beers," she answered, swaying off to the side before I grabbed her hand. "I don't remember."

"How many glasses of wine did you drink?" I demanded, alarmed. My mind was racing back to high school health class and everywhere else we'd studied alcohol consumption. I hadn't realized at the time that I'd ever need to apply the information to practical life.

"Um..." Caitlyn nearly walked into a parking sign. I yanked her out of the way just in time. "I don't know," she said absently, staggering under the force of my pull. "Two?"

I feverishly tried to conjure all the calculations I'd learned about percentage of alcohol in beer versus wine and how long it took the liver to process it, etc. I couldn't recollect anything I'd learned, except for the mental picture of old Mr. Zangari, our cranky, crusty, disillusioned driver's ed. teacher, bellowing "Coffee does *not* make someone sober! Sticking them in the shower does *not* make someone sober! Gotta let the liquor run its course!"

We were nearly up the stairs to the hallway when Caitlyn mumbled, "I think I'm going to be sick," and detoured abruptly into the girls' bathroom.

I trailed after her, wincing at the sound of vomiting coming from one of the stalls.

"Caitlyn?" I called, rounding the corner to where the toilets were lined up. "Are you okay?"

"Ugh," I heard her sigh and the toilet flush. "Yeah, I'm okay." She emerged pale-faced from one of the stalls, clutching a tissue. She steadied herself against the wall. "Just remind me never to do that again."

I got her some water and helped her into bed, figuring that if she had upchucked the alcohol the dangers of any potential poisoning were fading. I was so tired I slept straight through the night and remembered nothing I dreamt. I awoke around six to hear Caitlyn grabbing the trash can and running out the door. I pulled the pillow over my head and went back to sleep, feeling smugly superior in my sobriety.

Chapter 8 – The Slippery Slope

The Caitlyn-Ryan romance ended just as quickly as it had begun. When he neglected to call for the next two days, we knew something had changed in their brief liaison. She later found out through a series of informational tidbits leaked by various people that Ryan had met another freshman girl the night of the Theta Chi party who had swept him off his inebriated feet, and apparently, that was that.

Caitlyn initially was crushed and spent all of that following Sunday moping around the room and sighing, until out of the blue one of the guys from her Sociology 101 called and asked her to go with him to Mookie's, on the corner across from the football field, for ice cream. The invitation evidently revived her back to health, and she hugged me quickly before she sashayed out the door.

"If Dave calls, tell him I'm at the library," she called over her shoulder as she shut the door behind her.

I made no reply, but grabbed my books, figuring I'd go to the library myself so as to avoid that awkward scene.

Walking across campus and gazing at the beautiful structures and grounds that had been standing there for over two centuries, it always made me think of the many, many souls who had come and gone before me. What mark – what imprint, was mine to leave – on the school and on the world? How fortunate indeed I was that the answer to that question for me didn't involve the pressure of relying entirely on myself to figure it out. I had a Great Big God who would lead me in the way He had planned for me since before I was born. All I had to do was to be faithful.

Entering the library gave me a sense of awe at all the knowledge packed in the endless volumes that dominated the space. The portraits of gray-haired men lining its walls stared out sternly at me, as if they already sensed I was a misfit on their campus. I vowed then and there that if ever someone were to do a portrait of me that was to hang in a place of academia or other somber institution, I would be sure to strike a pose that would make people stop to read my name and find out who on earth was *that* lady with those crazy eyes and that maniacal smile? I would not be another mug that nobody so much as glanced at before walking on.

Before finding a cubicle to invade for a couple hours of quiet, I decided to check my e-mail at one of the computers available to students for 15-minute intervals. My stomach did a tell-tale flip-flop at the sight of "Graeme Reddig" in the Inbox. I opened it to find a brief message professing the fun he had at the Guys and Dolls party Friday night, and asking me would I want to get together for dinner Tuesday night.

My heart began to slam loudly in my chest like one of those bass drums at high school football games. Its strident beating was so audible, in fact, that I looked around the stillness of the library to see if anyone might have heard it. All my life I'd been warned against the pitfalls of dating non-Christian guys. I was familiar with the command not to be unequally yoked with nonbelievers, and it wasn't hard to figure out some of the reasons why it might be prudent to heed such advice.

In another part of my mind, though, I was acutely aware that taking this very same advice is what had led to my almost non-existent dating social life. I had never had a boyfriend throughout high school, having deftly evaded the pursuits of the dubious elect that had conveyed their interest in me through varying times and methods. There had been the football coach's delinquent older son, Jeff, whose interest I'd somehow garnered quite unintentionally and whom I'd effectively run from when he tried to kiss me behind the stadium once. There was Shawn Curtis from youth group (whom I always called Curtis Shawn in my head whenever I saw him), a nice kid but who raised the sentiment of pity, not affection, in my heart, and whose deep, open-mouthed breathing I could never quite get past. There had been Trevor Merret, a self-proclaimed motor head who had shared a shop class with me freshman year and beyond that, with whom I had absolutely nothing foreseeable in common. The more I resisted Trevor, the more he doggedly hung on and kept re-surfacing throughout freshman and sophomore years (until he finally dropped out mid-way through junior). There had been my well-meaning friends, Lee Smoker and Thad Legume, who had, within a week of one another, asked me to the senior prom and who had both been dolefully rejected out of a secret determination that it would be either Hank or else going stag with my girlfriends to mark that momentous occasion (and so it had been the latter, lending strain to both these male friendships after I'd gently declined).

Yes, the parade of y-chromosomed admirers through my adolescent life had been both scant and questionable. Of course, I had no intention of letting a relationship with a non-Christian guy like Graeme get serious. I just wanted to have a little bit of harmless fun – go on a couple dates, gain some experience – before I hit my twenties. What was wrong with that? After all, all I really wanted was to have a taste of youth like any normal teenager.

A voice spoke out quietly in protest somewhere in my mind, but I extinguished its reasoning before I hit "reply" and wrote the single word "Yes."

*****

After trying for an hour without success to concentrate on the text I was supposed to be reading for world history, I departed from the deafening hush of the library and headed out into the open air. I felt troubled. Perhaps I just needed some perspective, and from someone more erudite than I.

Anise and I had become close friends over the past couple of weeks since the bleaching incident. It surprised me because we had – at least superficially – so little in common. Our backgrounds and lifestyles were as different as Country Mouse and City Mouse, and I secretly wondered why someone who was so sophisticated and worldly found sufficient common ground in my company. Perhaps it was that we shared the same wicked sense of humor, or maybe it was because Anise seemed so grounded despite her more entitled lifestyle.

Anise didn't have a campus job – nor did she apparently have any need for one, as her father supplied every material thing that she possibly needed – but she expressed that she wouldn't mind getting one so long as it didn't involve interacting with stupid people. She supposed that this limited her options quite a bit.

"My idea of customer service is leaving off 'damn it!' at the end of 'what do you want?'" she explained unapologetically one day while we were standing in line at the deli. "I have no patience for people who are rude or who can't make up their minds. I'm not exactly the customer service rep type."

She spoke frankly about her family's wealth, yet without boasting. She was grateful for what she had, accustomed to it as she might be. I knew that her father was making millions with his plastic surgery.

Anise often relayed stories of some of the work people had had done through her dad's practice. I would listen in silent shock as she prattled away about additions or subtractions to various parts of their bodies– some more critical than others – that were for her, as routine as an orthodontist applying or removing braces.

"I think for my graduation gift from college, I'm going to ask my dad for new breasts," Anise had announced matter-of-factly once while we were in the cafeteria.

I had stared at my chicken sandwich for a full four seconds before I was able to form a reply.

"Oh?" was all I'd finally managed. It was difficult to imagine going under the knife in the first place, but having that particular procedure done by your *father?*

"Yep," she had said decidedly. "I hate how tiny I am up top."

My thoughts on plastic surgery were splintered. I was vain enough not to rule it out for myself some day – when I was old and saggy and say, 40 years old – yet I believed there was far too much attention paid to the exterior, and not what was going on inside and coming out of the mind. I had read somewhere that girls my age were the largest group getting plastic surgery, and that had disturbed me.

"Personally, I think what your dad already gave you *naturally* looks great," I had offered drolly after a few moments. "You're beautiful *and* proportional."

"Well, thanks," Anise had said. "But, when I'm twenty-one, there'll be a little more of Anise than there used to be."

Anise answered my knock at the door dancing in rhythm to some techno-sounding music. She smiled and continued dancing and echoing the lyrics as I wandered into her room. Her place always *smelled* so good, too, with some exotic fragrance of an expensive perfume perpetually hanging in the air.

She kept dancing until the song finally came to an abrupt end, and she hit the "stop" button on her stereo. "What's up, woman?" she asked.

"I'm not really sure," I replied truthfully. "I need some advice."

I proceeded to tell her about Graeme's e-mail invitation to dinner, my admitted attraction to him, and the dilemma of feeling it was already somehow a big mistake.

"Why couldn't he pick up the telephone and call you?" Anise asked. "How hard is that? Seriously, what is it with men these days?" She sank backwards across from me on Jill's empty bunk, shaking her head woefully like an eighty year-old, rather than an eighteen year-old. "They really could make a little effort."

"Well, at any rate, I told him I'd go," I said, trying to get back to the heart of the matter. "I don't know...I just feel somehow...like I'm *betraying* someone."

"To tell you the truth, I don't understand this hold the kid from high school has on you," Anise said point blank, picking up my implication purely to mean Hank. I had mentioned him to Anise once when she'd asked if I had a boyfriend, regretting how juvenile it sounded the moment it left my lips. "I mean, I get the idea from listening to you that he walks on water."

I was silent, feeling a faint, tell-tale blush stealing up my neck and ears.

"So, what's so great about him?" Anise asked genuinely. "I mean, he must be really something. Tell me."

How could I describe to someone who'd never met him all the charm and originality that comprised Hank Bobek? There was no one like him, simply stated. Never could be again in this era, I was sure. He was genius without a hint of dorkiness, he was riotously funny yet possessed a definitive subtlety that added volumes to his appeal. He had one of those rare "old souls" that made him before his time and yet ahead of everyone else. He was a maverick, yet fit in easily with the mainstream herd around him.

In school he had been popular across the various cliques, the one that the snooty females in homecoming court didn't necessarily possess the brains to wish to date, yet with whom they all wanted to be friends. He was athletic although not a superstar, with his sport of choice being golf. Even the teachers had been subject to him.

Although he didn't always let on, Hank understood people and what motivated their behavior, and he had the gift of being able to read them like pamphlets. It had therefore genuinely surprised me just as much as it had caused my well-regulated heart to palpitate that night in August, when he had confided to me that I was one of only three people from home whom he'd truly miss.

"The rest are just clones," he'd admitted drearily, naming some of the more popular people who used to throng him. "They'll get by in life with bachelor degrees and four-bedroom homes and two-point-five kids and the occasional trip to Europe, and they'll imagine that's all there is."

It was beyond even his perceptiveness, though. Hank and I were fashioned from the same discontinued metal, cut from the same vintage fabric, and it was so rare to find it in someone else. It was as though he and I had been destined for a former generation, yet had somehow mistakenly ended up in this one, a foreign world in which we were forced to function and survive among the bleating masses, yet meant for another place and time.

What it came down to was that Hank understood me, and I believed I understood him – far better than those silly popular-bots that paraded before the stands during the football games, or even the artsy girls, with their pencil-thin figures, affected quirks and variations of grunge. They wanted so badly to be seen as deep and unique, but they weren't really. Not in the way that Hank was. His singularity did not stem from nor mask a stark insecurity, nor did it depend on any one factor such as the way he dressed or the fact that he was a natural artist. He was simply Hank.

To love someone seemed a simple enough task, but to *understand* another person...well, that was quite a different depth. Therein lay his appeal for me.

"So you've said you guys never dated, right?" Anise asked.

"N-no, not in the true sense of the word," I admitted.

"He never asked you out or told you anything to believe he has a thing for you?" Anise continued.

I shook my head, feeling suddenly humbled and unusually dejected.

"Well, then I'd say it's time to redirect your affections somewhere else," Anise surmised. Her tone lowered and turned gentler as she read my expression. "Why waste time in life liking someone who may or may not like you? Besides, maybe this is your big chance to find out that the hometown boy isn't the only starfish in the sea."

I pondered this wisdom throughout the rest of the evening and well into the night, long after Caitlyn had returned in high spirits from her date, filling me in on all the details of her latest male fascination. Anise was right, I believed. What were all those sayings about unrequited love? What if Hank never gave me any indication he wanted to pursue a relationship with me other than an ambiguous, offhand note sent whenever it occurred to him to cast a passing thought towards me? What if I waited year after year for an epiphany of his affection until I slowly turned into a stodgy, decrepit, old maid in her late twenties, living at home and watching reruns on television with her parents? What if I never experienced "rapture before the rapture," so to speak, and died celibate? The mere thought was haunting enough to compel me to start dating immediately in true Caitlyn fashion.

Of course, forgetting Hank's existence would not be an easy accomplishment under any circumstances. I'd been secretly dreaming about him since I was fifteen, and had already made up my mind to marry him some distant day after college, probably when I was twenty-five. Anise was right, though. Since he had never given me any encouragement or indication that he felt the same way –it really was madness to go on dreaming about someone who wasn't dreaming of me. If I couldn't entirely forget Hank, I could at least try to distract myself.

My uneasiness had to do with a lot more than just Hank, though, and I couldn't possibly have expected Anise to answer with wisdom the other side of my doubts that related to the fact that Graeme did not share my beliefs. Lying in bed, I rolled over and flipped on my back, then reversed to my stomach, before repeating this pattern several times. I breathed deeply several times, trying to relax away the restlessness. It was two-thirty in the morning the last time I remembered glancing ruefully at the thin, red numbers of the clock.

*****

"Tomorrow night, right?" I heard the voice say. I looked up to see Graeme standing in front of me on the other side of the dessert counter in the cafeteria, tossing an orange up in the air and catching it. Wow, in the three days since I'd last seen him, I'd forgotten how cute he was.

It felt deeply humiliating to be standing there in my paper hat and hideous white apron, holding a spatula. Caitlyn could have made it look sexy for sure, but not me. I wondered for a moment if I'd find another e-mail from him later, revoking our date.

"Tomorrow night," I agreed, feeling my heart thump rhythmically.

He smiled. "I'll meet you at seven-thirty at your dorm." He took a step backwards, still looking at me and smiling.

"What should I wear?" I called after him. "I mean," I mumbled, lowering my voice as I noticed some stares in my direction from other tray-bearing kids. "What kind of place are we going to?"

"You know, casual." He grinned, a malicious twinkle in his eyes. "But better ditch the hat and apron."

I winced as he walked away, fiddling with my paper cap that made me look like some sort of reject from the Navy. I wondered anxiously what I even had in my wardrobe that passed for "casual" and not "frumpy." Perhaps Caitlyn would let me borrow something.

Chapter 9 – First Date

Apparently, I was not the only rookie who was experiencing masculine advances around campus. Kendra shot me an e-mail detailing her own little school soap opera.

"There's a senior – a red-headed, freckled guy – who approached me yesterday on the way to Chem and told me that as soon as first semester was over and the dating ban lifted, he was going to ask me out. When I told him that I wasn't interested, he said that God told him to pursue me," she wrote. *"Unfortunately, I felt no attraction to him at all, and in fact, was kind of repulsed by the whole experience."*

Her e-mail made me snort out loud in the computer lab, jerking heads all around me to my direction. I inched down in my seat before hitting "reply."

"God *told him?*" I replied scornfully. *"If he comes up to you again, you should tell him 'If God told you to ask me out, then He'll most certainly give you the grace to understand when I refuse.'"*

I decided not to tell Kendra about Graeme. She would only chide, and I didn't need to hear that right now. I knew what I was doing.

*****

"Casual or upscale casual?" Caitlyn quizzed me, as I prepared for the dinner date with Graeme. We were looking through her closet.

"What's the difference?" I asked doubtfully.

Caitlyn began to explain, giving me a crash course in Fashion 101 as she sifted through skirts and tops. Her clothing was trendy and much nicer than most of my outfits, but I secretly preferred Anise's more daring, flamboyant style, with its flair for the extraordinary. As I could not fit into anything petite Anise owned, however, I felt fortunate enough to be able to borrow from Caitlyn.

After pulling numerous items and me modeling them, we finally selected a simple white stretch fitted shirt and a plum-colored, tiered skirt to go with it. I had to smile when I viewed my reflection in the full-length mirror on our door. I looked nice, I thought, but I didn't look like me. If Hank had been there, he would have made some flippant remark about my being all set to vacation in Martha's Vineyard or something. Hank always had a gently smart quip for any situation.

Anise walked in just as Caitlyn was helping me straighten my hair.

"*Very* nice," she drawled. "If *I* were a man…"

As Caitlyn continued her transforming handiwork on me by applying eye shadow and powder, Anise went to retrieve some "bling" for me – a fuchsia, spiral bracelet and a woven, beaded handbag – in order to spruce up the neutral tones of the outfit.

After Caitlyn had applied the final brushstrokes, and Anise had sprayed me with one of her costly fragrances, the two of them stepped back and gazed at me like some exotic painting that they had taken great pains to touch up and were hoping would sell on auction.

"Wow, Molly," Caitlyn said. "You look fantastic. Like a different person."

"Thanks," I said slowly, receiving the compliment with some uncertainty.

"Hot," Anise remarked, nodding her head slowly up and down. "Graeme's gonna fall flat on his face in a daze."

Since I was ready a full half hour before Graeme was expected, I tried to busy myself with something to do. I was suddenly worried that we'd have nothing to talk about and we'd sit there and stare into our plates. The Guys and Dolls party hadn't been a problem because there had been stuff to do and other people were present. I wondered if I should jot down a listing of potential topics of interest to keep in my purse and refer to in the event there were any awkward silences. Nah, that would be entirely too nerdy.

When Graeme buzzed our room twenty minutes later, Anise ran to unlock the door. "Wait here," she instructed me. "You don't want to appear too overeager or like you've been ready for a long time. Make *him* wait."

Obediently, I sat where I was, running my hands over my now perfectly-straight hair for about the thousandth time, and checking my reflection for the hundredth.

Moments later, Graeme walked into the room, looking especially handsome in a black button down shirt, khakis, and wingtips. I gave him a nervous, little smile.

"Molly," he said, looking me over, his smile widening as took in my appearance. "You look great." I relaxed a little at the compliment. I *felt* as though I looked pretty great – I wasn't accustomed to wearing much make-up or dressing up for anything other than a special occasion.

The jittery feeling returned quickly as Graeme held the door for me, and the feeling that my pulse was doing sprints around the perimeter of my body continued as we drove to the restaurant in his black SUV. I didn't say much, and instead concentrated on staring out the window and breathing in the heavy, dizzying scent of his cologne.

Graeme had chosen a restaurant about five miles out of town called "Portofino." As we walked in my eyes adjusted to the candlelight and smoky mirrors and paintings of Tuscan landscapes and villas in gilded frames, and when we sat down, they widened as I saw the prices on the menu. I felt too nervous to eat anyhow, and figured I would get some soup.

"Their trout almandine is out of this world," Graeme said, taking a sip of his water. "So is their beef Wellington." I didn't ask him how he knew this, or on what previous occasions he'd dined here.

The courses were written in Italian and I had to read their descriptions in order to gain any clue as to what they might be. I'd been to a restaurant this fancy only once in my life – for a rehearsal dinner at a cousin's wedding. I felt out of my element.

When the waiter came to take our drink order, I requested a soda and Graeme ordered a draught beer.

"Didn't even flinch," Graeme whispered with a triumphant smile when the waiter had left.

I raised my eyebrows quizzically.

"He didn't card me," Graeme explained. "My last fake ID was confiscated, and I don't turn twenty-one for another month, so in the meantime, I have to take the chance. Most places around school check, but I guess this place doesn't get a lot of college kids."

I still didn't like the whole beer thing and being deceptive about one's age, but it wasn't quite the shock it had been when we first encountered the Theta Chi party. I was growing more accustomed to it, and knew that Anise had maintained that being raised in an Italian home, they had always had wine with dinner since she could remember, and she often drank it at mealtimes. *She* wasn't an alcoholic. I juxtaposed this information with Caitlyn's state of inebriation the other night and figured that there might be legitimate advantages to growing up in a cultural climate in which alcohol is accepted and even expected, as opposed to having it outlawed and forbidden for years in the home, and then suddenly available in an environment where there were few boundaries. Growing up in Anabaptist America was like growing up under Prohibition. I had always sort of assumed that alcohol was fundamentally evil, which never had quite aligned with the fact that Jesus' first miracle was to turn water into wine at a wedding, and at the request of his mother, no less.

Graeme was studying me. "You're beautiful, you know that?" he said suddenly.

My heart stopped for three seconds. I felt my face going from hospital sheet white to fuchsia pink in a matter of seconds. I wasn't used to getting compliments from guys, or at least, not the ones that you could trust as a reliable source.

"You must have had a hundred boyfriends," Graeme went on as I slowly chameleoned back to my normal color.

I wasn't compelled to tell him how very wrong that supposition was, nor did I feel a need to enlighten him as to the true line-up of males I'd had in my brief scope of eligible dating. Not to mention the fact that I consistently seemed to be a strange-guy magnet, like the needy, romance-deprived maintenance man at Shady Oaks nursing home – my high school job – who must have been ten years older than me and who, with his unscrupulous gaze and prominent thatch of protruding chest hair, thoroughly creeped me out each time I chanced to encounter him coming out of work. He had tried unsuccessfully but doggedly to entice me into dates with the allure of the fact that he drove a Swedish-manufactured car (used), and every time he mentioned this source of pride, I pictured my lifeless body being stuffed unceremoniously into its trunk at the end of the doomed date.

"Leprechauns," Kendra had termed these clingy, needy little men that I had a flair for attracting. I smiled as I thought of my dear friend.

Graeme and I managed to keep the conversation going pretty well throughout the evening, and I learned that his father had been a trader on Wall Street for many years before getting burned out and making the big decision to move to the Hartford area and start his own consulting business. Graeme's mother managed some storage units that the family owned, but she had never had any kind of full-time employment outside of that. Graeme and his older sister had never spent a single day in the public school system, but had gone to private schools all the way up through college. His sister was now vice president at some advertising agency and commuted to New York, having bought a house in West Chester.

Graeme informed me that in high school, he had played baseball but had no desire to pursue it in college. He liked pretty much every kind of music out there except for country and classical (I inferred that Christian tunes were not in that mix) and he told me all the television shows that he watched (another area of little common ground between the two of us, as I despised reality TV and was oversensitive to and disturbed at the scenes depicted in many of the crime dramas that dominated primetime).

Trips to New York City and Boston were standard fare for him, and he had been to Europe after graduation from high school with a group of his friends (the furthest I had traveled had been to Florida once to visit an aunt). He loved to ski (I had never even ventured out on a bunny slope) and had made various excursions to resorts in New England and Colorado.

My own background seemed comparatively drab as he extracted details of it from me. How to explain to someone like Graeme my affinity for old movies, classic television, and American literature? How to explain to him that a tune that was popular in the 1940s could stir my heart more than the insipid ballads of today, and that I preferred the scratchy sound of an LP to the empty perfection of an electronic download. I recognized the titles and tracks of music that were popular half a decade ago more so than I could have named any tune currently playing in one of the dorm rooms. To most people of my generation, I was aware that my tastes seemed positively eccentric.

Graeme listened politely as I answered his questions, with the look of one who is trying to decipher the tones of someone speaking in broken English, grasping only pieces of what I was trying to articulate of myself. He attempted valiantly to find common ground for my vintage predilections by asserting his fondness for Frank Sinatra. I nodded, thinking it best to refrain from telling him Sinatra was one of the few entertainers from the big band and silver screen era whom I simply couldn't stomach.

As Graeme speared his steak and I set my attentions to finagling my pasta around my fork, I thought back to a social studies class in which Hank had been sketching a caricature of the teacher when four of us were supposed to be working on some group project, and he had randomly turned to me, saying, "I was trying to remember the fourth member of Sun Studio's million dollar quartet...Elvis Presley, Jerry Lee Lewis, Johnny Cash, and...?"

"Carl Perkins," I had added easily.

"I'm impressed," he had said in awe, smiling broadly and giving me one of his looks that disintegrated my bone structure to mere gelatin. The supreme novelty of Hank, however, was not that he had that kind of old school knowledge, but that he could easily adapt to the shallow waters of today's pop culture and be just as charming, witty, and charismatic to the insipid minds around us as he could to the more profound (*like mine*, I thought truthfully). Of course, no one in our generation could have appreciated his singularity like I did. Of this, I was certain.

The food itself was outstanding (I had taken Graeme's recommendations for the entrée, and we'd split an appetizer), and by the end of the meal, I had managed to relax considerably, only to be wound up tightly in a ball of nerves as we got back in the car.

If I had been nervous before the date, I was even more skittish anticipating its conclusion. My heart began pounding again in wary anticipation as Graeme walked around the front of the vehicle to open my door and help me out.

"Thank you, Molly," Graeme said, turning after he'd walked me to the door, "For a delightful evening." He leaned in and kissed me on the cheek. I was rigid as a birch tree. He paused, and then I felt him leaning in to kiss me on the lips. I took an abrupt step backwards, dodging the kiss, and causing him nearly to fall. I stuck my hand out and grabbed his.

"Thanks for dinner, Graeme," I said quickly, shaking his hand, unwilling to meet his surprised look. I turned and fled into my dorm.

*****

You are such *a dork, Molly.* The voice in my head was relentless. I blushed every time I thought about the way the evening had ended, and since I was thinking about it all day, I was pretty sure that my skin had permanently changed to red.

I was dreading having to face Jon in German class the next day. It was very tempting to skip, even though I had predetermined not to skip *any* class at Durst short of landing in the emergency room. My parents were paying way too much in tuition.

Ugh, but Jon was friends with Graeme, and surely Graeme had told him about the unorthodox and awkward finale to our date. Recounting the evening's events to Anise and Caitlyn, I could only focus on the end.

"I wouldn't worry about it," Caitlyn assured me when I told her about my reluctance to see Graeme's friend in class. "Guys don't compare notes *nearly* as much as we girls do."

"That's very true," Anise weighed in. "When they *do* kiss and tell, they usually lie and exaggerate in the *other* direction. No guy is going to say a girl actually *ran* the other direction." She grinned, and then burst out laughing, falling back on the bunk. I blushed.

Caitlyn stepped in quickly, seeing my troubled expression. "I think it's kind of cute what you did, and I admire you for it," she affirmed. "You should never do anything with a guy or go any further than you want."

I went back and forth over whether to skip class. The temptation was mighty. But sooner or later I'd have to see Jon, and of course I'd run into Graeme. The campus was too small to avoid him. Thinking what a single class at Durst actually cost outweighed my cowardice to avoid it. I had to go. There was a quote I'd once read: "If you can't be brave, act like it. No one will know the difference." I decided to use that as my mantra, pushing it ahead of me like a banner into German class.

Frau Bund greeted me as I tip-toed into German to the beat of my own runaway heart. In her brightly colored floral dress, she resembled a maypole. I avoided Jon's gaze as I slid into the assigned seat next to him. Like most classes at the college, we were allowed to choose where we wanted to sit, but were mandated to stay in the same seat after the first day.

"What up," Jon said as I took my place.

"Hi," I mumbled back, unwilling to meet his eyes.

"Hey, I saw Frau last night with her husband out at the store," Jon whispered. "As skinny as *she* is, he's even thinner. In fact, I bet he weighs half of what she does and she could easily take him out."

"Is he German, too?" I asked, relieved to be talking about anything other than the subject most on my mind.

"Nah, he's a scrawny little American dude. Looks like a total wimp. I bet ya they role play in the bedroom and she dresses up in *Gestapo* drag and barks orders at him in German."

Inadvertently, I guffawed out loud at the mental picture. Frau Bund turned to me at once.

"*Naja*, Molly," she said. "Why don't you give us a summary of *die Aufklärung* from pages 16-24.

I had not read the homework assignment on "The Enlightenment" in its entirety. I had meant to read it, but was so worked up in trying to get ready for the date with Graeme that I kept putting it off for later. When I had returned late last night, I hardly felt like reading.

"I only read up to the part about *Sturm und Drang*," I confessed slowly. It sounded better than admitting I'd only read two pages. "Do you want me to summarize that?"

"I see," Frau said icily. "*Studenten,*" she turned to address everyone. "It is your choice of course, but if you do not bother with the homework, there is little purpose in you attending my class." She sighed heavily, sending the ruffles of her blouse fluttering. "Someone else who has *read* the assignment, *bitte*."

My face felt hot again, this time with a new humiliation. I was never one not to have an assignment completed.

Throughout the rest of German class until it finally ended fifty minutes later and we walked out into the warm September sunshine, Jon never mentioned or inquired about my date with Graeme. I began to wonder if Graeme just had such a rotten time that he didn't even want to *mention* our date?

Chapter 10 - Intolerance

After my morning classes were finished, I decided to skip lunch rather than chance an encounter with Graeme in the cafeteria. Instead, I decided to hole myself up in a cubicle in the back of the library. I was determined to do penance by completing not only last night's German assignment, but all the reading for the rest of the week. I had even used highlighters for areas I knew would come up in discussion. Frau would surely know I had not only read, but read with interest, when she saw my pages all marked up with fluorescent colors.

I read all about The Enlightenment in Germany, familiarizing myself a little better with Goethe and shuddering over the summary of the character in his work *Faust* – a doctor who promises his soul to the devil in exchange for knowledge and power. "Not a good trade there, ol' Faust," I mused aloud in my cubicle, wondering how anyone on earth could be foolish enough to pay with an eternal sentence for anything granted in this short life.

As I continued to read about Immanuel Kant and his attempts to define morality, I sighed. "'The Enlightenment' indeed," I mumbled, highlighting a final sentence before folding my textbook shut.

Walking back to the dorm, I saw Anise's roommate, Jill, hanging up posters with a guy I recognized as living in the Allies' dorm – the dorm for the sexually beleaguered, I thought.

"Hi, Jill," I called out to her, straining to make out the words on the poster. All I could detect was the familiar rainbow-colored triangle turned on its head, standing out prominently at the top of the bulletin like some discolored "Yield" sign.

"Hey, Molly," Jill replied detachedly, glancing briefly at me without slowing her efforts with the poster.

"Now let's go plaster the HUB," her companion said authoritatively, ignoring my presence and gesturing with a ring-clad finger towards the main building.

Nearing the poster I could discern that it was for a rally to be held the following week on the lawn outside of Old Main, the most central building on campus. The poster appealed to tolerance and purported to promote "better understanding and awareness of gay, lesbian, bisexual, and transsexual issues and persons" on campus.

I mused over the poster and its proponents as I made my way back to Watson. I had had a friend throughout elementary school, Evan Hegley, who "came out" in high school. He had endured some ridicule at the hands of the same thuggish few who dished out most of the ridicule in the school. It pained me when he'd later testified about the words they'd assigned to him to make him feel less than human.

While my camaraderie with Evan hadn't ended or even altered much after his announcement, I knew that the homosexual lifestyle was a dead-end road and wished I could express my concerns without losing his friendship entirely. There just didn't seem to be any good way to approach that one, so I figured that the best thing to do was to continue to be his pal and pray for him.

Of course, I had suffered from some teasing and sullen verbal bullying as well intermittently throughout school days, primarily during the awkward Middle School tribulation. However, it had never occurred to me to organize "greater understanding and awareness for dweebs and geeks" demonstrations. Another missed opportunity for leadership, I thought drolly.

It was nearing dinner time as I reached the dorm, and I knew Caitlyn and possibly Anise would be waiting for me to accompany them to the dining room. Mealtimes were one of the things I was seriously enjoying at Durst. The food was great, for one thing, and there was so much variety. Living in South

Central Pennsylvania it was easy to get an overdose of Dutch cooking.

"Meatloaf?" Anise had asked in bewilderment once when I mentioned our weekly household staple. "Never heard of it, but I can tell by its name I wouldn't touch it." I had not defended meatloaf nor extolled its virtues. Many a mealtime I had wished that my family had been of Italian descent, and not German.

"Hey Molly, where have you been?" Caitlyn asked as I opened the door to our room. "Graeme's called here twice for you."

"Really?" I asked, feeling my face flush again.

"Mm-hmm. He asked you to call as soon as you get in."

I dropped my books on my bunk and sat down, heaving a deep sigh.

"Apparently, you made quite an impression after all," Caitlyn teased.

I looked up at her. "How was your day?" I asked, pretending not to be deeply concerned with the topic at hand.

"It was good…" Caitlyn picked at her the nail on her left pinkie. "David's coming up this weekend."

"Your boyfriend? Really? That's great," I replied, searching Caitlyn's face. She looked troubled.

"I know," she said slowly, staring at a space on the carpet. "I'm really excited to see him."

"What's wrong?" I asked.

"Oh…nothing!" Caitlyn said brightly, dropping her hands at her sides suddenly and forcing a smile. She paced around the room a couple times before returning in the next instant to looking gloomy. "I'll just have to think up an excuse not to go to the football game with Jared."

I formed a quick mental picture of Jared out of Caitlyn's inventory of doting males. He was the tall one who wore grunge and wrote poetry. He had already penned a few adoring stanzas just for Caitlyn, which she had read to me breathlessly in our dorm room, and which I'd secretly found unintentionally funny and overwrought. I hadn't said this, though.

"I didn't know Shakespeare was a football fan," I remarked, invoking my nickname for him. I had monikers for all Caitlyn's legion of admirers.

"He's not, really. I was mostly the one who suggested it."

Probably out of interest for some guy on the team, I thought wryly. I had to hand it to her. The juggling skills were adept as ever.

I was about to ask more about David's arrival when the phone rang. Caitlyn picked it up. "For you, Moll," she said, handing me the receiver with a knowing smile.

"Hello?" I asked, heart getting ready to beat out a march again. I wondered for just a split second if one could develop a cardiac disorder just from nervousness around the opposite sex.

"Molly?" There was that deep voice.

"Ye-e-s," I answered slowly, as though Graeme could have been any man out of a thousand calling me.

"It's Graeme."

"Hi."

"Hey, did you get the e-mail I sent you?"

"No," I replied. "I didn't get around to checking it today."

"Oh. Well, I wondered if you wanted to hang out tonight and watch a movie?" he asked.

I hesitated. My homework for the next day was finished, but I was reluctant to accept his offer on such short notice. Another one of my mother's axioms sprung to mind. "Easily attained, lightly esteemed," she'd say. "Never make yourself too available to a man, or accept an invitation on a moment's notice when you're first getting to know him. It makes it look as though you have no life outside of him."

"I'm afraid I can't tonight, Graeme," I responded, heeding my mother's preemptive advice.

"Oh." He sounded deflated. "Well, how about tomorrow night?"

I thought about it for a moment. "I'll have to see what kind of workload I have tomorrow," I answered truthfully.

"Alright. Cool. Just message me then, okay?"

I agreed to do so. I wondered how the world ever got along without e-mail or texting. I figured I was one of the few who could still live without it if I had to. Sterile, impersonal electronic stuff that it was.

"So, what did you do today?" Graeme wanted to know.

Hid from you, I thought to myself. I did not say so, of course. We chatted for several minutes before I finally ended the conversation, citing going to dinner with Caitlyn.

"Alright, well I'll wait to hear from you tomorrow then," Graeme said.

As I hung up the phone, I could sense that small voice of warning in my mind telling me I was starting to venture into hazardous waters which belied unknown riptides and undercurrents. I shrugged the intonation and its caution out of my conscience. Graeme was a nice guy. He wasn't some brutish jerk or insensitive creep. I could handle this.

*****

There was a low buzz of electric energy on campus the next morning that was almost tangible. Caitlyn was the first to tip me off on what was going on, having had an earlier class than I did. Apparently overnight someone had penned certain Biblical references on plain white paper and stuck them alongside the Allies' promotional posters.

"They had written stuff like 'homosexuality is an abomination' and 'homosexuality is contrary to the laws of God and of nature' and had taped them right next to the gay posters," Caitlyn explained breathlessly. "Can you believe it? The newspapers were here and everything, interviewing people and taking pictures of the signs."

"What?" I exclaimed.

"Yep," Caitlyn nodded, "But you won't see any more of the Bible verses. They took them all down."

I continued to get dressed in silence, pondering this news.

When I arrived for Calculus II, the usual pre-class banter was going on, although none of what I could discern was centered around the Allies' efforts or the written opposition. It felt, as usual, like high school all over again, with everyone taking advantage of the few minutes before class to gossip, talk about parties, and slyly flirt.

Professor Jankowski was nearly ten minutes late getting into the lecture hall. When she finally arrived, she set down her book-laden bag and turned to address the class with an air of heightened gravity.

"We need to talk about something today more pressing than calculus" she said solemnly, looking intently into individual faces as she scanned the room. "Last night, there was a targeted attack of *hate* made on a group of people on this campus." She paused dramatically, her words hanging in the air over the seats of the lecture hall. All eyes were on her, expectantly. "For those of you who may not be aware, some anonymous *bible-belting* person or persons posted speech decrying homosexual and lesbian individuals next to the Allies' announcements all over campus." Professor Jankowski pushed her glasses back on her face and then crossed her arms, her eyes flashing out fury as well as a challenge to our sympathy.

"The offensive postings have already been removed," she continued, striding down one side of the small stage on which she stood. "An investigation into the person or persons responsible for this verbal assault is already underway." Professor Jankowski resumed her pacing towards the other side of the stage for full dramatic effect, before stopping suddenly and holding her arms out towards us in an imploring gesture. "A forum will be held this afternoon in Wakefield Hall for anyone interested in discussing this incident as well as sensitivity and tolerance in general. I would urge all of you to attend."

"Durst is a community in which *everyone* should feel safe and free from attack," she continued, pacing again. "It is frightening to discover that there are those out there with radical, fundamentalist ideas who would take us back to the Dark Ages, if allowed, in both their attitudes and ideals towards those with sexual preferences unlike their own." She threw out a harrowing look of warning, which I suppose was intended to instill dread into any would-be "radicals" out in the crowd who did not share her viewpoint.

"At this time I would like to open it up to you for any questions and concerns you might have about last night's incident." She stopped and stood still, looking expectantly – eagerly – into our faces.

The hand of a guy a few rows in front of me shot up. From where I was, I could only see the back of his head. He had dark hair and was wearing an orange-and-blue striped shirt.

"Yes!" Professor Jankowski said eagerly, pointing to him. A hundred pairs of eyes turned to focus on him.

"Yeah…uh…I saw some of the postings before they were taken down and I didn't see anything on them that personally attacked homosexual people," the boy said slowly and evenly. "It seemed more like whoever wrote those things was disagreeing with promoting homosexuality in general, and simply stating what the Bible had to say about it. I mean, isn't that freedom of speech?"

The huge room of students was completely hushed as they looked from this voice of dissent in the middle of the lecture hall, then back to our instructor.

Professor Jankowski was visibly vexed. She stared back at him for a few moments as if pondering from what planet he might have originated, then cleared her throat. "Whoever posted those statements did it covertly, without any authorization," she replied finally, finding her voice. "If they wanted freedom of speech they should have spoken up in daylight, just like the Allies did. The fact of the matter is that these homophobes had to *hide* who they really are and launch their assault *anonymously* when no one was around."

"With all due respect, Professor," the striped-shirt guy continued, not bothering to raise his hand this time, "Seeing as how whoever this person is who had a different opinion on the positive effects of homosexuality has already been labeled, ridiculed, and tagged a 'hater' and a 'homophobe,' why would he or she ever want to come forward and publicly show themselves? I mean, they might as well volunteer themselves for a campus stoning."

Professor Jankowski was silent for a moment as she stared hard at this unforeseen opposition. Finally, she spoke again, this time as though she were addressing an unruly child who, with enough patience, might eventually understand mature speech. "We encourage tolerance on this campus, and the persons responsible for showing themselves *intolerant* of homosexual, lesbian, bisexuals and others on this campus are creating an environment of hostility."

"Again, Professor, I respectfully disagree," Striped Shirt continued. "These remarks did not threaten or degrade homosexual people. They simply stated what the Bible says about homosexuality and its effects on society. What you're naming 'homophobia' is what someone else might term 'holiness,' and that likewise creates an environment of hostility towards Christians and anyone else for that matter who holds a different viewpoint.'

A girl in the very front row with curly red hair and rectangular glasses, who had turned around to hear the dialogue, spoke up suddenly. "I thought *Christians* were supposed to be tolerant towards their neighbors," she threw back accusingly at Striped Shirt, emphasizing the word "Christians" in such a way that left no doubt that the word itself was a bad taste in her mouth. "I also thought they were told not to judge."

"Christians are commanded to love one another as they love themselves," Striped Shirt answered back without hesitation or emotion. "Christians are *not,* however, told to be tolerant of sin itself. Speaking up for what someone believes in and standing up for truth does not equate to violence or even hatred, just because you disagree with it. Nor is agreeing with what God says about something the equivalent of "judging" someone, as only God can do that." He leaned back in his chair. "People who are militantly opposed to hearing the other side will do anything to discredit it and trash it," he added quietly.

"I think the forum this afternoon is a better place to discuss this," Professor Jankowski announced, bringing the debate she had introduced to a sudden end. "Again, I invite everyone present to attend." She turned and walked over to her satchel of books. "Alright, let's turn to page 23 in your textbooks."

Those militantly opposed will also do anything to silence it, I thought, seeing the truth firsthand in Striped Shirt's last remark.

Chapter 11 - Philosophy

"This place makes me want to drive into oncoming traffic," Anise grumbled, as we walked to where a campus film was being shown one evening. The air was taking on that coolness that speaks of crisp, autumn days ahead. It was just the two of us, as Caitlyn had opted to skip dinner, instead working frantically on a paper due the next morning. Anise was having a generally bad day, and having gotten a poor grade on her Environmental Science paper topped it off.

"Why's that?" I asked, chuckling at her remark.

"Fake people make me nauseated. And this school is infested with 'em.'"

She kicked a stone ahead of her and looked off, scowling, towards the road that ran through the main part of campus.

"I don't know. I'm just used to New York, I guess," she continued. "People there can be really rude, but at least they're real."

I didn't say anything. Durst was a different world from where I'd been all my life, but I didn't have any campuses to compare it to as far as how students behaved. The people here were generally wealthier than at home, but they weren't much different in behavior than the high school kids I'd known.

"Part of it too is I'm used to the city and city life and places to go and clubs and theatre and museums and *real* shopping venues with *real* clothing. This place is just so…*boring*."

It was something to hear that Anise found Durst so dull, when I found every aspect of it to be an entire wild, new adventure. I loved college and just about everything it entailed. It had been six weeks since I had waved good-bye to my parents and sister and essentially life as I knew it, and everything here was so unexpected and thrilling and *liberating*. It was unthinkable after just a little more than a month of this newfound freedom to recall those days of being under daily parental control again, not to mention school scrutiny.

Dancing in the dorm with Caitlyn and some of the girls on the floor to the *Grease* soundtrack till late in the evening and laughing ourselves unconscious, laying out with a textbook in front of Old Main and soaking up late summer sunshine, making a spur-of-the-moment midnight munchies trek over to the college store, goofing off without dignity in the dining hall…I was having the time of my life at Durst. To not have to answer to a strict authority at home felt like breathing deeply for the first time.

I had begun to understand in high school that my parents' tight reign all my life on things such as curfews and allowing me to attend certain social events and overruling others had been to protect me, but in the last few years I had often felt suffocated. Yes, the base they'd given me was needful, but my spirit wanted adventure and challenges like any other teenager. Finally, here at school I was experiencing the liberty of not having to answer to a set of ordinances and the scrutiny of every single movement. It was the fun of college that I enjoyed, to be sure, but even more, it was the freedom.

I still had not found a church. But then, my Saturday nights were quickly filling in with so many late-night social events that I was finding it easier simply to sleep in on Sundays. I was a member of the campus fellowship, after all, although I had missed the last couple meetings because of other campus happenings that had gotten in the way.

Then there was Graeme. We'd started hanging out together on a fairly regular basis since the dinner at Portofino. Strangely enough, the more aloof and detached I tried to remain from him, the more it seemed to attract him. After I had initially declined a couple dates because of school work, I came back to my room to find a bouquet of a dozen delicate pink roses on my dresser. When I didn't respond to an e-mail from him immediately, the phone rang instead. I didn't want to think about where a relationship with him would lead, so I continued to ignore the quiet-but-persistent voice of reason in my mind, holding Graeme at arm's length as well, trying to walk in that nebulous middle ground.

Had I been honest with myself, I would have admitted that I liked the attention I got from Graeme, more than I actually cared for him. It was nice having someone spend money on me, open doors, shower me with flowers, throw me an admiring glance across the dining hall, and surprise me with unexpected little notes in my mailbox. It was not only very agreeable, it was the first time I'd ever experienced this.

Graeme was also a welcome distraction from Hank, with whom there had been no contact since that sparse, initial letter. Whenever I thought of Hank off at art school, it was in an aching, bittersweet sort of way. I missed his conversation and his one-of-a-kind outlook, but I was weary of merely *thinking* about him for so long.

Anise and I were passing one of the college tour groups. A perky college senior was glibly explaining all the selling points of Durst and enthusiastically pointing out its many architectural structures. Anise looked up as we approached them.

"Don't ever come to this place," she said forcefully to the strangers, shaking her head in gloomy admonition. The parents and their eager, prospective teen-aged kids stared back at her in dumbfounded bewilderment. The student guide's smile froze and then crumbled in a moment of instant horror. They continued walking, now in a shroud of uncomfortable silence.

"At least I met *you,* thank God," Anise said, already oblivious to the impression she'd made. She slung an arm around my shoulder and gave me a quick hug as we made our way towards the hall.

*****

"So you're telling me that a person who is good his whole life, treats other people well, volunteers, even donates his money to charity, is going to go to *Hell* when he dies all because he wasn't a Christian?" Zach asked me incredulously.

"Yes," I answered him quietly, uncomfortably.

"That's so unfair that people who live the best they can would go to Hell," Zach responded, picking up a scoopful of egg salad and plopping it back into its tub.

"It sounds like it, doesn't it?" I answered quietly, "Until we look at God rather than each other for the standard. Because He is perfect and holy, He cannot stand to be in the presence of sin. Since every single one of us has sinned, that creates instant separation from God. The good news is that when Jesus died, his blood made a bridge between us and God, so that now when God looks at us, we're perfect in His sight. Kind of like looking through a prism – because of Jesus, we no longer have any sin in His sight."

We were working the deli this evening, making sandwiches for those students who preferred that to a hot meal. I saw Harry – the fifty-something-year-old cook stationed nearby at the grill – glancing frequently in my direction. Harry, like his grill, was perpetually greasy. I hoped he would keep his distance tonight. Last time Zach and I had been on delicatessen duty, every time Zach went to get a drink or to the back to get a refill on an item, Harry would come over and tell me all about his favorite pastime –swinging.

"You have no idea, *no idea,* what goes on in this little town at night!" Harry had told me, eyes gleaming as he relayed highlights of organized promiscuity to my unwilling ears. "It's a whole underground life with doctors, teachers, mechanics, realtors, you name it! I was at this house last Saturday-"

"I'd really rather not hear," I'd interrupted him then. Harry hadn't listened, but continued in his sordid litany of depraved details until he'd finally been called away to fry up some more chicken patties. I had been mortified by the tale, feeling nausea at the description he'd insisted on giving.

"But I don't think there is just one way to get to God," Zach argued, shifting from one foot to the other. "That's just too restrictive. And if God is loving, like you say, why would He send people to Hell who have different ideas about who He is? I think it's all about how you treat people and trying to live your life right."

I considered what he said and then answered, "The Bible says that 'there is a way that seems right to a man but in the end it leads to death'... Jesus said 'I am the Way.'"

"So you're telling me that if some dude pulls a gun on a little kid and shoots him dead and then later confesses it and asks forgiveness, he'll go to Heaven, while a guy who has never once broken the law and is a good father and citizen and gives his time and his money can go to Hell simply because he didn't believe in Jesus?"

"Yes," I replied evenly.

"That's crazy!" Zach exclaimed incredulously, now attacking the egg salad with a spatula.

"Yes," I agreed. "It is crazy. There is something definitively unfair about grace. Otherwise, it wouldn't be grace. It would be justice. What's really crazy, though, is that a perfect, just, all-powerful God would be willing to die for a bunch of bums who generally don't concern themselves with Him, only their own petty interests, and who insist on ignoring him and doing things their own way time after time, and relentlessly He pursues them and forgives them over and over." I thought about my own statement for a moment. "Yes, that really is crazy."

Zach switched the subject then and began relaying some bizarre forensics he'd seen on television the night before. I half listened, praying for him even while he described the morbid dissection of a cadaver. I prayed that the blinders would fall off and that the light of truth would shine into his life.

*****

"Look how skinny she is," Caitlyn said incredulously, staring at the supermodel's twig-like limbs. "She looks like a stick figure!"

"I'm surprised that purse doesn't just snap her arm right off," Anise agreed, eyeing the photograph.

"Do you think she's anorexic?" Caitlyn wondered, still gazing at the image.

"Of course she's anorexic," Anise replied. "Probably has a nasty little cocaine addiction, too."

"That's so sad," I said, studying the woman's whippet-thin frame.

"That's fashion," Anise answered simply.

We were paging through one of her many *haute couture* magazines, taking in the various images splashed across the oversized pages, many which struck me as outlandish. I had never paid an extraordinary amount of attention to fashion (my own wardrobe of course reflecting this) but Caitlyn and Anise especially had an awareness of every new trend and would not have considered neglecting their attire any more than I could forget going to the cafeteria to eat. Even their 'casual" clothing was always conspicuously trendy.

We flipped through page after page of downtown New York backdrops, where a three thousand dollar handbag was thrown out on the margin of a page as casually as coffee might be listed on a diner's menu. Evening gown and bracelet-bedecked models shot off spacey glances as they strode down runways, and celebrities and socialites were listed in boldface and depicted smiling demurely at some benefit or gala. Gazing at them I couldn't help but think how incredible it would be to have a lifestyle full of parties and penthouses and purchasing expensive new clothes.

At that moment, Anise's cell phone rang.

"Hello?" I watched her comb her cranberry-colored nails through her dark hair as she answered. "Hey, Luke," she said to the deep voice that came through the speaker.

Caitlyn and I listened with interest to the one side of the conversation that we could grasp, watching her until she finally snapped her adorable little cell phone shut and turned to meet our stares.

"*That* was Luke," she announced.

"Luke from sociology?" Caitlyn asked.

"Yep. He asked me if I wanted to go see a movie this weekend.

"So, what did you say?" Caitlyn wanted to know.

Anise shrugged. "I told him I'd go." She returned to where we were sprawled across the bed and sat at the foot. "He knows I have a boyfriend, though." She thought for a moment. "I like Luke. In class he's smart, but such a clown. Very different from Joe."

"Are you going to tell Joe?" Caitlyn challenged her.

"I don't know," Anise replied truthfully.

At that moment the heavy door pushed open and Jill's head appeared from around the other side of it.

"Hey," she greeted us, struggling to get her book-laden bag through the doorway. Her face lit up as she saw Caitlyn to the side of me. "Hey-y-y, sista!"

"Hi, Jill!" Caitlyn said brightly. Jill sauntered over to where we were sitting and I watched as Caitlyn – giggling – accepted a big bear hug from her.

"How ya doin'?" Jill asked Caitlyn.

"Good!" Caitlyn answered enthusiastically.

"How do you get your hair so straight and shiny?" Jill asked her as she picked up strands of Caitlyn's hair in her hands and then let them fall gently back to her shoulders. I glanced at Anise, who was watching the exchange intently, then down at Jill's sandal-clad toes.

As Caitlyn explained about her anti-frizz serum Jill continued to study her but didn't appear to be listening. I felt uncomfortable and didn't know why, so then I felt uncomfortable with myself for feeling uncomfortable.

"Well, I'd better get back to studying for physics," I announced, with a forced lightness in my voice. Jill didn't appear to hear me anyway, and I left her and Caitlyn to their conversation. Anise followed me to the door.

"See ya," she called after me, her slight eye roll telegraphing a sentiment that I wasn't exactly sure how to read.

When I got back to the room the phone was ringing. It was Graeme, wanting to know if I wanted to go over to the HUB for a game of pool. The physics quiz I was supposed to be studying for materialized and faded in an instant in my mind before I grabbed my key ring. I could cram later.

Chapter 12 – Mean Girls

One evening I was hanging out in the dorm with Caitlyn, a soccer player named Chris, and Chris' teammate and pal, Tad. It was Chris' room, and he evidently was waiting patiently in line to be Caitlyn's newest flame. I had no doubt he would realize his goal, but I hoped he didn't have his sights set on being the exclusive object of her affection.

The walls of Chris' room were papered with the same generic college posters every guy seemed to have: Jimi Hendrix with a reefer, the John Belushi black-and-white reproduction from *Animal House,* the one about beer as a historic resource in helping unattractive people have sexual encounters. In the back of my mind whenever I saw these repeat themes I always thought of how Hank would have quietly spurned such obvious uniformity. He would have seen it for what it was, a cloned lack of creativity masquerading as individualistic expression. I wondered what Hank's room was like at art school. I could see him furnishing his walls with some bizarre abstract or some outlandish and obscure post-modern work, and then hanging a Norman Rockwell illustration intermittently to add some irony.

Chris' roommate, Adam, was out. I knew Chris didn't care for Adam, nor did most of the kids in our dorm. Adam was short and talkative and plump and always overeager to join in whatever conversation was happening outside of him. While he was academic, he didn't possess athleticism or outstanding good looks or any tremendous sense of humor. I felt a mixture of pity and discomfort whenever I encountered him because he perpetually gave off the aura that he was *trying* so hard to fit in. Since I was one of the few who would patiently listen to his ramblings, he often latched on to me for an earpiece, until many a time I was forced to excuse myself on a flimsy premise and hastily vacate his presence.

Since college had begun, there were a number of people who flat out did not get along with their roommates, a couple in our freshman dorm in fact who had switched. Rumors would circulate about alleged bad behavior or habits of said roommate, or even some fetish deemed intolerable by the other, like one girl whose roommate attested that she was forced to fall asleep every night to Barry White's crooning and the air conditioning blasting directly on them, even with the temperatures now occasionally dipping below forty at night. Whenever someone moved out, I dubbed it a "roommate divorce."

"That kid's getting on my last nerve," Chris scowled, talking about Adam.

"Well, no wonder. I'm surprised you haven't gone freakin' deaf by now," Tad observed.

"It's not just the fact he won't shut up," Chris said. "It's all that kosher crap of his. I was trying to be nice the other night and offered to split a pizza with him. Well, how the hell was I supposed to know he can't eat pepperoni? When it came he just turned his nose up. He won't even *use* our refrigerator, which is fine by me." Chris laughed derisively. "The other night, I microwaved a couple bratwursts just to irritate him. He left the room so it worked. Probably went somewhere and called down holy Heaven on me."

Tad snorted at this last remark. He pulled himself up from the beanbag chair he was sprawled across and walked over to the desk closest to Adam's bunk and sat down in the chair.

"What are you doing?" Chris wanted to know.

"I'm gonna program his computer so when he turns it on, it flashes 'Hey, Jew Boy!' on the screen," Tad answered. "Watch this."

Caitlyn glanced at me, covering her face in a guffaw as if it were the funniest thing she'd ever heard. I snickered. I knew I shouldn't have, but I did.

As Tad fiddled around with the keyboard, Chris reached over from where he was sitting across from Caitlyn and me and opened the door to the miniature refrigerator that recently had been the topic of conversation.

"See, this is the best part about Adam not using this fridge," he told us, smiling. He swung the door open widely so that Caitlyn and I could see the full stock of bottled beer that lined each of its four shelves. "Do I maximize space or what?" he asked smugly.

Caitlyn giggled before affirming him on his resourcefulness. I just smiled.

Chris grabbed two bottles by their necks and swiftly uncapped both with an opener that hung on his keychain. "Ladies," he said, holding out one to each of us.

"Oh, Molly doesn't drink," Caitlyn said hastily, coming to my defense.

"Really?" Chris asked incredulously. "How come?"

"I just choose not to," I replied evenly. I was getting a little tired of having to explain myself any time I went to a social gathering.

"*I* live by the motto 'a day without a buzz is like a day that never was,'" Tad informed us from where he sat by Adam's computer. "Here, I'll give that one a home," he offered, gesturing to the bottle Caitlyn had rejected for me.

Tad raised his bottle in a toast and swallowed down about half of the brew in one gulp before slamming it down on Adam's desk. Chris laughed and said to Caitlyn and me, "I've watched that guy funnel faster than anyone I know. It's a *gift*."

"Are you guys going to pledge a fraternity?" Caitlyn wanted to know.

"Oh, yeah," said Tad, washing down the rest of his beer. "Greek life is half the reason I chose this school."

"Consistently ranked in the top ten party schools in the nation," Chris said exuberantly, uncapping a second bottle and handing it to Tad.

Durst had a policy that freshmen couldn't pledge fraternities or sororities. They had to wait until sophomore year and then choose which ones they wanted to pursue. I imagined that this was in place out of fear of higher party-induced dropout rates among freshmen.

Caitlyn had claimed she was not fond of the taste of beer, but lately she hadn't been refusing any when they were offered. Typically, alcohol manifested itself with her by louder and more frequent giggling fits, as well as a general increase in all-around goofiness. I had noticed, too, she became much more touchy-feely around both sexes when her beer count went above two. To her credit, since the night of the Theta Chi party she hadn't had any further incidents of upchucking or passing out. I was not yet learned enough in my observations of the effects of alcohol to know what constituted real worry when it came to possible poisoning. I was still leery of the scene I had imagined that first night, of Caitlyn's parents tearfully crossing paths with me at the hospital after various doctors had tried – too late – to pump her stomach. I had envisioned her mother's wrathful accusation as she jabbed a hanky into her eyes- "You –*you* were *supposed* to be her friend! You could have prevented this if you'd just taken her *immediately* to the hospital!"

On the other hand, Caitlyn had told me the morning following the party, in between making known her need for cold compresses, Tylenol, and dead quiet, that she would have simply died of humiliation if I had taken her to the emergency room during her first intimate encounter with alcohol.

"It wasn't *that* bad," she'd stated defensively when I had explained my worries.

As I watched the three of them cradling their beers, and listened to their banter, I began to think about my stance on drinking. It seemed since the beginning of college like it was one of those things that set up an immediate barrier between me and the other kids in whatever setting I was in. Even though no one openly ridiculed me or even gave much more than a questioning glance when I declined, I hated the awareness that I was instantly cutting myself off from a circle just by the slight and ever-so-subtle suspicion that I sensed whenever I did not partake. It reminded me of a conversation I'd heard between my dad and a friend of his, who had at the time recently returned from a business trip to China. This buddy of my dad's had made the point that many in the Far East lit up cigarettes immediately upon a business introduction, and it was a kind of bonding gesture to them, of strangers establishing a quick trust simply by partaking in the same activity.

Just as much a factor as the isolationism I felt from abstaining from social drinking, I was genuinely curious to know how beer tasted. It certainly seemed to be the lifeblood of the campus. Being a teetotaler at Durst seemed like taking a trip to Italy and not sampling its pasta. "When in Rome…" There was a difference between trying a sip of it and *drinking,* after all.

"Caitlyn," I asked tentatively. "Do you mind if I just have a taste of that?"

"Oh, here – I'll get you your own," Chris said quickly, opening the refrigerator.

"No-o-o, I don't want a whole bottle, just a taste," I protested.

"Too late," Chris said brightly, as he popped the lid off of a bottle and handed it to me. He held up his own beer. "Cheers."

The bottle was icy cold in my hand. The same sour smell that greeted me every time I stepped into a fraternity house wafted out of it when I held it closer to my face. I held my nose with the thumb and finger of my left hand as I pressed the rim of the bottle to my lips and tilted it.

The liquid was cold and bitter, and after I'd swallowed it, my stomach felt warm. I thought back to high school health class and tried to remember if that was the lining of my digestive system being eaten away by the alcohol.

"Well?" Tad asked. He, Chris and Caitlyn were watching me expectantly, as a parent might observe a child reluctantly taking its first bite of solid food, making sure it actually swallowed the stuff.

"Tastes terrible," I answered truthfully, making a face.

"Don't worry, it'll taste better the more you drink," Chris laughed.

"Definitely an *acquired* taste," Tad agreed. "Speaking of 'acquired,' I'd like to acquire myself another, Chris."

As Chris obliged him on his third, there was a rap at the door.

"Knock, knock!" said a husky, familiar voice. I glanced up morosely at its owner.

Sure enough, it was Taylar, poking her head around the door. "Can I come in?" She slipped inside without waiting for Chris' reply. "I see you're having a party!" She narrowed her eyes. "You should have locked the door. Nathan could totally come in here and bust you guys."

Or some other unwanted guest, I thought gloomily.

"Lock it behind you," Chris ordered.

Taylar turned the bolt in the door and then turned around to face us. Her gaze fell on me. Throwing me a look of affected surprise, she exclaimed with a tinge of mockery, "Molly! I don't *believe* it! You're having a beer?"

"She's taken the plunge!" Caitlyn chirped up merrily, already starting to show the effects of her first beer. I wished she wouldn't have said it.

"I never thought I'd see the day," Taylar shook her head, settling onto the side of the bed next to Chris. Her patronization made me writhe. "Chris," her pitch went up an octave. "Can you hook me up?"

Wordlessly, Chris retrieved a beer for her from the mini-fridge.

I took another sip of the forbidden beverage in my hand. This time, I didn't hold my nose. Yep, it was lousy alright...but I kind of liked the stomach-warming aftereffect.

"So...I heard you guys had an awesome game yesterday," Taylar said to Chris and Tad in her nightmarish voice.

"It was okay," Chris answered.

Taylar continued to talk, addressing Chris, Tad, and Caitlyn, but never so much as glancing at me. After a few moments, I tuned out her incessant drawl, balancing my discomfort in her presence with sipping the beer before me. It gave me something to do, and despite the annoyance of her company, I was starting to feel strangely relaxed. I studied the endless pattern of lines and colors in the psychedelic abstract on the opposite wall.

"Molly, you're dating Graeme Reddig, aren't you?" Taylar said suddenly. I snapped out of my reverie.

"Well, I guess we've kind of been hanging out together," I replied uncertainly.

"'Hanging *out* together'?" she mimicked, the patronizing pitch audible again in her voice. "What exactly does *that* mean?"

"To tell you the truth, I don't know," I said smiling, determined to meet her accusatory gaze with equanimity. "I guess we're mostly just friends."

"You mean to tell me, you two haven't *slept* together yet?" Taylar asked incredulously.

I could feel the blood rushing up through my neck and face, my ears burning in a deep blush – from anger as much as embarrassment as all four pairs of eyes in the room turned to me. Of all the inappropriate things to say, I was completely caught off guard that Taylar would ask such a thing – as if she had perfect right, no less – in mixed company, and in front of two guys I barely knew! *The gold ring was secure in this pig's nostrils, alright*, I thought humorlessly.

I took a deep breath and smiled at her, as Tad, Caitlyn, and Chris watched with curious expectation. I detested confrontation, but when I reached my breaking point, there was little I could do to restrain my emotion. "Not *all* of us believe in going all the way on the first date," I parried calmly.

From where he still sat at Adam's desk, Tad made a kind of a choking sound as he removed the beer bottle from his mouth, quickly smothering the sound with his hand and turning it into a cough.

"Good night, and thanks for the beer," I said quickly, setting down my nearly-empty beer bottle and walking over to the door.

"See you back at the ranch," I told Caitlyn. I didn't look at Taylar as I unlocked and walked out the door. I could see out of the corner of my eye that she had a purplish hue to her cheeks, and that she was fuming.

Chapter 13 – Nietzsche's Shadow

"I just don't know what to do," Anise confessed, sighing heavily as she finished reading aloud to me the letter Joe had written to her. His correspondence had been full of his profession of adoration for Anise, and also heavily peppered with sexual innuendo, which had secretly floored me a bit. Granted, sexual activity was rife all over the campus and on television and the Internet, but to hear it detailed in such language to a close friend of mine was new for me. Anise had read it to me without dramatization or much emotion.

"What's wrong?" I asked now, watching her anxiously clutch the gold cross that hung at her neck as she paced back and forth in her room.

"I'm really liking Luke," Anise sighed, pausing for a moment in her pacing to face me. "He's just so funny, so easy to be around. He's so different from Joe." She picked up Joe's letter, which she'd cast indifferently onto the dresser. "Joe certainly knows how to treat me as far as wining and dining and he's a great dancer and he dresses better than I do. I mean, he treats me like a queen." She glanced at the letter another time before tossing it to the dresser again and then covered her forehead up with a bejeweled hand. "Why am I so confused?"

"Does he treat you better than Luke does?" I asked.

"Actually, Luke has always been the perfect gentleman, too," Anise admitted. "He holds doors, insists on paying my way…he's really sweet. And he's so laid back. I really like that. Joe can be so damn uptight about stuff. Like one time when our waiter brought out the steak overcooked and you'd have thought Joe's life was ruined because of it." She thought for another moment. "Luke doesn't have all the money and maybe he's not quite as sophisticated as Joe, but I'm so attracted to Luke's personality that I really don't care about the money and all. He just cracks me up – *all* the time! Don't you think a guy with a great sense of humor is just a major turn on?"

I nodded in agreement, thinking Hank had to be the patron saint of such males.

"Luke is so down-to-earth, too," Anise continued, smiling slightly as she thought more about him. "He can switch from joking around to listening to what I have to say and talking to me like he really understands. That's so different than what I have with Joe. Despite his clothes and his car and his looks, Joe's a very insecure person."

"So what's keeping you from giving ol' Joe the heave-ho?" I asked.

Anise began pacing again. "Well," she said finally, tugging again at the cross around her throat. "I guess the real reason is the fact I lost my virginity to Joe." She studied the floor for several moments. "To break up with him now would mean that I gave away such an important thing to me for nothing."

I couldn't think of anything appropriate to say, so I sat in silence, waiting for her to finish her thought process. She continued extolling the virtues of Luke and then comparing them to Joe's for another twenty minutes or so.

At last, she sat down on Jill's bunk across from me, forcing a troubled smile to take the place of her worried expression. She looked me in the eye. "Molly, why does life have to be so complicated?"

*****

"You're looking at a rich man," Jon said pompously when I walked into German class one Monday morning and took my seat next to him.

"Oh, yeah? How'd that happen?" I asked. Cooler temperatures had not discouraged him from wearing sandals, and the odor of his feet was more powerful than ever today.

"Hit the *jackpot* yesterday," Jon said smugly, little beads of spit flying from his mouth. His watery blue eyes contained more excitement in them than I'd ever before seen.

"Was this with your sports gambling?" I wanted to know.

"*Wagering,*" Jon emphasized. "Gambling, like they say, is when you lose." He cleared his throat self-importantly. "I hit it *big* last night on two games!"

"Congratulations," I told him. "So what are you going to do with all your money?"

"Well, I've gotta buy cases for the fraternity, of course," Jon said, grinning. "Also getting a new stereo system for my pad at the house, some new DVDs. Of course, I have to save part of it to re-invest back into next weekend's match-ups. I'm on a *roll!*"

I congratulated him again, secretly hoping he would consider buying some foot spray with his winnings.

"*Guten Morgen,*" Frau Bund said, marching into the room and overriding our conversation. The paisley had been surrendered today in favor of a bright purple crepe dress. With her pencil-thin figure, she looked like a grape swizzle stick.

"Ve - have - vays - to - make - you -*speak!*" Jon whispered, doing his best *Hogan's Heroes* imitation. I burst into a low laugh. Frau Bund looked at me. The grin on my face evaporated into a straight line. I sat frozen, wondering if she'd heard what Jon had said. She glowered at me for a moment. For a split second I pictured her in the Gestapo garb, smacking a club against her open palm.

She looked around the rest of the class, which was silent. "Today, class, we are continuing our study of the German Enlightenment with the perspectives of Nietzsche and the philosophy of nihilism. "Who can give me the definition of nihilism, in your own words?"

One guy jabbed his pencil in the air. Frau pointed at him. "Life is pointless," he said.

Frau gave a short laugh. "Okay, *ja*. Can you elaborate on that a bit?"

The boy thought for a moment. "It pretty much is a philosophy that there's no point in traditional values or hope for an existence beyond this life."

Frau nodded exuberantly. It occurred to me as I watched her that it must be very disheartening to spend one's entire life pursuing higher education in a particular subject, write and defend doctorates and theses, and then spend one's time getting such pat answers from apathetic rich kids at a private college.

"Nihilism," she reiterated, "comes from the Latin word 'nihil' which means 'nothing.' Nihilism purports that values and absolute truths are without any foundation, and that life itself is meaningless."

She walked over to her laptop and tapped a button. It projected onto the far wall the following quote:

"After Buddha was dead, his shadow was still shown for centuries in a cave - a tremendous, gruesome shadow. God is dead: but given the way of men, there may still be caves for thousands of years in which his shadow will be shown. -And we-we still have to vanquish his shadow, too." - Friedrich Nietzsche, *The Gay Science*

Frau Bund read the statement aloud, enunciating every word in her distinctive, German accent. When she came to the words "God is dead," I flinched.

I stared at the photograph of Nietzsche in my textbook. I had seen pictures of him before, and with his wild eyes, out-of-control moustache, and chronic sideways glance, he looked in my estimation like a pretty strange individual. His facial hair alone appeared as though it might be possessed. I couldn't imagine that he was the sort who got invited to many beer festivals in the local German bergs back in the day.

"Ol' Friedrich there's a real killjoy," people probably said of him. *"Don't ask him to come, or he'll start philosophizing about how pointless life is and kill your buzz."*

"Studenten, what do you think of this statement?" Frau asked, searching the blank faces before her. "What is he saying, and do you agree? Disagree?"

No one said anything. One girl yawned. I could hear the second hand ticking on the wall clock behind me.

Frau Bund looked exasperated. "Ladies and gentlemen, *what* is Nietzsche suggesting with this statement?"

"God is dead," Jon answered, stretching his arms out in front of him as though he'd just awoken from a nap.

"Ja, okay," Frau conceded. "But what else?" She looked around the room at the comatose figures supporting their heads on the desks.

I felt my heart starting up like a war drum, the way it always did before I knew I'd inevitably be drawn into a battle. I raised my hand. Frau nodded at me.

"He's saying that God no longer exists, and that it's simply we human beings who have propped up the notion that He's alive by giving life to a mere shadow all these centuries." I paused, "Nietzsche also, whether intentionally or not, seems to be affirming that Jesus Christ indeed is God."

Frau's expression, which showed she was following me at the beginning, indicated that she could have done without the last part of my explanation.

"Ja, well, he is definitely suggesting that human beings are simply not aware of this notion that God does not exist. As for the claim that Jesus is God, I do not follow where you are deriving that."

"Because for God to be dead, Nietzsche is suggesting He would have at one time had to exist. He's also drawing a parallel between Buddha and God. Nietzsche is proclaiming as God the one True God, even though he does not realize it, and even though he is pronouncing him dead."

Frau Bund did not appear to be convinced. She answered, "I believe that what Nietzsche is saying in the greater context of his work is that God does not exist, except for in the minds of those who continue to prop him up."

I was pretty sure that I had read somewhere back in high school that Nietzsche's philosophy had been instrumental in fueling Hitler's idea of a race of super-humans, and whether intended or not, Nietzsche had offered grounds for the reprehensible ideology of a superior race which led the Nazis to their existential murder.

Now, as I sat there pondering whether to point this out or just be silent and let it go, another thought struck a dark chord in me – that Charles Darwin, whose theories on the origins of life had never been proven and were increasingly discredited, had been even more instrumental in the rise of Nazism than anything else. Darwin was still gaining ground, despite his scientifically bankrupt theories, in a society which previously had largely viewed man as created in the image of God, and therefore found all life valuable.

Darwin, I knew, was revered by Durst – indeed, they were celebrating his gruesome legacy with some kind of "Remembering Darwin" celebration, which I had seen advertised to take place the following month. Of course, they weren't commemorating his ties to Nazism – in fact, I felt sure that the connection would never even be cited.

It was one thing to study history in hopes of not repeating it, but I wondered as I stared with glazed eyes at Frau's paisley patterns – which bobbed up and down as she wrote on the whiteboard – what was the point of studying history if we weren't going to examine the implications of making such statements? If we were only going to study half-truths? What about the fact that elements of Nazism were alive and well in our society with the barbaric practice of abortion?

My experience with academia in the weeks that I'd been at Durst had reinforced one very important truth that the Bible stated: "Knowledge puffs up," or knowledge makes one arrogant. These same professors who daily made evident their unbelief in – or rather their rebellion towards – an Almighty God, also no doubt fancied themselves wise beyond the rest of the mere mortals who did not have doctorates or write books or sit around lecture halls discussing theory and philosophy and life. Yet they were not deep at all. They were shallow and superficial and barely breathing. They were well-rounded intellectually, to be sure, but that was only a sign of breadth, not depth. I suddenly felt sick at the thought of them blindly leading so many young people astray, not even aware of their destructive impact.

I did not volunteer any more opinions on Nietzsche or nihilism throughout the rest of the class. It occurred to me that in the brief time that Frau Bund had known me, I had not exactly demonstrated myself to be a shining example of a follower of Christ, someone who shattered the accusations and prejudices of Nietzsche. To present the truth now might be to disparage the name of Christ through my actions. This thought left me severely dejected. Nor did my spirits lift when I finally exited her class, escorted by the seemingly uncomplicated Jon.

"Better watch out for that God stuff," he whispered to me as we assimilated into the mass herd rumbling down the stairs in the language arts building. "Remember, talk up 'women's issues.' You don't want to get a bad grade in her class!"

*****

Kendra and I had been corresponding a little less frequently as the weeks had gone by. I found my time so consumed by other prospects and activities that I simply put off replying to her immediately. Opening my mail and seeing her name pressed in between a bunch of risqué and even raunchy forwards was always disconcerting. More alarming should have been the slow dawning that Kendra's communications were beginning to produce more of a feeling of discomfort in me than were the messages containing lewd innuendo that were dished out regularly and in endless supply by a few of my newfound college friends and peers. Some of the messages that I opened, and then even read, I knew I shouldn't. There had been one in particular that was so graphic that I couldn't stop thinking about some of its content for the next two days. I wished I hadn't read it. I hadn't really intended to, in fact, but just seemed to get sucked right in.

Perhaps it was the fact that there was becoming less and less in my personal life that I felt I could relay to Kendra, even while she was telling me all the ways God was working in her life and on her campus. I still had yet to tell Kendra anything at all of Graeme, who was rapidly consuming more of my time and attention. And how to answer the questions she posed me of my own ministry and faith? It had been weeks since I'd been to the Christian fellowship, and I couldn't even remember when the last time was that I had sat somewhere alone and spent time in devotions. True, in the first few weeks that I'd been at school I had openly professed elements of my faith to Caitlyn and Anise

116

and tried to impart Biblical wisdom for some of what they were experiencing in life, but since then, I'd really faded. In the back of my mind, whenever I read Kendra's amazing accounts of God's goodness and power demonstrated actively in her life, a tinge of envy towards her situation seeped into my heart. How great would it be if I had chosen a conservative Christian college where the atmosphere was one in which everyone generally believed in the Lord and His truths? How much easier it would be!

Whether Kendra sensed this cooling in our friendship I couldn't tell. A place in me mourned the widening gap in our relationship, but a larger part of me passively sensed that it was necessary either to falsify reality or else loosen ties with her. The other alternative was to come face-to-face with her scorching assessment of the current direction my life, candid and loving though it would be...and *that* would not be agreeable at all.

*****

Graeme and I were talking about God one evening when he walked me back to the dorm. I had asked him about the subject early on in our acquaintance, and he had informed me that if God was out there somewhere, he sure hadn't heard from Him.

"I don't discount that there is such a thing as God," Graeme had stated. "I just haven't given the whole thing a lot of thought. I guess I think of Him more as a force – an energy – and I believe that when we die we're all just absorbed into this universal positive energy."

I had given him a wry, sideways glance, thinking suddenly of *Star Wars*. Then I had responded, "Well, *I* believe that Jesus was who he claimed to be, and that is God's Son. And since I believe that, I believe everything else that he said was true. And one of the things that he said was that there is only one way to God, and that is through him – through knowing him and believing in him and trusting him for our salvation."

"I don't know," Graeme had argued skeptically. "I read a bumper sticker once that I thought made a good point. It said, 'God is bigger than any one religion.' I liked that. I think a lot of the problems in this world were caused by organized religion."

His remark turned me off. If I had a dime for every time an atheist or agnostic used that cliché about organized religion I figured that I might have paid my way through the first year of Durst without any assistance.

Graeme had continued. "I live my life the best I can, never hurt anybody. To me, that's what it means to be a Christian anyway," he had said.

The scripture popped again into my mind, "There is a way that seems right to a man, but in the end it leads to death." However, I did not argue with him further.

For the past couple weeks I had tried several times to make up my mind what to do about Graeme. I knew I should stop seeing him, but each time I resolved that I would inform him of this the next time I saw him, he'd catch me off guard with some surprise shower of affection and flattery and I'd lose my nerve all over again. It was just so hard to put an abrupt end to all that. So, I kept delaying it.

Perhaps it would have been easier if I had had more serious male relationships in high school. Being a relational female and spending my adolescence in singlehood had only augmented the desire now to experience what every other girl out there my age seemed to have as standard fare. I wanted someone of the opposite sex to share my feelings with, to laugh at my jokes, and to look out for me. Of course, the physical aspect was always, always in my mind, but the gate on that particular dimension was fastened firmly shut until I was with the man I'd marry.

I shivered in the crisp evening air, concentrating on the leaves crunching beneath my feet. I detected the delightful smell of wood smoke, which always reminded me of childhood and the wood-burning stove that we had had in our family room. Graeme put his arm around me. He always smelled so good – so masculine. I shivered again.

"Well," I said, turning to face him as we reached my dorm. Perhaps now was a good time finally at least to hint at the news to him.

Well," Graeme said, loosening his hug around my shoulder. We stood staring at one another for a moment, and then he gripped my hand and gazed deeply into my eyes. He stared at me intently, and then inclined his head toward mine and kissed me gently on the lips. His mouth was incredibly soft, and the kiss ultra sensuous.

"When I saw you the first time at that party, the very first weekend of school, I thought to myself, 'I'm gonna kiss that girl.' I've been waiting a *long* time to do that," he whispered quietly. "I'm so lucky."

His words deepened the sensuality of the kiss, and I had to remind myself to breathe.

"Good night," he said in a low tone, kissing me again.

I floated up to my room in a kind of confounded haze of giddiness and confusion. Caitlyn was out and I spent the next 45 minutes parachuting down from my cloud, feeling as the initial euphoria wore off that I was actually being pulled into a tailspin.

I was so tired of this ceaseless, day-to-day tug-of-war between my hormones and my head, my vanity and my virtue. I felt very much as though I were caught in the middle of some dreadful battle in which taking a side of my own would mean certain misery in either case. Yet not to choose the side would mean this endless discomfort of being torn in half.

Lately I'd been having increasing difficulty falling asleep at night, and tonight was no different. A thousand thoughts trooped through my mind as I lay there in the darkness, contemplating what I should do, and how I should do it. I was awake long after Caitlyn slipped in with her Shakespeare wannabe suitor, and I could hear the smacking of lips as they kissed in the darkness, assuming I was fast asleep. I was very much awake after Shakespeare tucked Caitlyn in and then reluctantly left, and I was still wide-eyed when the sullen red numbers on the alarm clock rolled past 2:30 A.M.

Finally, my racing thoughts must have run out of steam as I relived the magical sensation of Graeme's first kiss over and over in my mind, at last slipping into the world of the subconscious.

Chapter 14 – Tug of War

"These make my butt look like a giant red planet, don't they?" Anise asked me. We were in the dressing room at the mall, trying on an array of sweaters, pants, skirts and tops.

"They look fine," Caitlyn replied, eyeing the red corduroys Anise was wearing.

Anise turned to me. "Say it; they make my rear look like a spaceship could land on it, right?"

"Everything you put on looks great on you," I answered truthfully. I wasn't exaggerating. With her pixie-like frame and beautiful face, Anise could have donned sackcloth and ashes and with the right accessories started a new trend.

Caitlyn preferred the neutral tones of khaki, white and gray, but everything looked wonderful on her as well, more in the girl-next-door classic way than Anise's full-blown glamour.

I liked going shopping with Anise because she wouldn't hesitate to give me an honest assessment of whatever it was I was considering buying.

"You look *hot*," she'd say when I tried on a particular flattering cut of jeans and coupled it with a tight, one-size-fits-all baby tee. (If my dad had seen it, he would have dryly described it as "one size fits nobody.")

"Nope, doesn't do anything for me," she'd answer truthfully when I'd emerge in a style or color that wasn't particularly flattering.

Having Anise and Caitlyn shop with me was so much more beneficial than the occasional trips I'd venture out on with my mother. My mom was much more concerned about secondary things such as necklines and jeans being too low-cut. I could never get from her an unbiased opinion of the fashion itself.

"Hey, don't look now but there's Heather Smush-Face," Caitlyn said in a low tone.

I turned my head slightly, pretending to check out a rack of belts, and glimpsed a skinny, well-dressed little stick figure, with perfectly highlighted hair and an expensive looking handbag, perusing an array of knit tops on a nearby table.

"*That's* the one who was all snotty to you?" I asked Anise.

"That's Smush-Face alright," Anise nodded.

Had it been an SAT question, the answer would have been Smush-Face was to Anise as Taylar was to me. Though I'd never seen her, Anise had informed me that the said Heather routinely rolled her eyes and made other faces whenever Anise would speak up in their philosophy class. She had earned her nickname because Anise claimed that her profile was flat, as though someone had driven an anvil into it.

"Speaking of philosophy class, I'd like to tell her my philosophy about her nose," Anise had said. "It needs some major reconstructive work. Maybe I'd better leave my dad's card in her mailbox."

I could hardly imagine anyone being brazen enough to give Anise attitude. It seemed like a hazardous endeavor.

"I heard that she's really, *really* stupid and that her dad is paying double tuition just so that she can go to Durst," Caitlyn informed us eagerly.

"*Double* tuition?" I repeated. "What is he, a multimillionaire?"

"Probably," Anise said. "She'd better hope that she gets her MRS degree while she's here. God help the man who ends up taking care of *her* for the rest of his life!"

"She wishes that man were Luke," I observed. "*That's* why you're the target on her radar. It's so obvious whenever he's at a party and she's there."

"I heard that she never, ever leaves her room without all her makeup being perfect. And she *never ever* goes without lipstick because her lips are collagen and they look freaky without it." Caitlyn abruptly turned away. "Don't look. Here she comes!" I dropped my eyes and pretended to study the price tag on the cardigan in my hand.

"Hi!" I heard a voice say. I looked up, and Smush-Face was before us.

"Hey!" Caitlyn turned around, acting surprised and delighted to see her. Anise said nothing, just staring at her.

"Rolling out the fall wardrobe, I see," Smush-Face observed with high-pitched, overexerted cheerfulness. I thought that her voice sounded like Beaker from *The Muppets*.

"Yep, getting some great bargains," Caitlyn played along with the act. "How about you?" I detected Anise darting a quick look of reproof towards Caitlyn.

"Well, I'm not really looking for *bargains* necessarily," Smush-Face said with an air of condescension. "But I'm hoping to find something here that doesn't look like what all the locals are wearing." She laughed unpleasantly.

I waited for her to turn her head to the side so that I could examine the claim of her two-dimensional profile for myself. She did not cooperate, however, and after an uncomfortable pause, she at last said to Anise in her *falsetto*, "Well, see you in Philosophy!"

"Yep," Anise answered shortly, offering nothing more. We watched Smush-Face flounce away.

"She makes my skin crawl," Anise asserted tightly, racking her rejected corduroys with a vengeance.

I tallied my new treasures and took them up to the counter, watching with pleasure as the cashier scanned the items of costume jewelry, blouses, blue jeans, and the tee-shirts my dad would have equated with the size and durability of postage stamps. The new clothes cost me practically everything I'd earned through working all those hours in the dining hall, but it was worth it not to look like frumpy ol' maid Molly of the not-so-distant past. I felt an urgent need to banish her and her lack of sophistication to a dark closet somewhere.

*****

Professor Day handed our labs back with an aura of detachment. I was still getting used to how different college was from high school in that manner. Even our senior high teachers had fussed over or lectured us, or even praised our grades; college was a different story. With rare exception, little comment was made about a class's general progress. Apparently, nothing was said about an individual's progress or lack thereof either, unless that individual took it upon himself to contact the professor.

This was a good practice, I thought, encouraging us to be independent. I was particularly grateful for it on this day when Professor Day dropped my paper on my desk, adorned in red lettering with a large red "C" and paragraphs of more red lettering explaining why my lab stank. Quickly I shoved the paper out of sight under my physics book.

****

Later that week, Caitlyn and I got all dressed up one evening and decided to dine out, rather than slum it in the cafeteria. We had agreed to push our luck in trying to pass for 21 years of age and see if we could get away with ordering alcohol.

"More make up," Caitlyn suggested as I posed for her approval. "It'll make you look older."

I took her advice and slathered on more foundation and rouge, then applied a berry-colored lipstick.

Arm in arm we traipsed through the middle of campus, taking in the smell of fall that hung in the air, and chattering incessantly. We were so absorbed in our conversation that I didn't see the figure in front of me, and ran nearly headlong into Jen Houseal. I pulled back, a little uncertainly.

"Hi!" Jen said.

"Hey, how are ya?" I said, a little too cheerfully, hoping wildly that the discomfort I felt in seeing her wasn't manifesting itself on my face.

"Good to see you, I've been hoping to catch up with you," Jen said eagerly.

"Yeah, me too," I said, feigning a bit more exuberance than I felt. "Um, this is my roommate, Caitlyn."

Caitlyn and Jen exchanged pleasantries, and then Jen said quickly, "Well, it looks like you two are going somewhere, so I don't want to hold you up. But I really hope we'll get to see you at Fellowship soon."

I assured her I would try to make it to the next one, although that was tomorrow night, and I already had plans with Graeme.

Finally, we left Jen and continued walking the couple blocks into town. There was a popular off-campus bar and grill where a lot of the older students went for dinner and drinks, and we wanted to try it out. I had had a powerful, unanswered craving for quesadillas with guacamole for the past three days and knew that the restaurant served this. We had been informed that if we got there early enough, we would not have to risk rejection by a bouncer.

Our waiter was a guy who looked to be in his mid-twenties and who, naturally, took an instant interest in Caitlyn. (I envied the tremendous power she wielded with her looks alone). After we'd looked over the extensive beverage menu, Caitlyn announced her desire to try a strawberry margarita, while I decided upon a Long Island iced tea. I couldn't get over how many different types of drinks there were, and I figured I'd better try to educate myself on them with a crash course if I didn't want to look like a complete cultural imbecile all my life.

College life had taught me the basics, and I was self-taught on the rest. "Beer before liquor, never sicker," was the mantra upper classmen had repeated often enough, and "Liquor before beer, you're in the clear." I also knew something of the "four food groups" of alcohol and what beverages were categorized in each. As for my personal tastes, I was still a novice and eager to learn.

When our waiter returned, I gave him my drink request and held my breath, waiting for him to card me. He wrote it down without batting an eye, and then took Caitlyn's order for the margarita. He smiled at her and told us he'd return momentarily. We both breathed a sigh of relief and did a silent cheer across the table as he walked away

When my drink arrived, I cautiously took a sip. It tasted like something that might be able to cure me of an infection. I coughed, my eyes watering a bit. "Whoa," I said. "I thought it would be more like – I don't know – an iced tea."

"Oh, I don't think Long Island iced teas have any tea in them at all," Caitlyn informed me. "Try my margarita."

Over the next hour, Caitlyn and I chattered about everything inconsequential we could think of, laughing riotously and generally oblivious to those around us. I did notice a couple times several glances cast our way from neighboring tables, sometimes from young guys and occasionally from a group of men sitting near the bar who looked older than my father. I wondered if these older men were questioning and disapproving our ages in regards to the alcohol. We didn't pay anyone much attention, though. I satiated my quesadilla craving and our drinks both disappeared as well. That warm, relaxed feeling was settling over me again, growing as the moments went by, and I felt merry and unencumbered.

When the check arrived, Caitlyn insisted on paying it in full. I felt bad, thinking that her main reason for the generosity was probably because she was much more intoxicated off that margarita than I was from my Long Island iced tea.

Our waiter said, "Come back and see us again," pointedly to Caitlyn as we got up to leave. She assured him, giggling, that we would.

As we walked out the door, one of the older men followed behind us.

"Hello," he said to me as I held the door behind me. He had dark hair that was graying near the temples, and he was wearing a tie that had been loosened around his neck. "I'm John. It looks like you're about to leave, but I was hoping to buy you a drink."

Thoroughly taken aback, I was at a loss for words.

"We were actually just leaving," Caitlyn interposed, slurring a little.

"I'd like to take you out for dinner some time," he added, his gaze still fixed on me. His confidence disarmed me.

"She has a boyfriend," Caitlyn jumped in immediately, grabbing my hand. "C'mon, Molly, let's go!"

"Thanks, anyway," I mumbled to the gentleman, still astonished. Yep, he had to be more than twice my age.

We left him standing there watching after us. When we were sufficient distance from the restaurant doorway we took off sprinting down the street for a block. When we finally ran out of steam, we collapsed into the side of an ancient brick building on the main street, panting and laughing.

"Molly's getting hit on by *geriatrics*!" Caitlyn hollered, bursting into a fresh peal of riotous laughter.

"Stop it," I laughed, trying to catch my breath.

"Bet you he'd take you somewhere where they offer a 'senior special' for a date!" she screamed, doubling over against the wall of the house in hysterics. "And they'll have to puree his food before he can eat it!"

I grinned. "Alright, alright, so an older guy hit on me."

"Your nickname for him will be 'Gramps,'" Caitlyn snorted, clutching her stomach. Tears were actually spilling over the corners of her eyes.

"And his kids will all hate me because even *they* will be too old for me!" I finally added, succumbing to the spirit of it.

The door to the house we were standing near suddenly opened abruptly and a curly, gray-haired head poked out around it and glared at us. It belonged to what I determined to be a woman, after it spoke.

"Shut up or I call the cops on ya!" she hollered. "Yer makin' too much noise!"

Caitlyn and I stared at her, flabbergasted, until she slammed the door shut with resounding force. We looked at each other and burst into fresh guffaws, then took off running again as fast as we could, laughing the entire way back to the dorm.

*****

Graeme called me late the next afternoon, his voice thick with a cold. "Ugh, I feel awful," he said. "This always happens to me around the change of the seasons."

"Do you want me to get you anything?" I asked, disappointed to miss out on our date.

"No, I'm fine. Just wanna sleep."

"You sure? Don't want me to come over at all with some soup or something?"

"The last thing I want to do is get you sick," Graeme said. "Believe me, I'm bummed we can't go out, but I promise I'll make it up to you."

I told him goodnight and hung up. Caitlyn had already left to go out with one of her devotees, and Anise was trying out for some dance team that was forming. It occurred to me that my evening was now free to attend the Christian fellowship. I paced back and forth in my room for a few moments, trying to decide what to do. I wasn't entirely comfortable with the idea of going; on the other hand, I wouldn't feel the need to avoid Jen and the others every time I saw them around campus if I showed up and made an appearance. I threw my sweatshirt on, said goodbye to Caitlyn, and started in the direction of the building in which it was held before I had time to change my mind.

When I walked into the room we used to meet in for fellowship, I was greeted with an overwhelming response.

"Molly, hey! Good to see you!" Jen was the first to hurl herself onto me in a hug, followed by several others. I hung back a bit sheepishly, but found myself propelled forward by all the greetings.

The lost sheep has returned to the fold, I thought wryly.

The chatter eventually died down as the familiar faces of the worship team took the stage. As we sang the well-known songs, I felt as though I were viewing them as a stranger might, as though the words were somehow vaguely recognizable, but from just where I did not know…almost as though I were suffering a mild form of amnesia. I knew them, but they didn't strike in me the same tone that had once given them their meaning.

Finally, we got to my favorite song, called "It's Amazing," and the lyrics went like this:

> I have searched the whole world over,
> Looking for the things I thought would
> fill my heart and ease my pain
> I can climb the highest mountain,
> Or sail beyond the seas,
> And it always brings me back to you again.
>
> It's amazing how you love me;
> It's amazing how you care,
> It's amazing how you're always thinking of me
> All the time, everywhere.
>
> There are times when I feel lonely and twisted up
> inside
> On who I am, what I want to be
> There's a yearning deep inside me, and a longing to
> be free
> And it always brings me back to you again.
>
> It's amazing how you love me;
> It's amazing how you care,
> It's amazing how you're always thinking of me
> All the time, everywhere.

I have lived my life an outlaw on the run
Leaving broken hearted dreams for everyone
No matter what I do and no matter what I've done,
It always brings me back to you again.

I can look the whole world over thinking that I'll find
Another one who'll know me like you do;
But no matter where I go and no matter where I
search,
It'll always bring me back to you again. *

I felt the rigidity of my heart starting to lapse as I sung the words, really feeling the weight of their meaning this time. Mournfully, I recognized the bitter truth of their reality in my own behavior in the last several weeks. Repentant, I felt the tears squeezing out of the corners of my eyelids.

When we broke up into smaller groups for prayer, I confessed to my group what I'd been going through, how I'd been ignoring the voice of the Spirit and how I'd been following along my own path instead of His. Some of them shared how they could relate, and Jen – who was in my group – prayed for me that I would give myself over to the Lord and that He would guide my path from that day forward.

When I left the fellowship meeting and walked outside into the night air, I felt refreshed and more at peace than I had since the first week of my arrival at Durst. Jen asked if I wanted to go get milkshakes at the HUB, but I wanted to be alone for a bit and think. As I made my way back to my dorm, I passed clusters of kids laughing loudly and all dressed up in their party apparel, most likely on their way to various fraternity functions. I was relieved rather than remorseful for the first time in quite some time not to be among them, but instead to be heading the opposite direction towards my room, and solitude. I needed some time to think.

Chapter 15 – Homecoming

My parents' expressions when I walked in the door that night mirrored the ones I had seen a few hours earlier at the Christian fellowship.

"You're *home!*" my mom shrieked as I walked in the door. "Is everything okay?"

It was almost eleven o'clock at night when my ride pulled in front of the house and dropped me off. I hadn't told them I was coming. Everything had come together so quickly that I hadn't even had time. Detouring to the HUB after fellowship I had called three of the names on the board outside the mailroom that listed who was available for any carpooling. Of the first two names which lived in the general direction of my home, the first was unreachable and the second had already left. The third person I called who had advertised on the board had been detained due to finishing a paper, and so I lucked out in being able to hop a ride with him. He was a freakishly quiet, sandy-haired kid who explained to me that he drove home every weekend to see his girlfriend. It took about half the car ride to get that piece of information out of him, as it was like a tug-of-war to get him to speak.

I hope your girlfriend talks, I thought to myself as we drove along in labored silence. I pictured the joyous reunion of the two of them being wordless, and them just sitting there on a date staring at their food.

I hadn't been home since I'd started school. Truth be told, I hadn't *wanted* to go home or anywhere else off campus for fear I'd be missing out on stuff.

It was strange to be in my old room. I looked around at the shelves holding my paperbacks and the artwork hanging on my walls. I opened the top drawer of my dresser. The caricature of Elvis that Hank had sketched for me that day in math class was still tucked away in there, along with all kinds of notes and knick-knacks. High school seemed like such a very long time ago.

It seemed so *quiet* being back home, too. After the constant noise and energy of dorm living, I wasn't used to the silence. I slept fitfully, dreaming about my parents' neighbors playing "Redlight-Greenlight" outside my bedroom door and of Professor Bund coming to see my way of thinking as we raked leaves and talked worldviews under the giant oak in my parents' back yard.

The next day, my family wanted to hear all about my time away in the last ten weeks, and I was careful to share with them the items I knew would not overly alarm them. Anne listened in with interest as well as I described campus goings-on, professors, and the workload that was so much heavier than what I'd ever had in high school.

"You've changed," Anne said suddenly when we were alone together in the living room Saturday afternoon. The point blank statement caught me completely off guard.

"In what way?" I asked.

"I don't know," she said thoughtfully. "You don't seem quite as…relaxed…as you used to be."

"I feel plenty relaxed," I retorted, a bit defensively.

"No, I mean overall," she answered. "I don't know how to describe it exactly. Just like, well, you're not quite as carefree."

"Yeah, well, living among the world jades you," I replied in an off-hand way, and deftly changed the subject.

Being home again intensified my longing to see Hank. I missed his one-of-a-kind outlook on everything, and would have given just about anything I possessed to be able to hear what he thought of college and to be able to share with him my own observations. Throughout high school I'd always felt so naïve and inexperienced compared to Hank, and perhaps now he would realize I'd gained some ground, had caught up to him a little. I wondered how he would react to hearing about Graeme, what he'd say in response. I wondered if he'd even care that I had been seeing someone.

That evening, I walked alone outside for about an hour, circling the block, reflecting on my decisions over the last couple months, and praying. What a backslider I'd been! Numb-in-the-*head*. I wanted to live for God every day, and to be a living testimony to His truth on campus, and instead I'd been a stumbling block! How could I so quickly have faded away? How could I have turned my back on my First Love? How could I have traded Truth for frivolity and insistence on my own way?

"God, please forgive me," I murmured, walking under a streetlight, my head down towards the pavement. "Let me start all over again. Let this all be as though it never happened. Help me to be the person *You* want me to be."

*****

I would have liked to have stayed for church Sunday morning, but my mute-like carpooler had informed me in no more words than were absolutely necessary that he was swinging by before noon to pick me up. There was reading waiting for me back in my room anyhow. I had left Durst in such a hurry on Friday night that all I had had time to do was scribble a note to Caitlyn explaining that all was well but that I had decided to go home. I hadn't called Graeme at all to see how he was feeling Saturday, a gesture which no doubt made me looked like quite the cold-blooded brute in his eyes. The fact of the matter was that I was scared to call him, afraid that a conversation with him might derail me from my quest to seek out God.

Waving goodbye to my parents and Anne in the doorway, I sighed. I was eager to get back to school, but also scared of what it would bring.

"We missed you!" Anise cried, giving me a huge hug as soon as she saw me. It was hard to believe someone as tiny as she could squeeze that hard. I felt one of the vertebrae in my back crack as she released me. "It was so boring here this weekend without you!"

"It was creepy being in the room alone Friday night," Caitlyn told me. I kept hearing noises and waking up. (I inferred from this statement that she possibly had remedied the problem Saturday night by having one of her gentlemen friends stay over).

"By the way," Caitlyn continued, "Graeme called here and left a couple messages on Saturday, so I went ahead and called him back and let him know that you had gone home for the weekend."

"What did he say?" I asked nervously.

"He seemed surprised, but just said to tell you that he called."

I nodded. I planned to delay calling him as long as I could, as I was dreading it. I knew that I had to break off ties with him, and that was going to be tough.

I skipped dinner that evening to avoid running into Graeme and instead got take-out with Caitlyn. Finally, around eight-thirty, I figured I couldn't delay calling him any longer. It would be better just to get it over with and deal with the aftermath. Fingertips sweaty and my heart protesting rapidly, I dialed his room extension

"Graeme isn't here," his roommate Jeff informed me when I called. He was so seldom in their room that I was amazed to have caught him at all. "He went to the emergency room."

"What?" I asked in disbelief. "What happened?"

"His cold got worse over the weekend and by this evening he had a fever of 104.1. Medicine wasn't touching it so he figured he'd better check in to the hospital. One of the Theta Chi brothers gave him a ride there about an hour ago."

I hung up the phone with jumbled emotions. I had really hoped to get this ordeal over with; on the other hand, my concern for Graeme's health was real. Offering up a fervent prayer that he would be alright, I read my Bible until my eyelids grew heavy. I had opened up randomly to the strange account in Genesis of Noah getting drunk and passing out naked, and his one son checking him out. *Weird,* I thought.

As I turned out the light, it occurred to me that I should ask for a Bible commentator for Christmas so that I could understand the deeper significance in what I was reading. No doubt I was missing out on some major stuff because I didn't always understand why certain things had made it into the Bible.

Caitlyn was on the phone with David for well over two hours, infusing giggles and tales of her classes in between professing to him how much she missed him and couldn't wait to see him again. I wished she would use her cell, but knew that she had run over her minutes the month before and that the bill had been over two hundred dollars. With the phone line being tied up, I wouldn't be getting a return call from Graeme, and I drifted off to sleep, partially glad to put off facing the dreaded issue another day.

*****

I stopped by Graeme's room mid-morning the next day. I figured that it really *would* be insensitive not to pay him a visit as a friend.

"Come in," I heard his voice call, muffled from behind the door. My heart began thumping at the sound of it. I stepped into the familiar surrounds, which were darkened by the drawn shades and dimmed lights. Instantly, the scent of his cologne, now identified forever with him, greeted me.

He was lying on the sofa, facing the television. A light came into his eyes when he saw me, and he smiled broadly.

"How are you feeling?" I asked, a little stiffly.

"Awesome now that you're here," he said, stretching.

Inwardly I groaned. Did he *have* to make this that much more difficult?

"Um, I'm not getting too close, just because-" I faltered.

"Oh, believe me," Graeme interrupted, "I wouldn't wish the fever I had last night on my worst enemy. Better keep your distance for now." He grinned. "Later, I hope to get contagiously close to you."

"Are you feeling better now?" I asked, my voice coming out wooden.

"Much better. It was one of those weird, random things. By the time they finally saw me last night, the fever had peaked and broken. Man, emergency rooms *suck.*"

"Well, can I get you anything?"

"You being here helps a ton," he said softly.

Oh, dang it all, I thought hopelessly. *Why don't you just carve my heart out using a knife and fork?*

"By the way," he said, a note of teasing in his voice, "why'd you take off like that? I mean, I get sick for one night and cancel a date with you and I thought I was with Cinderella – just took off without any warning. *That'll* teach me."

"I guess I was restless," I said evasively. It was not in me to tell him the full truth at that inopportune moment. "And, it was the first time I'd been home since school started. You know how parents can give you such grief."

"Oh, yeah. No one can lay on the guilt like your average WASP," Graeme chuckled. He had used the acronym before, and in fact, since coming to Durst I don't believe I'd ever heard so much slang to designate groups of people. I of course had heard of this term for Caucasian Protestants, but brand new to me was JAP, which I learned stood for Jewish American Princess, something which Anise and Caitlyn had taught me, apparently because such a term was relevant in New Jersey.

"We don't have much ethnic diversity where I live except in the inner city," I had told Anise and Caitlyn truthfully. "Mostly, we just have livestock."

"Well, I hate to run but I do have class in forty-five minutes and I have some reading left to do," I said, coming back to the present.

"Aw, sure you have to go?"

I nodded, feigning more remorse than I felt.

"Hey, Molly?" he called, as I reached for the doorknob.

I turned around.

"I missed you," he said softly.

I put a smile on my face, inwardly thinking what a pleasant thing it would be if the Lord would just return *now* and swoop me away to Heaven.

Chapter 16 –Blurred Lines

"If a guy gives you his phone number, would you ever call him first?" Caitlyn wanted to know. She, Anise and I were hunkered down along the far wall in the cafeteria.

"Nope, wouldn't do it," Anise stated, spreading a slab of butter all over her bread.

"Molly?" Caitlyn asked me.

I shook my head. "I'm old-fashioned when it comes to stuff like that," I said.

"In sociology we have to write a paper on whether or not it sets feminism back half a century by the fact that women generally don't make the first move when it comes to approaching a guy or putting the moves on a guy," Caitlyn explained.

"Who cares?" Anise shrugged. "Why should I risk putting my neck out there when the guy can do it?"

"Well, here's another scenario. What if you've been on five dates and the guy hasn't even tried to hold your hand," Caitlyn suggested. "Say he's really hot, too. Would you grab his hand first in the movie theater?"

"Only if it was holding my drink," Anise said. "Then I could make it look like a coincidence."

"How about you, Molly?"

"No way," I said, shaking my head. I could picture Taylar doing something like that. "I wouldn't want to appear desperate."

"Oh, yes she would!" Anise laughed, teasing. "If he was really hot, she'd be all over him!"

I blushed, staring down at my spaghetti.

"What about the double standard between a girl who sleeps around a lot, as opposed to a guy who does the same thing."

"Well, *that* is unfair not to judge them the same way," I agreed. "It's gross either way."

"You get diseases either way," Anise chimed. "*That* doesn't discriminate."

"Well, my sociology professor was saying how despite the progress they've made as far as voting and equal rights, women are still socially captive when it comes to traditional gender roles. They're still not on the same playing field when it comes to things like approaching the guy first."

"I don't know," I replied. "My uncle is pretty old and he was telling me once that when he was our age, women controlled everything socially and that the men had to snap to attention. Now, he says that men treat women like dirt because women have stepped down from expecting to be treated respectfully and have settled for being equal to men. The men have no standard to shoot for any more, and so they're all confused."

"No matter what, I personally think that being a lady never goes out of style," Anise agreed.

"Me, too," I said. "I don't want to be treated equal to a man – I want to be treated much better than a man!"

"Here's to that," Anise toasted my chocolate milk with her tea.

"Speaking of gender roles…" Anise trailed off. I turned around. Jill was walking towards our table, her eyes zeroed in on Caitlyn. "I'll bet someone's here to promote her latest cause."

"Sister!" Jill exclaimed exuberantly, coming up from behind Caitlyn and giving her a long hug, which Caitlyn returned to the

140

best of her ability from where she sat. I watched Anise, who was observing the two of them, a sort of half smile on her face.

Caitlyn ought to pose the same question to Jill and see where she comes down on the guy or the girl making the first move, I thought sardonically.

"Hey, everyone," Jill turned to address me and Anise. "We're having an educational session on gay marriage next week on the steps of Old Main. We need your support, so please come. Here's the information." She placed a stack of flyers on the center of the table in front of us, the trademark triangle at the bottom. "Pass these out to your friends and the people in your classes." She gave Caitlyn another long hug. "See you, sister!"

The three of us watched Jill's ample figure shuffle over to another table.

"I don't care what people do behind closed doors, but I'm not all gung-ho pro-gay either like she is," Anise finally said. "I wish she didn't push it so hard all the time. When she's around, I feel like all she talks about – all she thinks about – is being a lesbian and getting other people to focus on that, too. It's like, get a hobby or something!"

As I continued to watch Jill, I was suddenly flooded with an overwhelming sense of God's love for her. I wasn't thinking about it, just contemplating my own morose views on the subject, but I was bowled over by the unsolicited wash of love that I sensed coming from Him for Jill. He cared for her so very much, longed to be with her and to fellowship with her heart. Tears sprang into the corners of my eyes as the floodgates of His mercy opened on me, and I pretended again to be absorbed in my spaghetti so that Anise and Caitlyn wouldn't see. Right then and there, I made a silent commitment to God to pray for Jill every day until I was sure that she came to know this Great Love that was in store for her. Political views weren't unimportant, but they were secondary to that for sure.

*****

"What do you mean 'you think we should stop seeing each other'"? Graeme's face was ashen. "You're kidding, right?"

I shook my head mournfully. I had only ever heard of breaking up in rock songs. I'd never attempted it myself nor had it dished out on me. No wonder it was so often likened to death by slow torture.

"Molly, I don't understand." Graeme covered his eyes with his palms, breathing in deeply. He took his hands away from his face. "I thought things were going so great between us. I thought we had so much in common..."

Next to nothing in common, especially the most important thing, I thought regretfully, staring at my fingernails, unwilling to look him in the eyes. And now, how to make him understand a concept that he was totally blind to. The failure in trying to break up gracefully with a non-believer was as good a reason for not dating them as any other.

"Did I do something wrong?" Graeme wanted to know. "Are you seeing someone else?"

"No, no, no," I sighed. *Wish that as I might.*

"Then what is it? Tell me what I did wrong and what I can do to fix this!"

"Graeme," I drew a breath. "I just – feel – that I can't continue to see you and devote myself one hundred percent to God as well. I've tried to explain how important He is to me"-

"So, in your religion does God require that you be a nun?" Graeme interrupted, a little derisively.

"No," I answered drearily. "Of course not. It's just since I came to Durst I've been involved in some things I never thought I would do and it's interfering with my spiritual life."

"Like what?" Graeme wanted to know.

"Well..." I hadn't thought entirely through giving him an explanation. I guess I had figured he'd show up, I'd tell him it was over, and we'd part ways without much further discussion. "For one thing, remember at that party when we had the conversation about alcohol? And I told you how I wanted to be obedient about the laws that were in place and not drink it? Well, I've been drinking alcohol on a regular basis lately."

Graeme looked puzzled. "*I* didn't ask you to drink, nor would I care whether you choose to or not."

"No, I know," I said hurriedly, mind racing about how better to articulate myself. "But my whole life has gotten off track and that's just one of the ways."

"So how is being friends with me and us hanging out together getting your life 'off track?" Graeme demanded, a note of bitterness in his voice. "How am I this terrible hindrance to your life goals? Do you think I'm a bad person?"

"No I don't think you're a bad person," I sighed again, frustrated. "It's more that I don't trust myself not to compromise when I'm with you."

"Compromise *what?*" Graeme wanted to know.

I looked away, fumbling with my keychain. Boy, would I make a horrible litigator. I made a mental note never to go to law school.

"Compromise what?" Graeme repeated. "What is it you feel is going to be compromised by us being friends?"

From somewhere down the hallway, I could hear the sound of riotous laughter. At least somebody was enjoying life. I wished I were anywhere but where I was standing. "I can't go any further with you physically," I blurted out.

Graeme looked at me, appearing as though he knew I was speaking English but as though he were trying hard to decipher meaning in my words.

"Have I *asked* you to?" he questioned.

"No," I admitted. "Not yet."

Graeme dropped his head. He looked at me. "Is *that* what all this is about? That's you're not ready to sleep with me?"

"I'm not *going* to sleep with you," I emphasized, finding boldness suddenly and clinging to it. "Or with anyone else until I get married."

"Why didn't you just say that in the first place? Do you honestly think I'm such a jerk that I would have broken up with you over that?"

I gazed at him, unsure of what to say.

"A lot of guys would, but not me," Graeme said. "I'm content just to stay wherever you're comfortable." He held out his hand to me. "We can still be friends, can't we?"

I stood there for a moment, a flurry of thoughts whirling through my head, and at the center of them, blank space. What was I to reply to that – "No, we can't be friends"?

"Molly, please answer me. We can still hang out together as friends, right? Just have fun, enjoy each other's company?"

I felt like I was melting like a huge popsicle onto the floor, and that one by one each of his words was a ray of warmth that was thawing me into a puddle. The hardness with which I had bolstered myself before coming to see him had softened to slush. I took his hand. He drew me next to him and squeezed me tight in a hug. Even that simple gesture provoked my mind thinking in a sensuous direction, and I tried to block out the physiological response. A strange sort of relief settled over me as I sat there at not having made a clean cut of it, yet the longed-for freedom that I had hoped to fly away with when I left his dorm was not present. I felt cagey, compromised.

*****

I tried going to bed early that night but couldn't sleep. The riot of emotions that had passed through me over the previous four or five days seemed to have capsized my equanimity, and once again I felt as though I were headed for deep waters with fogged direction. It was not my wish at all to give up Graeme's friendship entirely. Like he said, what was the harm in just spending some time together? After all, I had made clear where I stood on things. In fact, I had drawn the boundaries better than some *Christian* kids I'd known who were in a relationship. I comforted myself with that thought for a moment, then tossed onto my side.

If only I had someone to open up to and share my heart – someone who would truly listen and understand. I felt as though Kendra had never stood in this spot and therefore couldn't possibly relate to the struggle taking place within me at that moment. She would have a list of "thou shalt nots" for me – and granted, they would be founded in love – but she wouldn't really fathom the complexity of what she was telling me to do.

Anise and Caitlyn were great friends, but neither of them could possibly understand the dilemma of the faith aspect of all this. My mom would be the last person with whom I'd share any of this (I could just picture her and my father arriving under cover of night and whisking me away from college, perhaps locking me in the basement – or worse, sending me to an all-girls' school). Anne was too young and plus I wouldn't want to burden her with this kind of stuff.

As I shifted around in my college-designated bunk, I suddenly thought of Hank. It had been over a month since he had sent me the letter and I had never replied to it. That was more than sufficient time to contact him now without my infatuation appearing too obvious. I glanced at the clock. It was only nine-thirty. Caitlyn was out with Brendan from her sociology class and wasn't expected back any time soon. *Studying sociology,* I thought ironically, *or perhaps practicing it.*

Hank had given me his number at art school the night before he'd left, and I had it tucked into a page of our high school yearbook where he'd written a typically humor-ridden, slightly ambiguous message summed up by telling me not to be a stranger after high school.

I picked up the phone and dialed the first three numbers of the area code. My heart was slamming again, and my breathing was as though I'd just taken the stairs. I put the receiver down. I took some deep breaths through my nose and tried to think about something else. Whenever I was nervous or dreading something, I would try to picture eternity and then comfort myself in the fact that my lifespan might be 75 years if I were lucky and that 75 years into eternity was zero and that any embarrassment suffered in this life was utterly meaningless. This rationale could get quickly depressing if I dwelled on it too long, but it often gave me just enough courage to go through with whatever scary task was at hand.

I dialed the number. Each ring of the phone seemed in itself a mini-eternity.

"Hello?"

His voice! I didn't realize until just that moment how much I had missed the sound of it. My throat instantly dried up while my palms turned to puddles.

"H-Hank?" I stammered.

"Yeah?"

"It's Molly."

Silence. "Molly? Oh. Hey, how ya doing?"

I wouldn't have nominated him for a welcoming committee or anything with that greeting.

"I'm fine, Hank. How've you been? How's everything at art school?" I hoped wildly that my voice sounded casual.

"Super," he drawled, sounding more like his old self now but not offering any more information on the matter.

"Oh." My heart sunk a little at his enthusiasm.

"What's going on?"

"Well," I began, forcing airiness into my voice. "I got your letter and never wrote back....you know how crazy things can get at school and all...and anyway, I wanted to give you a call and just let you know I hadn't entirely forgotten about you...wanted to see how you were and what you were up to."

"Well I thank you for the call," Hank said with his easy-going, mock formality. "I'm doing great and life is grand."

There was a pause. "What classes are you taking?" I continued, trying to keep the floundering conversation alive.

"Uh..." Hank seemed to be searching his mind. "Literature and the arts, intro to metal fabrication, fundamentals of ceramics, and a philosophy course."

I only half listened as he rattled these off. I was too conscious of my own nerves. "Well, I'll bet you're meeting all kinds of interesting people there in the far out world of art."

"Actually, I am," Hank answered. "In fact, I hate to cut you off but I was just on my way out the door to go meet someone right now. My girlfriend's waiting for me at a café down the street."

The breath caught in my throat. His words stopped and hung there in the air. In my mind I could see the words spelled out. *My Girlfriend.*

I had heard it said that you don't feel pain when a bullet hits the heart. Amazed at my own poise and self-possession I calmly – even jokingly – wished him well and managed to get off the phone.

I stood there in the darkness of my room, oblivious to the things around me, except for the cold that I felt all over. How long I stood there I don't know, nor do I remember thinking a single thought. I felt paralyzed in both mind and body, as though I knew somehow – faintly – that I was still breathing and had a pulse, but was helpless to move or feel anything. It was as though I were existing on life support, but had no interest or will in the matter myself.

Some time must have gone by and I became aware of the girls on my floor goofing off and gallivanting through the hallways. It occurred to me that life must go on – *would* go on – and that I must somehow be a part of that, utterly immaterial as it now seemed.

Slowly, I climbed back into bed and lay motionless as the minutes crept by, staring at the ceiling. I thought about this new girlfriend of Hank's, imagining her to be pretty and petite and probably artsy and ultra-cool. I pictured her wearing thumb rings and tiny t-shirts and walking around with a detached air of boredom. I wondered if she felt anywhere near the same way about him that I did – that he was the most wonderful male creature ever to be imagined by the mind of God, and that she was the luckiest human being in the world to be the object of his affection.

I was awake when Caitlyn returned to the room but feigned sleep to avoid having to talk with her. I wasn't in the mood to hear about her date and all its glory. For the first time, I even felt resentment towards Caitlyn. If she cared for her boyfriend David a fraction of what I did for Hank she would never treat him so carelessly and cruelly.

The minutes cumulated into hours and I dismally watched them roll by one after another, wondering if this night would ever end. I thought of the verse from Psalms, "Weeping may endure for a night, but joy comes in the morning." Not for me. I had no desire for the morning, because I would wake up and realize that this nightmare of Hank being with someone else was not a dream, that it was altogether real, and that somehow I must still go on living, not only without him, but now without even the *hope* of him.

Chapter 17 – The Games People Play

Life, of course, continued in spite of the tornado that had touched down upon my own small world. It didn't feel like life, though, so much as life support.

As I went through the motions of the day-to-day I learned that I was truly masterful at disguising my real sentiments and that people generally were too busy and absorbed in their personal cares anyway to notice the wilting away of my own vivacity.

My course load was getting harder and although I was zapped of the will to succeed for the sake of success itself, I poured myself into the work because it was a distraction from my pain. I began locking myself away in the library for hours in the evenings, seeing it as a welcome sanctuary from the rest of the campus.

Afternoons, when classes were finished, I'd head over to the piano rooms at Weiss and sit down and play anything from Simon and Garfunkel to the old chords of a Wesleyan hymn. The music soothed me a little after a while, but inevitably when I had to leave my former gloom would slowly envelop me as I left the building and returned to routine.

My appetite dwindled and as the days went by I began to notice that my clothes were growing looser on me. Graeme complimented me so ardently on my weight loss that I counted this as one of the kickback blessings to being completely miserable inside.

Despite our having "broken up" we soon lapsed back into the physical part of the relationship. The first time that Graeme kissed me since my "break up" with him I thought immediately of Hank and burst into tears. It was the first time that I had cried over the situation. I managed to come up with a glib excuse for this absurd reaction, and Graeme seemed to buy it. I was becoming quite an artist of fabrication.

Prior to the unhappy realization of Hank's new relationship status I had already stumbled upon the discovery that alcohol was a remarkable remedy for instant relaxation of my already high-strung nature. I never knew that switching from an introvert to an extrovert lay in two cups of beer, or a double shot of vodka. Now, my desire to dull the perpetual ache that weighted me so heavily to the earth stirred in me a new inclination for the substance. Although I had written off the forbidden liquid, I found myself again "having a glass or two" when I was hanging out with Graeme at the house or when Caitlyn and I ended up at some party per the invitation of one of her many admirers. It was amazing how a few sips could miraculously brighten my outlook.

My daily range of emotions was downright manic, but there were plenty of distractions to keep Hank out of my mind, and to dissipate that nagging feeling that things were not right in my life; that I was "dipping my big toe" in Christianity but not following the Lord with my whole heart. There was no shortage of organized events hosted by both the college and its Greek life, including dances, socials, talent shows, a male beauty pageant, film showings, and a bevy of near-celebrity status guest speakers. The less "quiet" there was, the easier it was to ignore my restlessness.

Dreading the shadowy blue-gray of nighttime and its fearful loneliness of unshared thought, I was making an effort not to be alone in my room any earlier than I had to be most nights. The party atmosphere at Durst served as a willing accomplice to this need for escapism, and a weekend for me could start as early as a Tuesday night. While I generally was doing well at getting up the next morning despite my late nights, by Friday I was pretty well worn out and it wasn't unusual for me to sleep through my morning classes. Lunch would serve as breakfast many a morning and I'd hit a class in the afternoon before grabbing a quick dinner with Caitlyn and Anise and then preparing to party all over again Friday night.

On Halloween, the three of us went trick-or-treating around the town. It was comforting to relive a childhood practice, even though we were way too old to be garnering candy from the locals. We dressed up as three pregnant nuns. It was Anise's idea, and I suggested we murmur, "Bless you," to everyone that gave us candy. Along with the candy, we were given a lot of strange looks, and we weren't sure if that was because of our choice of costuming or our ages.

Living with Anise and Caitlyn and the multitude of Durst's cosmopolitan had made me much more aware of my appearance and the way I dressed, and I found myself studying fashion magazines with a sudden fervor. Dissatisfied with the contents of my own wardrobe, I began signing up for extra shifts at the dining hall so that I could poke some funds into my undernourished bank account for new clothing and accessories. For the first time I started paying attention to brand names and designers, and became conscious around campus of who was properly outfitted, and who was not.

My taste in music was shifting as well. I had gradually stopped listening to my Christian praise and worship and even the rock, and was starting to acquire a penchant for some of the variety that Anise liked. Whether in the dorm or at parties, I found dancing to be a great release, and when fueled with alcohol I found that my energy could last well into the wee hours of the morning.

The restlessness never went away completely, though, and I found that I became much more aware of it when I was alone and it was quiet. So I made every effort not to be by myself.

One evening after Graeme and I had been watching a movie in his room, he pleaded with me to stay over. It had grown late and I admittedly had no desire to venture out into the cold. The prospect of returning to my bleak room was equally unpalatable. I agreed to stay. I didn't have any pajamas, so Graeme gave me a pair of his mesh shorts and a tee shirt to sleep in, which were remarkably comfortable in their oversized proportions.

A little uncertainly I climbed into bed next to him. It was the first time I'd ever shared a bed with someone of the opposite sex, and as I settled into the cramped single bed I felt uncomfortable. I was unaccustomed to having someone sleep that close to me. Graeme wrapped a big arm around me and fell asleep instantly, but I lay awake, acutely aware of the unfamiliar sounds and shadows of his room.

Eventually I relaxed, and when I awoke suddenly in the gray dawn and glimpsed him next to me, breathing deeply in his sleep, I felt comforted. Snuggling in close to his masculine warmth, I fell into a deeper sleep than I'd had in a long time.

****

"You have no idea how lucky you are," Anise told me one day as I was sitting in her room, listening to music with her while she smoked a cigarette through the screened window. She smoked only when she was unusually stressed, opening the dorm window to the crisp, November air to blow out the smell of it. "To have your parents still together, still in love..." She shook her head and savagely dabbed the heel of her hand at her eyes. "All the wealth mine have can't save their own marriage."

I had been crushed to walk into the room an hour earlier and find Anise in tears, pleading plaintively with her mom on the telephone. Her piece of the conversation informed me clearly what was happening on the other end of the receiver – that the cruelty of a pending divorce was looming for her parents.

"I guess they were holding out all these years for me to graduate and leave home," Anise said tearfully, fiercely swiping a hand at the tears and mascara that mingled and made a trail down her cheek. "They stayed together so they wouldn't rock the household for me and my brother, and now...now that we're both out of the house, they don't see anything worth staying for."

I sat there mutely, listening to her words, studying her face. I felt helpless – impotent – to help her with her problems. I wanted to ask her if I could pray for her right then and there, but I couldn't bring myself to do it. My own relationship with God was in disarray – fragmented – thanks to the weeds that had grown over it. Because I could not see His face, I didn't know how to begin to help myself, and was equally powerless to come to Anise's aid.

*****

"The rules of the game are simple," Chris stated. "Bounce the quarter into the glass. If you make it, you drink the beer and go again. If you hit the rim, you get another try. If you miss, you pass it along to the next person."

"*And*, if you make three in a row, you can make a rule," Tad added. "Like, everyone else has to do a shot." He grinned. "We don't want anyone feeling left out."

"This should be good," Caitlyn whispered. She, Anise and I were sitting huddled around the cheap coffee table in Chris' room along with him, Tad, and Adam. The look on Chris' face when Adam asked to join displayed his clear disdain, but since it was Adam's room, too, Chris had little choice.

"Low-ball glasses courtesy of Durst's dining hall," Chris said grandiosely, pouring a juice glass half full for each of us.

"Variation: if you miss three times in a row, you gotta guzzle a whole can," Chris added.

"Hey, trade glasses with me," Anise said to Chris.

"How come?" he asked.

"Mine has a chip in it," she complained.

Chris did as he was told, a self-deprecating smile on his face. I continued to marvel at the ease with which Anise could command men. It was entirely different from Caitlyn's art, which was more manipulation by charm, giggles, and the occasional feigned flooziness. Anise was more this tiny power figure, with her disarming beauty and spitfire spunk. She had zero interest in or apparent awareness of her own popularity, so she was utterly devoid of that obvious fear nearly everyone else had of losing it. I had never witnessed her embarrassed or self-conscious, and guys seemed to eat out of her hand within seconds of encountering her. I could picture her in another time intimidating and subsequently charming Mussolini.

"Ladies first," Tad said coyly, placing a shiny quarter on the table in front of Anise. I knew he liked her, but I also knew that he didn't stand a chance with her.

"He reminds me of a newt," she had said plainly when Caitlyn and I made known to her Tad's affection one day at the lunch table. "That small head and those beady eyes. I'll bet he kisses like one, too, with his tongue darting in and out like this-" She had done an imitation that had left Caitlyn and me doubling over with our hands over our mouths, trying to keep the food from flying out. Tad was considered kind of cute by the standards of some at Durst, including himself, and I wished someone could have relayed to him Anise's remark so I could watch his ego deflate like a slashed tire.

Anise took the quarter and spit-shined it on her shirt. "Better make sure this is clean," she said. "Who knows where it's been."

Anise bounced the quarter and it went flying off the table. "*Oh-h-h*, that was just a practice shot!" she exclaimed, snatching the quarter back before Chris could touch it. She wiped it off and poised to bounce it again. Chris gingerly withdrew his hand and said nothing as she made her second attempt.

"Aw, *man!* This game is rigged!" she complained as her quarter bounced off into the opposite direction again. "Maybe it's your coffee table, Chris."

"My turn," I said, holding out my hand for the quarter. I held the coin by its edge, Washington's pigtailed profile facing up towards me. I gave it a quick bounce and it flipped head-over-tails into the hocked cafeteria glass.

"Nice shot!" Chris applauded. I fished the quarter out before throwing back the brew. Chris refilled my glass, this time a little past the halfway mark. "Go again!" he said.

I bounced the quarter a second time and again I watched it sink to the bottom of my glass. A cheer rose up from the assembled. I plucked the quarter out again and drained the glass. Mindlessness was on its way.

To my dismay, I missed the third attempt. The round went on to Caitlyn, then to Chris, Tad, and finally Adam and then repeated. As our motor skills faltered and we all grew progressively uncoordinated, the invisible fill line in the glasses seemed to get higher each time around.

Adam grew red-faced and even more talkative as we played. Chris would give Caitlyn a look of undisguised disgust after his roommate made some admittedly dumb joke, and she would smile knowingly back. I felt kind of sorry for Adam, but didn't want to risk the label of nerd by association for laughing at any of his remarks.

Tad hit three in a row and let out a holler. "New rule, new rule!" he shouted exuberantly. You'd have thought it was the greatest day of his life. "Everyone has to do a shot of tequila!"

Adam groaned and Caitlyn let out a little squeal. I watched with only slight apprehension as Chris withdrew a gold-labeled bottle from behind one of his shelves and slammed it on the middle of the coffee table. My stomach turned as I glimpsed the corpse of

156

the worm inside the bottle, reminding me of a high school biology specimen in formaldehyde.

"Oh, gross, no way," Anise said, shaking her head and covering up the mouth of her glass as Chris went to pour her some.

"It's the rule," Chris insisted.

"Not *my* rule," Anise retorted. "I'm not drinking that shit."

Chris acquiesced and turned to me. "Just a bit," I said, laughing a little. He filled the bottom of the glass an inch, then did the same for Caitlyn, Tad, and himself. Grimacing, he splashed some in Adam's glass before capping the bottle.

"To higher education!" he crowed, raising his glass. All of us, with the exception of Anise, clinked glasses and tilted back our heads.

The smell of the drink alone was vile. When the liquid hit my throat I sputtered, eyes burning. Oh, it was bad!

"Good stuff," Tad gasped, finishing his in a gulp.

It took me three attempts to finish my tequila. My nose, taste buds, and stomach all recoiled at the acerbic fermentation. Next to me, Caitlyn was coughing.

"You okay?" Chris asked, laughing. She nodded, tears rolling out the corners of her eyes.

Adam took his turn at quarters next, and I began to wonder how much longer the game would continue. A strange feeling suddenly came over me like a chill, and I felt uncertain in my stomach. It occurred to me that my body might not be welcoming its first introduction to tequila. I tried to ignore the unsettled feeling and concentrate on something else.

Suddenly, Adam was sputtering and hacking, thumping a closed fist on his chest.

"Oh, my word, he swallowed the quarter," Tad said in disbelief.

"Adam, you okay man?" Chris asked him. "Can you breathe?"

Adam nodded, his eyes closed, but he continued coughing, water streaming down the sides of his cheeks.

"He's coughing, it must not be blocking anything," Tad surmised.

"I can feel it right *here,*" he articulated painfully, his voice barely audible. "It feels like when you get a fishbone caught in your throat."

"Oh, shit," was Tad's comment.

"I guess we'd better get him to the hospital," Chris muttered.

"Yeah, but how? *We* can't drive," Tad pointed out. "If we call the RA, we're totally busted."

The feeling of nausea was spreading over me like a wave. I wished that I could think straight, but it was hard to ignore the sickness.

"Maybe we should call an ambulance," Caitlyn piped up.

"It's not that kind of an emergency," Tad said irritably, "And besides, an ambulance would only attract all kinds of attention."

"*I'll* take care of this," Anise said, shaking her head. Foggily, I wondered if her exasperation came from listening to the two of them or from the entire situation. She opened the door to the hallway and in seconds was back with Eric, a shaggy-haired, self-classified computer geek who lived on the floor.

Anise entreated Chris to grab Adam's wallet and ID. "You've gotta go with him," she said sternly. "Make sure he's okay."

I watched bleary-eyed as Adam walk down the hallway, the long-haired, creature-like Eric on one side of him and the clean-cut Chris on the other making for a mixed escort team.

As a kid I remember I had accidentally swallowed a penny once when I was lying on my back holding one of those little plastic money purses over my head. I had thrown it up immediately, along with the chocolate ice cream that I'd had.

Now, the memory of throwing up sent another wave of nausea over me. "I gotta get back to the room and lie down," I groaned, heading towards the stairwell.

"I'm coming, too," Caitlyn said. "I don't feel so good."

Behind me I could dimly hear Tad asking Anise a question, and then Anise's demure tones insinuating a refusal.

I had some difficulty getting my key into the lock. When I finally sank onto the bed, easing my head onto the pillow without removing anything but my shoes, I realized that the ceiling and walls were spinning around and round.

"If you ever get the spins, put your foot on the floor," I had once heard someone advise. I decided to try this, and unsteadily swung a leg over the side of the bed. After about fifteen seconds, the room was still tilted and moving.

I didn't want to stand up again, but I knew that I had to do it. The sickness enveloped me from head to foot as I staggered towards the door. Caitlyn was already passed out in her bed, I sensed dimly. It occurred to me that I should make sure she was alright, but I was too sick to help her at the moment. Placing one foot in front of the other, I tottered down the hallway, never realizing until now how long it seemed. I finally broke into the bright fluorescent light of the bathroom. I felt a vague sense of relief at the cold tile beneath my feet. I'd made it.

Dreading the coming sensation, I clumsily forced open a stall door. How I hated getting sick to my stomach! I knelt before the bowl and waited. A sweat broke out on my forehead as I wretched over the toilet. The sickly smell and texture of vomit induced more heaves, until my innards ached from the motions. I averted my eyes and flushed, grabbing some tissue at the same time.

I sat for several minutes on the cold floor, waiting to make sure that my stomach wasn't planning an encore performance. I leaned my head back, dabbing at the sweat with my tissue. I didn't care that someone was in the stall next to me overhearing the effects of my ridiculous predicament, nor that this someone might have been Taylar. I didn't care about the shame of being hunched over a toilet nor groveling on dirty tile. All I cared about was not feeling sick any more.

Chapter 18 – Gossip

The next day I felt like one of those cartoon characters that gets hit over the head full force with a hammer, and its head vibrates back and forth for several seconds before a giant lump sprouts from the top of it. I wondered if I would ever walk upright again, or if I would spend the remainder of my days crawling. As someone in a movie had once described it, I felt "like the inside of a sow's stomach." That pretty much summed it up.

Caitlyn was in equally bad shape, having awoken me with the sound of her tossing in the trash can. The wiser Anise (who had abstained from the folly of tequila) paid us a visit as we both lay wounded in our beds.

"Joe's coming the weekend after next," she announced grimly as we both gazed at her, bleary-eyed, from our respective bunks. "I feel like I should miss him more. I don't know how it's going to be, or how I feel about it."

She informed us that Adam had recovered nicely from his unfortunate coin-swallowing incident, recounting the sequence of events leading up to it over and over, detailing with pride the surgery performed (for which he remained awake and observed all the action). His antics had earned him a new nickname in the dorm: slot machine.

"By the way, Chris is a creep," Anise told Caitlyn candidly. "I know he likes you, but personally, I think you should forget about him."

"Why's that?" Caitlyn frowned from her pillow.

"I just get this sense he's a jerk," Anise offered. "Put it this way: better not swallow any quarters and expect *him* to come to your rescue. He'll stand around debating whether or not it's serious while you're croaking there on the floor in front of him."

"I thought he acted responsible last night," Caitlyn protested meekly. "Besides, it was Adam's fault in the first place that he ate a quarter."

Graeme came by to see me later in the day as well. He seemed to think it was the most hysterical thing in the world that I had a hangover.

"First hangover *ever?*" he asked incredulously, sitting on my bed. "That's a special occasion. I should have brought flowers or something. Or better yet, a six pack."

I groaned. "Don't even mention that. Would you please hand me my water?"

As he gave me the glass, Graeme asked me if I knew the best cure for a hangover.

"What?" I asked hopefully.

"Hair of the dog," he replied. "Drink beer."

"Ugh, I don't want to even *think* about beer ever again," I moaned.

"I'm telling you, it'll work," he laughed. "Best thing to cure a hangover is drinking."

Graeme was not exactly pleased when I told him how I'd come by the hangover.

"You were playing quarters with three guys?" he asked suspiciously.

"It was no big deal," I answered. "Besides, Chris is smitten with Caitlyn and Tad likes Anise."

"What about this other dude?"

"Adam?" I repeated. "You have to be kidding. Adam is a short, nerdy little Jewish kid who talks too much."

As soon as the words left my lips I felt bad. I sounded so cruel – *anti-Semitic*, even.

Graeme, however, harped so long on my hanging around other guys that I finally gave in and promised I'd invite him the next time I was with them or any other male of the species. Between him and the throbbing in my skull it was just easier to agree and let it at that.

*****

Two days later my hangover was no more than a distant memory, and I was back to partying again.

At Theta Chi I earned the title of "Mistress of Beer Pong" for my skills and accuracy in being able to throw a ping pong ball into a pyramid of opponents' plastic beer cups at the opposite end of a table. The person on the other team had to guzzle the contents of the cup that contained the ping pong ball and then remove the cup from the lineup. The object of the game was to get the ball in your opponents' cups first. We played in teams of two and the winners advanced to play a new team.

More often than not the ping pong ball landed on the filthy, sticky floor of the fraternity house, and although it was given a quick douse in a cup of water before being launched again, it was disgusting to think of what was probably in the beer I was drinking. So I didn't think about it.

My higher education included becoming rapidly proficient in matters of alcohol. I had acquired a taste not only for beer, but for cocktails, wine, and champagne as well. Moreover, I could anticipate the kind of buzz I would get from the type of alcohol I was imbibing; for example, I knew that whiskey and coke would give me a dull ache right in the back of my head, whereas wine would make me pleasantly loopy and then wreck me completely if I continued with it. I was discovering that I was capable of alternating between liquor such as vodka and another "food group" such as amaretto without it making me ill (so long as I stopped drinking the moment I felt myself hit that wall of no return – if I went past it, I'd be sick). I was reluctant to return to the formidable tequila, and so that was the one beverage I avoided.

Almost joyfully I would look forward to an evening of drinking and its promise of instant relaxation and universal merriment. Having the choice between my own introspective, abstemious disposition, or a light-hearted, fun-loving outlook that brought straight to the surface my dormant humor, it wasn't difficult to trade over one nature for the other. The exchange was simple, too, like removing one article of clothing and putting on another. The first nature dissolved with every sip I took, and the carefree one came eagerly and without fail to take its place.

Of course, inevitably, morning would come and with it the demands of payment for the exchange made the night before. Depending on how big the transaction from one persona to the other, I came to expect the price the next day to be in accordance.

My stalwartness in holding out physically with Graeme, meanwhile, was starting to crumble. I had set certain boundaries that I had made clear would never, *could* never be crossed. Although I continued to patrol those boundaries and he consistently complied, it was not without continual and more eminent frustration on both our parts. We would reach the same old place and know that we had to stop, and the force that had propelled us along that far had entirely different notions. It was monumentally frustrating. How many clowns had I heard suggesting through one statement or another in my adolescence that women didn't have hormones, that they simply were creatures of emotion, and devoid of physiological drives? As certain utterances sprang to mind it occurred to me that they had been made predominantly by either men or menopausal older ladies. If only it were true that we women weren't wrestling the same volatile impulses! I could feel the chemicals raging and protesting in every nerve of my body when we'd suddenly come to the usual screeching halt, and there was no way it could have been any less maddening for me than it was for Graeme.

Short of committing murder, I had been brought up to believe that the worst thing a person could possibly do or dream of doing was to fool around before their wedding night. Growing up in the church, I had always been given the vague impression that the only people who ever did such a thing before marriage were folks who lived Somewhere Else, like in a big city perhaps where lawlessness abounded. It was this mortal dread of committing the ultimate cardinal sin that now upheld my floundering resolve to remain chaste.

In high school, of course, there had been the handful of girls who had gotten pregnant and usually dropped out, so I knew that some sort of fornicating existed locally. Pieces of conversation I'd overhear in the hallways and in the locker room tipped me off to the fact that I was hardly attending a nunnery. There had also been that girl I'd befriended from across the street who was a foster child and had detailed to my naïve ears some of her clandestine trysts – but then, it was expected that she might be involved in such sin. After all, she smoked and I'd caught her in a couple of lies so it was entirely conceivable that she might have done some Unknown Unmentionable Thing with her boyfriend. Generally, however, all the circles I moved in were with "good girls" like me, and so I never gave much thought to the reality of what was going on around me, nor the fact that "decent" people might have fallen into this kind of sin.

Anise had also filled in for me the remaining gaps in sex education that my public school had omitted. I would ponder some of her accounts with secret astonishment, and she, Caitlyn and I often engaged in lengthy conversations about the subject, speculating and relaying tales of hearsay.

Of course, being in a co-ed dorm it was nearly impossible not to be confronted in every direction with sexual innuendo and sometimes overt obscenity. Some of the guys had plastered on their walls provocative posters of airbrushed, tanned female bodies with certain parts of their anatomy covered just enough to give you an easy guess. Conversations among roommates produced tales of escapades taking place regularly in the rooms surrounding us, and jokes were routinely made about needing oil spray for the squeaky bed frames. Once, Potion Pete had attracted a small crowd in his room by pulling up a photo on the Internet of a pornographic image so grotesquely bizarre I wondered how anyone in the world could have imagined such a thing to do in the first place, not to mention willingly participate in it. Immediately I regretted having succumbed to the savage curiosity that persuaded me to take a glance at it. When certain things got into your mind, it was impossible to make them leave.

The college itself promoted its own values through forums and courses, not only on "sexual diversity," but also on every conceivable topic besides. There were posters outside different halls announcing various upcoming lectures such as Sex and Socialism, Sex and American Ideology, Keeping Kosher: Judaism and Sex, Sex and the African American Female, and even a symposium discussion entitled Pleasurable Sex for Your Partner and Yourself. The campus health center had mandated a video on sex and venereal diseases shortly after freshman orientation, and it was forever promoting its literature detailing the proper usage of condoms, which were issued free of charge for those brave enough to walk in and grab them out of the plastic fishbowl inside the door.

The only department which seemed woefully neglected in the subject of sex was Mathematics. Surely they could have devised something for those poor left-brainers, I thought ironically. I imagined a poster reading, "Sexuality and Linear Equations: Debunking the Myths."

One Monday evening following my monumental hangover, Anise and I were hanging out in the TV lounge downstairs, just the two of us. We were talking more than we were watching what was on television, and the subject of our respective roommates suddenly came up.

Anise lowered her voice, "Jill definitely has a thing for Caitlyn."

"Gross," I said flatly.

"Yeah, but what I don't get is why Jill thinks she has a chance with her. I mean, clearly Caitlyn is straight."

"Maybe she's getting a mixed message from Caitlyn," I said dryly.

Anise looked at me quizzically.

"Caitlyn will do anything to encourage a little attention," I continued. "Or haven't you noticed? It doesn't seem to matter where it comes from, either."

Anise's face formed an expression I couldn't entirely read, but she said nothing.

At that moment I became aware of movement beyond the open doorway of the lounge. I looked up and there was Taylar, standing in the archway of the lounge, staring at me. She gave me a nasty little smile.

"Hello," she said in the same tone another person might use to curse.

""H-hi,"I stammered. I could feel the blood draining from my face. She had surely heard what I'd just said about Caitlyn. My voice tended to carry, and I hadn't used the same discretionary whisper as Anise.

Taylar stood staring at me, fists on hips, for another moment. Then she turned abruptly and I could hear her rapid footsteps as she paced briskly down the hallway.

"Oh, no," I breathed.

"What?" Anise wanted to know.

"Taylar totally overheard me, and she's going to tell Caitlyn."

*****

I wondered how long it would take for the recounting of my backstabbing gossip to reach Caitlyn. I was certain Taylar would tell her, but wondered if Taylar would embellish the story to make it even worse than it was. After all, here was her big chance for revenge after I had put her in her place of rightful humiliation in front of Chris and Tad.

Anise and I had returned to my room shortly after the ill-fated eavesdropping, and Caitlyn wasn't there. Anise was a true friend, offering to accompany me and help soften Taylar's ruthlessness by explaining to Caitlyn the context of what we were discussing. It was thoughtful of her, but I honestly didn't see how it would help the situation much.

It occurred to me that I could go over to Graeme's and spend the night at his place, but I had to face Caitlyn some time and I would rather that it be sooner instead of later. Besides, if I could get to her before Taylar, I could significantly deflect the blow by coming clean and making it appear as though I intended to confess my slander all along out of a guilty conscience.

Caitlyn returned after I had finally shut the lights off a little after eleven. From where I lay in the darkness, I tried to discern her body language for any clues that she counted me among her enemies. I wondered if I should just say something and break the ice. I opened my mouth, preparing to call out to her. But what if Taylar *hadn't* said anything? Then I'd be doing real damage instead of damage control.

I listened to her movements in the darkness, eventually hearing her climb into bed. My courage failed me and I kept quiet. As I heard her flip to her side in bed, I started to say something again, then stopped. After a few moments I figured she was probably sleeping anyway. I lay listening to the gloom of the room, once again wide awake until well after midnight, feeling completely and utterly alone save my anxious, shifting thoughts.

*****

Over the next couple days I had little contact with Caitlyn as she was working on a seven-page paper for economics. She seemed a little quieter during our interactions and I asked her if anything was wrong. She claimed it was stress from her workload. I wanted desperately to ask her if Taylar had said something to her, but I didn't know how to pose the question.

"Did Taylar tell you how she overheard me totally tearing down your character...to our mutual friend Anise, no less?" There was no good way to say it.

I avoided our room evenings and early mornings when I knew she would be there, sensing the tension but not entirely sure whether it was real or self-imposed out of my own fears.

Anise was a ball of nerves about Joe's arrival. She and Luke had been spending more and more time together, and she finally had told him about Joe's pending advent.

"He wasn't exactly thrilled, but he didn't give me an ultimatum, either," Anise explained. "Whatever time you need,' is all he said." She sighed. "That in itself was so sweet it made me just want to jump him right then and there and rip his clothes off."

I had met Luke on several occasions and liked him immensely. He was much more the rugged, laid back, man's man, and the fact that his personality and background were so vastly different from Anise's actually seemed to enhance their budding friendship. They complemented one another, and when I saw them walking together, they made a stunning couple.

"He's a southern boy," she had explained to me one time, although she could never remember whether he was from Alabama or Arkansas, a fact that used to make me laugh. Details were not Anise's forte, and it never bothered her to omit them from memory. "I used to think all southern guys were hicks, but he's definitely the gentleman type. If the whole south was full of Lukes, I'd transfer to Dixie. Yee-*haw*."

I readily agreed with her. Perhaps that should have been one of my criteria in choosing my undergrad.

"Ugh, what to do, what to do," she groaned, rummaging through her endless inventory of clothing as I sat on my usual perch on the bed, watching. Her wardrobe was always so impeccable.

"Dump Joe," I told her.

She turned around to face me, surprised, I suppose, at my bluntness. "You know why I can't," she said finally. "I can't bring myself to do it. Not yet."

*****

Graeme picked me up to take me out to dinner at a Japanese restaurant one evening. The air was chilly and I huddled my coat around my shoulders tighter as he helped me into the car. The sky was austere and the stars seemed cold and hard glinting down on us as we drove along. I had never eaten Japanese food and Graeme insisted I needed to try it. I told him that I was more of a steak and potatoes kind of girl.

"I'm committed to helping you get some culture," he said, only half-jokingly I suspected.

The restaurant was out of the way, in an area of the town where I'd never been. Just before we turned into the parking lot, we passed a quaint, old-fashioned little white church standing by itself, with a little cemetery directly behind it.

170

I peered through the car window for a moment at its architecture, thinking of the decades of history it had seen and the numerous parishioners that it must have welcomed, each bringing their individual cares and joys each Sunday through its double doors and into the sanctuary. As I studied the church, my gaze was drawn to the simple cross adorning its side. A momentary pang throbbed in my chest. Quickly, I turned my eyes away.

Chapter 19 - News

After hearing all the intimate details of his love letters – or lust letters – to Anise, it was somewhat bizarre the first time I was introduced to Joe.

I know every strange thing that tickles your fancy, I thought ironically, shaking his hand. *And all your shortcomings, too.*

Joe *was* strikingly good-looking, and I had never seen a male that well-dressed in person – the only guys I'd seen in threads that high-end were hosting television programs and usually were gay. Throughout the weekend, I overheard some of the guys in the dorm commenting on his car and his clothes, marveling at their probable price tags.

I didn't see much of Anise that weekend, and Caitlyn still seemed to be keeping distant. I was almost sure at this point that word had gotten back to her about my betrayal, but when she joked around with me a couple times I thought perhaps maybe I was mistaken, and had read too much into her previous perceived silence. The agony of not knowing for sure was wearing on me, and I longed to have our friendship back intact. I missed her.

Twice when we were in the room together I was on the verge of admitting to her my guilt, and both times I hesitated and the moment passed. This left me even more frustrated than before, and a sudden feeling of resentment seized me after the second opportunity passed.

After all, Caitlyn did *sort of bring this on herself,* I thought bitterly. *She* does *act the part of the helpless, doe-eyed damsel every time a "y" chromosome is in the vicinity. Plus, she has a boyfriend! Why should* I *be the one to give in to* her?

This resurgence of antipathy created a strain of stubbornness in me that overtook and drove out the former humility I'd felt over the situation, and I pursed my lips tightly in a resolve not to cast my pride by the wayside so quickly. It was, after all, just like Caitlyn not to *confront* me about what was said and instead act superficially.

Instead of going to lunch together as was customary on most Saturday mornings, Caitlyn said she had some errands to run around campus and downtown and apologized for not being available to accompany me. I shrugged off the subtle rebuff and told her that it was fine. I had work to do anyway.

Shortly after she left, Graeme called me up, asking me to come over and hang out. I told him that I had to go to the computer lab to work on a paper, but would come over after that.

A few hours later I entered Graeme's room. He looked so handsome in his rugby shirt and jeans, and the smell of his cologne was like pheromones. Feeling no need for small talk, we embraced and began passionately kissing. I had been contemplating the last week how important certain boundaries really were – how clearly it was spelled out – and what was and wasn't permissible. In my mind, I had already begun to make some rationalizations, and the solid lines that had been drawn previously were starting to waver and recede. As we moved over to the bed, the surge of my eighteen-year-old hormones was more than I could stand, and the rigidity of my former absolutes faltered under the intense force of something much larger that now propelled me forward.

*****

Graeme and I went to dinner together in the cafeteria that evening and I felt as though I were seeing the world through a different lens. The memory of the afternoon's events was a pleasant ember that my mind returned to and with which I warmed myself. I did not feel shame. Instead, I felt massive relief that at last I was no longer walking the test line. Being on one side of where the battle lines had been drawn was infinitely easier than standing right in the middle of the crossfire, getting pulled in two different directions for weeks on end, feeling like I belonged nowhere. I had felt for quite some time that I was on the verge of snapping. This massive tension had been alleviated by a decision to succumb to one side. I didn't spend a lot of time psychoanalyzing my choice. In my head repeated the notion that what I had done was not really so terrible.

*****

"So did you guys go all the way?" Anise asked incredulously. Joe had just left to back to school and we were sitting in her room Sunday night.

"No," I replied. "We didn't."

"Well, give me the details!" Anise demanded. She was beaming like a proud parent whose backward child had for the first time advanced to a new and unexpected level of progress.

I blushed, but dutifully recounted the sequence of events that had occurred since I first entered Graeme's room the previous afternoon.

"So tell me how things went with Joe," I said abruptly as I finished my tale, wishing to change the subject.

"Ugh," Anise groaned, stretching out across from me on Jill's neglected bunk with the ease and abandon of a tabby cat. "Honestly, I couldn't wait for the weekend to be over."

"Really?" I responded, settling more comfortably into my spot now that I was no longer on the stand.

"He made me feel *fat* when we were in bed," Anise said. Her voice was full of belligerence, but it was underscored by a note of definite hurt. "Seriously, Molly, I felt so *uncomfortable*. I felt like I was being compared to something – or someone. Then, the rest of the weekend, I just didn't feel like doing anything with him physically."

I was silent, secretly wishing I could see ol' Joe just one more time and tell him that his big bankroll was simply a substitute for his miniature manhood.

"I mean, I know I gained a *couple* pounds since summer ended and college started..." Anise trailed off.

"You have to be kidding," I spoke up defiantly, spurred to speak out of indignation. "You are one of the most beautiful people I've ever met, and you're so tiny you could fit in a suitcase."

Anise laughed.

"More than that though, you have a fantastic personality. And you're kind. Most gorgeous women don't have all three of those things. Maybe Joe should spend some time in a POW camp and find a girlfriend there if he likes emaciated bodies so much," I finished hotly.

"Aw, thanks, darlin'" she said, the smile lighting up her pretty face. "Guys are only good for one thing, right? And sometimes they're not even good at *that.*"

We laughed together mockingly before Anise cracked open her window to smoke another cigarette.

*****

Whatever had come between me and Caitlyn seemed to have dissipated a little since the weekend. She, Anise and I were goofing around like old times. Still, I wondered what she actually thought of me, and if things would ever be entirely the same between us if I didn't come clean with what I'd said about her. However, I determined not to fret about it. I was tired of taking on guilt and worry, so I decided simply to ignore it.

"Well, Jared is a person of the past," Caitlyn announced while I was stirring my broccoli cheese soup and Anise was contemplating a meatball on her plate. Caitlyn, apparently, had effectively broken ties with the once beloved poetic suitor the prior weekend.

"You dumped Shakespeare?" Anise exclaimed. "What happened?"

"He was a heavy breather," Caitlyn explained. "You know, one of those guys who breathes really loudly through his nose when he kisses. I just couldn't take it."

"How did you get rid of him?" Anise wanted to know.

"Well," Caitlyn chewed her BLT sandwich thoughtfully. "I told him that I thought we were young and that it was immature not to be seeing other people."

Anise guffawed, but I hid my smile, not yet feeling comfortable enough to be honest around Caitlyn.

"You mean he hasn't figured out that he's only one of about seventeen right now?" Anise asked incredulously.

Caitlyn ignored the jab and continued chewing her sandwich. "He pleaded with me for a while but I held my ground. He said he just couldn't bear the idea of sharing me. And that was it."

"What if he changes his mind and decides he can live with it after all? What will you tell him then?" I asked.

"I don't know. I'll think of something."

No doubt she would. If Caitlyn was anything, she was resourceful.

"Seriously, girl, I have no idea how you do it," Anise confessed, a note of awe in her voice. "I'd be mixing up names, calling one guy by the wrong name, forgetting who they are and which one had told me what the day before. Do you have them all listed out on a spreadsheet?"

Caitlyn blushed. "You only live once," she replied.

*****

One sleepless night in the middle of November, after staring into the dark for a couple hours, I finally got up and got dressed in the chill of Graeme's room. I was restless and felt a tremendous need to get outside.

Graeme didn't stir as I slipped out his door. He had given me his key and I double checked to make sure it was in the pocket of my jeans before I gently let the door shut.

The brisk air felt wonderful as it hit my face and I breathed in deeply. It smelled of leaves and of dampness and of the first hint of winter. The campus was uncannily quiet, so still it could have been a snapshot I was walking into. It was difficult to imagine that this was the same place that regularly swarmed with hormones and haute couture and bantering and obscenities.

Whenever I was alone somewhere on the Durst campus, my mind inadvertently crept back to the saga of lives that had trooped through it. The history was so heavy and full that I could feel it tangibly, an aura that a newer establishment did not exude. I often wondered about the students who had attended Durst in days gone by. Predominantly males, their photos hung in various corners throughout the campus, and I had studied those somber eyes many a time. I wondered if a hundred years ago the college kids coming through were as "bad" as we were. Was the language as rough and was the licentiousness as prevalent? Or did those starched clothes and neat crew cuts simply better conceal the realities of years ago?

Once, I had posed the question to my grandfather, "Were people as awful when you were a kid as they are now?" My grandfather had responded thoughtfully with the reply that "Human nature doesn't change. Society has, though." His reply puzzled me. I found it difficult to believe that people who lived a century ago didn't have more honor and overall decency than those of today, but again, maybe they just kept it hidden better because – as he implied – society didn't tolerate all that they do now.

I walked along the pathways under the amber glow of the lamps, studying the darkened windows of a dorm as I passed it. I pondered all the hidden hopes and dreams and fears of the occupants just past those limestone walls. I wondered if any of them lay in bed worrying about death and being afraid of the unknown like I did. I wondered if any of them had deep secrets that no one else knew about, and if life for them was sometimes a wrestling match with grief that went on round after round with no end in sight.

Studying the contours of Old Main always filled me with a sense of pride and awe that I was now a part of this school's legacy. It was rumored that the top floor of the building was haunted by the ghost of a professor who had killed himself, and as I looked up at its darkened windows, a slight chill passed through me. A single leaf scuttled across the path at my feet. I watched it, seeing if the breeze would take it all the way over into the grass again. Somewhere off in the distance a dog barked. The sound was desolate and forlorn.

The lines of a poem I'd read in high school – in an English class I'd shared with Hank – came back to me all of a sudden:

> For of all sad words of tongue or pen,
> The saddest are these: "It might have been."

I shivered, realizing all at once that it was much colder than when I'd first stepped outside. Time to be getting back to the familiar warmth of Graeme's room. He might even be awake, wondering what in the world happened to me. As I turned my back on the regal façade of Old Main and put one foot heavily in front of the other, I felt like the most lonesome creature in the entire world.

Chapter 20 - Problems

Since mid-terms had come back, I realized that I was getting a "C" in physics. If I didn't ace the final, it would be disastrous. My parents would have my head on a charger.

"Just withdraw from the class," Graeme advised me when I admitted it to him later. I was embarrassed even to mention it to him, but had to tell someone.

I considered this. To withdraw seemed like such a cop-out, for one thing, and then there was the whole issue of wasting an entire credit. All that time and money wasted! If I studied hard enough, perhaps I could earn a grade high enough on the final to pull up my grade point average to a "B." It was a daunting task indeed, though, since I was so far behind in what we were currently studying. The snowball was rolling and I didn't know if I'd ever catch up.

Beyond the discomfort of my present predicament in physics, I was nonetheless relieved that I had never challenged Professor Day on the finer points of his lecture on The Big Bang Theory. My apathy in his class and general poor performance would have discredited me, and would have more unfortunately brought even greater ridicule from him on Christianity.

Graeme had asked me to go home with him for Christmas Break (or as it was politically correctly deemed at Durst, "Winter Pause") and I had agreed. I would be home for Christmas, but gone by New Year's Eve. While normally Christmas was by far my favorite time of the year, the last thing I felt like doing right now was going home, where I would doubtless be sought out by Kendra, who would recognize me instantly as the backslider that I was once we began talking. More than that, Hank would probably be home and I remembered his farewell promise to see me again on break – at the time, I couldn't wait for it. Well, a lot had changed since that August night and I couldn't picture myself at ease around Hank under current circumstances. For all I knew, if we got together it would be an introduction to his girlfriend. No, I definitely wanted to get as far away from home as possible, as soon as possible. Besides, the idea of traveling with Graeme over break was exciting; I'd never been to New England, which would be an adventure in itself. How my parents would react to this news regarding their Winter Break profligate would be another matter, but there was no changing my mind.

*****

"Everything okay?" I asked Zack, picking up on his troubled expression. It had been a while since we had shared deli duty. My instinct to avoid Dirty Sammy the Cook at all costs generally kept me safely back in the dish room.

"Not really," he replied. He stared straight ahead for several moments while I waited for him to continue. I fiddled with the scoop that was in the macaroni salad and pretended to find interest in the dispersed herd of students around me. Finally, I heard Zack's voice come out low and quiet. "My best friend, Kevin, from high school was in a bad car accident over the weekend. He's in critical condition. I just found out."

"I'm so sorry," I said.

"Some idiot ran a red light and hit him head on while he was about to make a turn." Zack's voice cracked a little. "I talked to his mom. She said he's holding on for life."

I let out a deep breath. "I'm sorry," I repeated again, giving him a hug right there at the deli.

"You know how I feel about organized religion," Zack continued, sniffling a little and quickly jerking the heel of his hand across the corner of his right eye. "But at this point, if there is a God up there, I'll believe anything and give everything to see Kevin pull through."

I remained speechless for a few moments, feeling suddenly paralyzed. Ordinarily, I would have put my hand on Zack's shoulder and prayed for him and his friend right at that very moment, curious onlookers notwithstanding. I would have prayed with conviction and authority for Kevin, and Zack might have sensed the Spirit of the Lord as we came together in supplication. Instead now, I felt impotent. Like I had no confidence to proclaim such a prayer. How many times had I beseeched the Lord for an opportunity like this to minister? Yet now that it was here, I wished that I hadn't been asked. I was powerless.

"We'll just hope for the best," at last I answered lamely, putting my hand on his arm.

*****

"What in the world is *this?*" I demanded, my voice trembling with rising rage. I held the magazine with two fingers by its corner, as though it were contaminated with the Ebola virus.

Graeme looked sheepishly at it. "Oh, uh...where'd you find that?"

"Oh, so you admit then that it *is* yours?" my fury was rising as I cross-examined him. I was as much in disbelief as I was in outrage that he would do something like this.

Graeme shrugged. "Yeah, it's mine. Look, I knew you probably wouldn't be too happy about that-"

"Oh, really? Then why in the world would you *look* at this trash?!" I bellowed, cutting him off. I could feel my neck and ears slowly heating up and turning red like the inside of a toaster. "This is absolutely *disgusting!*"

Graeme sighed. "It's no big deal, okay? I'm a guy. Looking at porn is just something guys sometimes do."

I stared at him for a moment, dumbfounded. With fresh fury, I hastily turned to one particularly repugnant image. "Staring slack-jawed and slobbering at *this shit* is what passes for normal with you men?!" It was the first time in my life I'd ever used a curse word, and I was in awe of myself for doing so. I felt as though Anise had briefly overtaken my body. Though I hadn't meant to do it, no softer word seemed appropriate under the circumstances for getting my meaning across. Graeme looked away as I thrust the photograph in his face.

When I had initially let myself into Graeme's room before he'd returned, it had never even occurred to me that I would ever stumble upon something in there that I didn't want to see. Sitting down on his couch, I had noticed a corner of the publication sticking out from under it like a tell-tale beacon. When I pulled the magazine out in idle curiosity and was greeted by a topless female smiling provocatively on the cover, my heart had started up its quick, steady beat with disbelief. I had never even seen a porno magazine before, and as I had paged through it - aghast at some of the more extreme images - I couldn't even believe that such things were *allowed* to be distributed. No wonder our society was so screwed up, I thought as I flipped page after page, sickened not only by the obscene photographs but also by the titles and phrases popping out of some of the articles. No *wonder* there were so many problems with rape, kidnappings and domestic violence in this country. It suddenly made sense! This filth was feeding it all.

"These women are human beings that you're degrading like they're some kind of soulless objects," I continued dispassionately, ears still burning hotly like little torches on the side of my head. "And all the while *you* guys degenerate to nothing more than animals when you drool over them!"

"Look, they're not even real," Graeme shot back. "Besides, ask any guy. It's better to look at these fake, airbrushed silicone shots then think of your girlfriend that way."

"Is that right?" I asked sarcastically. "Yeah, well the next time I'm mentally unfaithful to *you* and I'm imagining being with some other guy, I'll reassure you with those same words and see if *you* buy it!" With that, I held out the obscene periodical in front of me with both hands. Gripping it with my left, I shredded its binding and then continued shredding page after page as Graeme looked on in a mixture of uncertainty and slight fear. "In the meantime," I continued, striding over to the trash can and disposing of the demolished porn, "You can forget about me coming to Connecticut with you for break."

"Aw, Molly, c'mon now! You don't mean that?" Graeme protested, jumping to his feet and propelling himself to where I was standing. "Look, I had no *idea* you'd be this upset. I'm sorry!"

I turned away, tuning out his feeble apology. I headed towards the door.

"Molly, *please* don't go!" Graeme begged, following behind me. His implorations grew louder as I continued to ignore him. "Look, you're right. It's insulting to you. Besides, I honestly don't need that stuff. You're more than enough for me."

I gave him a wry look.

"Listen, I'm not gonna buy something like that ever again, okay?" Graeme looked desperate. For a split second, staring at his wild expression, I almost felt sorry for him.

"Why buy anything at all when you have the Internet at your fingertips," I pointed out, gesturing towards his computer.

"Molly, please. Listen to me. I won't do it again, okay? Please believe me."

For a moment, I listened to his words, then the thought flashed in my mind that not only had he been looking at this trash, but the fact that it was stashed under his couch indicated that he never intended for me to find out. My wrath was instantly rekindled. "I need some space," was my reply. I bolted out the door before he had time to change my mind for me. Out in the hallway, I could hear his groan of frustration through the door.

Serves you right, booby-boy, I thought to myself as I stomped out.

*****

"Men are such beasts," Anise stated, shaking her head after I relayed the scenario in Graeme's room back to her. "Seriously, I swear getting laid is all they ever think about. It's like they're programmed."

"I don't know," I said uncertainly, still sullen but not willing to toss the whole species out with the garbage. "I've known some decent ones in my lifetime."

"Perhaps," Anise conceded. "Deep down, though, they probably were just as bad as the others but hid it better. I don't think men can *help* being dogs."

This thought occupied me as we sat downstairs in the HUB over a coffee that she had ordered, and a hot chocolate which dwindled to lukewarm as I stared sullenly into its cloudy depths. Anise spoke from more experience, plus she had an older brother. Men were still pretty much unclassified organisms as far as I was concerned. I *had* known a few Christian men who were as guilty as Graeme by their own admission when it came to porn and leering at women and such. To their credit, most of them had or were trying to overcome these strongholds. No, I couldn't believe that *all* guys were pigs. It was just too depressing.

"You know what *I* honestly think?" Anise said, lowering her voice so that it was inaudible to the scores of other students sitting around us. "I think that there's something missing in women's chromosomes that keeps us from realizing how foolish we really are to want to be with men so badly in the first place."

I grinned faintly, staring at her with an even mix of skepticism and acquiescence.

"No, I'm serious," Anise continued, dark eyes flashing faith in her own burgeoning philosophy. "Think about it. Who do you see arrested for violent crime all the time? Who rapes who? Who do you see walking out on their families because they met someone younger or because they had a kid born with a disability and they just couldn't handle the stress? Who makes it possible for sex clubs and strip joints to stay open in the first place? It's men who are at fault for our society falling apart."

"Well, I do think that women in general seem to have more of an inherent sense of responsibility when it comes to their children and their families," I agreed.

"Of course they do!" Anise exclaimed. "And we're living in a time period now when we women don't *need* men to support us monetarily or manage our finances, so what is the point of even dealing with them? I'm seriously starting to wonder if we're just missing some giant, obvious truth."

I still want one, though, I thought dismally, an image of Hank coming into my mind.

"*My* motto is, 'Use 'em for what you can get from them,'" Anise said, laughing.

"Except that then we're no better than they are," I said glumly.

"Damn, you got me there," Anise said, throwing down her biscotti in a gesture of surrender. "I'd hate to be on the same level as someone I don't respect."

*****

I finished my third beer and resisted the tremendous urge to let out a foundation-shaking belch that would have made the walls of the student lounge vibrate and possibly have drowned out the Macy Gray that was playing. Anise was chatting gaily with Luke and Caitlyn was juggling three unknown guys in an animated conversation in which she undoubtedly was the subject, and not wishing to disturb either one of them, I decided to beeline for the bathroom on my own.

A sea of faces floated in front of me as I made my way from the dark, crowded room and into the hallway. I felt happy and lighthearted and unencumbered, except of course for the pressing urge to use the potty.

I had been in need of a good night out with my friends, especially after steadfastly avoiding Graeme and his entrapments of phone calls and flowers for the past 24 hours. As he continued pursuing just a conversation with me, I wondered if perhaps I wasn't being a bit too harsh. It wasn't in my nature to hold a grudge for very long, and I used to find that even in high school when I'd fight with my mother, no matter how hard I'd try later to hold onto the anger, it evaporated much more quickly than I would have liked.

However, this was different. This was more than simply an argument. This, I told myself, was betrayal.

Mercifully entering the dorm's restroom at last, I swung open the door of an empty stall in the student dorm and absently took a seat. Gazing cross-eyed at the Red Zone poster tacked to the door in front of me, I tried to calculate how many times I'd actually read what it said. *If I have used the bathroom an average of three times per day since coming to Durst in August, times approximately* [I counted on my fingers]...*twelve weeks...with a few extra bathroom breaks factored in for party nights...ugh...that would be....um...never mind, forget it. This is why I'm not a math major...*

Someone's pen had fallen under the door of the stall. Normally, I was a germ freak when it came to public restrooms and wouldn't have touched anything in them other than what was absolutely necessary, even using my forearm to shove open the doors rather than make contact with the push-plate. In my current relaxed state, however, the idea of microorganisms didn't faze me. I carefully assembled my thumb and forefinger like a pair of forceps in order to grab the writing tool.

Microbrews override all fears of microbes, I thought languorously, then immediately believed it was the cleverest thought ever imagined.

I took the orphaned pen and spent a few moments "doctoring" the Red Zone poster, the irritated protests of a couple females waiting in line outside the stall only inciting me to take my time to make it legible.

When I was finished, the poster read like this:

The RED ZONE

The Red Zone is defined as the ~~time period~~
~~between Freshman Orientation and Homecoming, when a new~~
~~student is most likely to be date raped.~~
area between the 20-yard line and the goal line at both ends of the football field.
Excessive alcohol consumption is often a contributing factor to ~~this pandemic~~. **making bad choices with ugly people.**
Some tips to ensure your safety during this high-risk phase and any other time during your college tenure:

- *Use "the* **bed** *buddy system" when attending social events.*
- *Never leave a beverage* ~~unattended~~ **full**
- *Check in with your roommate before you* ~~leave~~ **get lucky** *as to your whereabouts and* ~~when you will return.~~ **whether he's cute**
- *Remember, No means NO!*

Satisfied with my handiwork, I flushed and exited the stall, making sure to place the pen carefully in the exact same spot I had discovered it.

When I returned to the party, Caitlyn was now juggling a fourth young man, and Anise and Luke were talking to another guy – one whom I didn't recognize. I was about to go up to the keg for another beer when Anise made eye contact with me.

"Oh, *there* you are!" Anise cried, grabbing me by the arm. "I was looking for you! Molly," her beautiful eyes were sparkling with a hint of undisclosed mischief. "I want you to meet someone. This is Robert, Luke's friend from Arkansas."

"Alabama," he corrected her politely in his lolling accent. He held out his hand. "It's nice to meet you, Molly."

I took his hand, studying his features. With his slick-backed hair and blue eyes, he reminded me a little of Hank. Perhaps his personality was similar to Hank's, I thought dreamily in my beer-state.

"Hi, Robert," I said, glad that I had imbibed enough fluids not to feel even a tremor of nervousness. The opposite sex tended to disarm me almost immediately, especially if the individual in question possessed better-than-average looks, as Robert appeared to have (if my three beers weren't misleading my vision). I wanted to ask him if he was into art and vintage culture and see what his sense of humor was like.

"So what brings you up here, Robert?" I asked, by way of starting a conversation.

"I was up in Washington, D.C. to see about a possible internship for next spring, and decided to rent a car for the weekend and come up to see my old pal from high school."

I got a kick out of the way he said "high school."

"Robert's a senior," Anise explained importantly. "He and Luke played football together."

Another plus, I thought, nodding politely and subtly trying to eye up what I could glimpse of his physique through his knit sweater. *Bet he's got biceps that could choke an alligator.*

"Well, I'm gonna go get a refill, we'll be back in a minute," Anise said, giving me a knowing glance as she walked away.

"Can I get you something to drink?" Robert asked.

Ah, that deep drawl! It made my stomach do a somersault. I felt like replying, "Why, fiddle-dee-dee, of course you can!" like Scarlett O'Hara.

"I'll have another beer," I answered, smiling.

"Be right back," Robert said, matching my smile with his own.

When Robert returned with my beer, he asked me all about myself, which of course was very agreeable. He wanted to know where I was from, what kind of music I liked, what I thought of living up north, had I ever been to the Deep South, and on and on.

"Ya know how you're always running into people you don't want to see at Wal-Mart?" he asked at one point. I laughed, and he proceeded to tell me about accidentally reconnecting a couple years after graduation with a teacher for whom he'd behaved particularly badly in school. "I tried to hide behind one of those aisle displays, but she saw me. So, I pretended to be all surprised and happy, and the whole time I'm wondering, 'Does she remember the time I super-glued the wheels of her swivel chair to the floor, and she kept pushing and pushing with all her might when she sat down?'"

Robert wasn't drinking, so I determined to pace myself to avoid looking completely ridiculous. I had learned once, upon a late arrival to a party, that there is nothing more annoying in the world to someone who's stone sober than a drunk.

As the moments trooped by and my fourth beer disappeared, I grew fonder by the moment of Robert.

What a fool I've been to imagine myself so ridiculously smitten with Hank Bobek, I thought at one point. *Robert maybe doesn't have* exactly *the same great traits that I've come to admire in Hank. But he's taller – and almost as interesting to talk to – and with a southern accent, no less!*

"Would you like another?" Robert asked, gesturing towards my empty cup.

"Uh...maybe just *one* more," I agreed, discarding my earlier resolve to stop at number four.

"Be right back," Robert said, grinning at me. My heart did a cartwheel. He was really cute.

"So, how are things going?" Anise wanted to know, flanking my side from out of nowhere like some ethereal being the moment Robert was gone.

"He's nice," I sighed appreciatively. "And those *pecs!* Betcha I could bounce a quarter off of his chest!"

"Sh-h-h," Anise admonished gently, covering her lips with her forefinger as she laughed. "You're a little loud, and Luke's right over there. I don't want him to hear."

"Well, his friend's hot," I stated frankly.

"Oh, no," Anise said. I followed her gaze, feeling too giddy to be disturbed by much of anything.

"Oh, no," I echoed. Just through the entrance of the student lounge was Graeme.

"Oh, for cryin' out loud, why did *he* have to show up *here?* Why didn't he stay in his little fraternity hovel tonight like he was supposed to?" Anise demanded to know.

"He's looking this way, too," I remarked, pretending to be interested in the goings-on behind me instead of Graeme.

"You want me to get rid of him?" Anise asked, annoyed.

"Nah, it's okay," I said. "Hopefully he has the sense just to leave me alone right now."

"I don't think he's going to be thinking too sensibly when he sees who you're with," Anise pointed out, nodding in the general direction of Robert, who was standing near the bar area.

"Yeah, well. That's tough," I said resolutely.

At that moment, from seemingly out of nowhere, I saw Taylar appear. I watched as she ran over to Graeme, all superficiality and smiles. My heart sank as I observed her hugging him as though they were long lost friends. *Why don't you just wrap your legs around his waist and drag him to the floor,* I thought. The conniving witch! I felt my blood beginning to boil.

"Oh, what a hooker," Anise snorted, watching Taylar. She turned to me. "Don't let her upset you. Okay? She's just some trashy broad that has managed to get a bad reputation even as a first-semester freshman. Seriously, remember, *you* are a lady...and you always have to *be* the lady." Her voice dropped an octave. "Here comes Robert."

"Your beverage," Robert said grandiosely, handing me my beer.

"Thanks," I replied, taking it from him. Despite the quantity of alcohol I'd had, I suddenly felt as though I were wound tight as a spring.

"Everything okay?" Robert asked me.

"Oh. Yeah. I'm fine."

I glanced over to where Graeme was standing. He was composed and still while she went on and on, throwing her head back and laughing ostentatiously at intervals as though she were the bearer of the most exciting news on earth. I couldn't imagine that anything that came out of her mouth was intentionally funny. Watching her, she reminded me of some bizarre cartoon – hyper-animated and completely unreal.

"So, I never even asked you," Robert was saying. I tore my gaze away from Taylar and Graeme and looked at him. "Do you have a boyfriend?"

"Uh, well…" I stuttered.

Robert's face collapsed a little, then he smiled. "I should have known. All the good ones are taken."

I considered telling him that I was single for as long as he was in town, but that didn't seem like the right response.

"Things are kind of on the rocks right now with the guy I've been seeing," I told him, slurring the words and hoping fervently that he hadn't noticed. "To be honest, I don't know where things stand right now." There, that was being truthful.

"Ah, I understand."

I felt lightheaded and foggy, and thinking was becoming too much work. I knew from previous experience that if I were to drink much more I would soon hit that cement wall, and then it would be too late to reverse the protests of my stomach and the dizziness in my head.

"How long are you here for?" I asked Robert.

"Just until tomorrow. I'll be leaving in the morning."

His features were starting to blur a little bit, but he was handsome alright. I wondered what it would be like to kiss him. I considered doing it right then and there.

"Hello, Molly."

I turned to face the familiar voice, and focused my eyes as much as they would allow. "Hi," I said in a strained pitch, higher than my normal range.

"Um…Graeme, this is Robert. Robert…Graeme." My hand gesture felt clumsy.

"Molly, can I please talk to you?" Graeme asked me lowly. My brain was focusing as keenly as my eyeballs. I turned uncomfortably to look at Robert.

"I'll just go see what Luke's up to," he said with decorum, excusing himself.

"Who is that guy?" Graeme wanted to know. I was about to tell him, when I caught Anise's cold stare from across the room. Instinctively, I checked my own naivety and answered with what I knew *she* would say in response.

"I can't imagine how that could *possibly* be any of your business," I slurred, mustering as much spirit as was feasible with my alcohol-induced speech impediment.

Graeme stared at me for a moment in disbelief. Finally he asked, "Is this the end of us?" I stared back at him, glassy-eyed. "Molly, please don't call it quits on us. Look at what a great relationship we have!'

I stared at the ground, unsure of what to think, let alone what to say. Our relationship was lukewarm at best, in my opinion, but I had missed its comfortable familiarity. It had consumed so much of my thought and my time, that the past few days without it had seemed frighteningly listless and empty. I looked around to see where Taylar was. Glimpsing her yapping in the distance with a couple of twig-girls, her eyes suddenly met mine. The Mickey Mouse grin on her face disappeared and her expression turned cold.

"Molly," Graeme repeated. "Listen to me. Please. I am *so sorry* for upsetting you. It won't ever happen again, I promise. *Believe* me, I don't need to look at that junk! You're more important to me than anything else, and the best thing that's happened to me this year. I don't want to lose you! I'll do anything in the world to make things right again."

Oh, to be able to manage one decisive, logical thought! I glanced over wistfully at Robert's muscled bulk and then remembered instantly that he would be gone in the morning. Truth be told, I didn't want things to be over with Graeme yet. I had grown accustomed to him and his attentions, and life had been intolerably quiet just these past couple days without him in it. My initial rage over the porn incident had faded, thereby weakening my resolve to avoid him. I was getting tired of deflecting his approaches. I was also aware that if I split up totally with Graeme at that moment, there would be no ticket away from home for me during our winter break. Besides, perhaps he really had learned his lesson.

"You want to go for a walk somewhere?" Graeme asked.

"I could really go for a burger from Jocko's" I answered truthfully, suddenly craving their charcoaled, greasy beef. Perhaps a midnight feast would absorb the booze and stave off payment in full tomorrow morning.

"Let's go get a burger," Graeme agreed quickly.

"You go ahead and I'll meet you right outside," I said. "I just want to say good-night to Anise and Caitlyn."

Graeme looked doubtful.

"Go ahead," I insisted. "I'll be right out."

Before he left, Graeme put his hand around the back of my neck and planted a massive kiss close to my mouth. When I turned around, I saw Robert silently watching the whole mini drama.

Darn it all, Graeme, I thought irritably, suddenly mad at him all over again. *You could have given me at least until tomorrow to make up.*

I walked over to where Luke, Anise, and Robert stood in a trio. Robert was watching me, then glanced away as I got close.

"Well, I think I'm going to head for bed," I said, again wishing that thinking a thought were not so much like walking through a dense fog. "It was nice meeting you, Robert."

Robert nodded, then stuck out his hand formally. "Nice meeting you," he said cordially. Mournfully, I glanced at his impressive build for a second before turning away.

"Want me to go with you?" Anise asked, studying me. I knew she had watched the whole scene unfold and was disappointed with my choice. Oh, well, nothing I could do, now.

"Nah, I'm good," I said. I took a couple steps backward, still watching the three of them. As I backed up I tottered – right smack into Taylar! She gave me the most miserably disdainful look I'd ever seen, as though by accidentally bumping into her I had purposefully and maliciously ruined her life.

"Oh, excuse me, Taylar," I said with exaggerated kindness. "I was just leaving. Graeme's waiting for me outside."

I left her staring, slack-jawed, looking very much as though she'd like to puke on me. Walking unsteadily out of the lounge and through the foyer, I at last burst past the double glass doors of the dorm and out into the chilly, early December night where Graeme was waiting.

Chapter 21 - Connecticut

It was a five-hour trip to Graeme's hometown in Connecticut, and I watched the miles go by with a growing sense of nervousness. I'd never been serious enough with a guy to be introduced to his parents before, and I wasn't really sure what to expect. I supposed they would look at me and size me up, but I wondered if some sort of subtle, cloak-and-dagger interrogation would ensue in which they would try to deduce my socioeconomic background, political views, and perhaps whether mental illness ran in my family.

Before we had left for Winter Pause four weeks earlier, Anise had gone to pains to help ensure that at least my appearance was fitting for the occasion, and had helped me procure the proper outfit for such an occasion.

"You want to look conservative but not stodgy; trendy but not cliché," she had said matter-of-factly during our mission to the mall. "First impressions should really be called 'Prejudice based on appearance.'"

"How about I arrive in a micro-mini and go-go boots," I had joked.

"Graeme's *dad* might like that," Anise had replied.

"Ew, *gross!*" I had gagged.

With Anise acting as my own Coco Chanel, I had found an outfit that fit the criteria she had suggested. I was attired in low-rise, boot cut jeans and a pale blue cashmere cardigan over a white button-down. For a pinch of panache I had picked out pointed shoes to wear with the jeans. An hour into wearing them, they were viciously assaulting my toes.

"We're about to cross the Tappan Zee," Graeme announced. "That means we're half way there."

A sense of adventure infused me as we began to drive onto the massive bridge and over the Hudson River. I stared with delicious trepidation at the waters below, and marveled at the distant houses dotting the green hills on the other side. I wondered at the people who lived in them, whether they worked in the city and were very rich, and if they took for granted such magnificent views of the river that they saw every day from their windows.

Graeme and I listened to the radio as I watched the scenery fly by, not talking much as we covered mile after mile of the Interstate. We had stopped in northeastern Pennsylvania to get some fast food, and conversation had lulled since then. Graeme was a fan of classic rock, and I recognized only a handful of the tunes that spewed from his radio.

We passed in and out of New York and then finally saw signs telling us that we were entering Connecticut. An image of my fifth grader teacher, Mrs. Brubaker, suddenly popped into my mind, teaching us how to spell the name of the state. "'Connect – I – Cut' is how to remember it!" she had intoned. I had never forgotten nor misspelled the fifth state since.

"Only about an hour away now," Graeme stated. I looked ahead, gripping the side of my seat for a moment, feeling like the bottom of my stomach might drop out.

"Relax," Anise's words came back to me. In addition to outfitting me properly she had also given me a pep talk "What are you so worried about? You're awesome! If his family doesn't like you for some reason, something is seriously wrong with them. They could only *hope* their son could catch a woman like you!"

I smiled, thinking of my brash, resoundingly confident little friend. Her words made me brave for about nine seconds, before I relapsed into nerves.

When we finally exited the Interstate, I looked around curiously. Connecticut didn't resemble much at all the scenery I was familiar with in my hometown in Pennsylvania. The houses were more upscale, the stores were different, and the traffic seemed much more congested. Funny how each state was its own little entity.

We drove down several multi-lane roads before eventually the streets thinned and the traffic lights appeared less frequently, and at last we turned into a residential neighborhood. I gazed at each property as it passed by, the homes some of the largest and most beautiful I'd seen. Yards were all carefully manicured, and hedges meticulously clipped. It was January, and a few houses still bore remnants of the Christmas season, with lights visible along rooftops, but other than that, they were entirely uncluttered by any kind of objects or children's toys.

No tacky lawn ornaments allowed here, I thought to myself.

"Here we are," Graeme said, and my heart instantly stepped up its rhythmic drumming as if on cue.

Graeme's house was a pretty, brick Colonial Revival. Situated between two palatial spreads on either side, its smaller dimensions made it look more modest compared to the rest of the neighborhood. After grabbing my bags and following him up the brick pathway and through the front door, I soon saw how my own humble digs paled in comparison.

The two-story home was quaint and cozy, and classical in its décor. Standing in the foyer, I stared wide-eyed at the formal living room to my right with its white sofas, Persian rug, and stone fireplace. To the left was a carpeted, cozy den, equipped with another fireplace, enormous flat-screen television, and bookshelves.

Graeme headed for the kitchen, leaving his bags in the hallway and instructing me to do the same. Following my slightly awestruck gaze, he gave me a guided tour of each object my eyes met. The countertops were a dazzling, dark granite and the cupboards went all the way up to the ceiling, their contents visible through leaded-glass windows. "Custom cabinetry," he explained, a little pompously I thought, as he showed me the soft-close technology built in to each drawer. "Mom wants the appliances upgraded," he continued as I stared at my mottled reflection in the stainless steel. Our refrigerator and oven back home were still of the blinding white variety, which I had thought an improvement over the puke green ones we'd replaced from the 1970's. "She also wants butcher block for the island top."

There was a breakfast nook at the far side of the kitchen, and French doors leading out to a deck. The large kitchen adjoined a spacious and elegant formal dining room.

"My parents' liquor cabinet is in here," Graeme explained with a wink. "I'll show you *that* after they go to bed."

I heard footsteps trudging down the stairway that we'd passed and I turned around.

"Hello, Graeme," said the deep voice belonging to a man in the doorway. He was considerably older than my own father, tall, with silver hair and glasses. Attired in a button-down and khakis, he looked exactly how I would picture a financial consultant.

"Hey, dad!" Graeme walked over to him and the two shook hands. "Dad, this is Molly."

"Hi, Molly," Graeme's dad stepped forward and gave me a hearty handshake. "Welcome to Connecticut." I smiled.

Having been warned never to arrive empty-handed to a hostess, I had picked up for Graeme's mother a winter bouquet, replete with white mums, burgundy roses, and ferns. Since she was nowhere to be seen, I held onto it, unsure whether to give it to Graeme's father instead.

"These are for you and Mrs. Reddig," I said finally, handing him the bouquet.

"Thank you," he said, glancing at it and setting it on the table. "You kids hungry?"

I looked at Graeme and he nodded. "Where's Mom?" he asked.

"She's at her therapist's," Graeme's dad said. "We'll go without her."

Therapist? I thought incredulously. *Wonder what's wrong with her.*

I knew that Graeme's family had a housekeeper, Marcella, from Curacao, but that I probably wouldn't meet her until later in the week. I was interested to learn from Graeme that she was "extremely religious" according to his description of her, and wondered what exactly that meant.

Graeme's dad had not given me his name by way of introduction, so I was at that awkward place of not knowing how to address him. To be on the safe side, I figured I would call him "Mr. Reddig," which made me think of that kiss-up Eddie Haskell on *Leave it to Beaver.*

Graeme's father's idea of dinner was to take us to dine at a four-star hotel situated just a few miles from their neighborhood. The prices for appetizers were more extravagant than what I was accustomed to seeing for the main courses at other restaurants, and I felt a bit out of my element. Graeme and his dad both ordered steaks, but I stuck with a burger and fries.

Mr. Reddig didn't say much throughout the course of the meal. He asked a few polite questions but mostly just sipped his martini and read a newspaper. I wondered if his mother had ever told him as a child that it wasn't polite to read at the table.

When the waitress whisked away his martini glass, he cordially rebuked her, pointing out that he wasn't yet finished. She gracefully apologized and set it back in front of him, whereupon I noticed there was about a half-swallow remaining in the bottom of it. Inadvertently, I laughed, and when Graeme and his dad looked at me with puzzlement and curiosity, respectively, I covered up my mouth with my linen napkin and coughed quietly.

When we returned to the house, another car was in the driveway, and my heart resurrected its marching band beat. I silently lamented not having had a martini or two of my own, or better yet, a triple scotch.

A cloud of perfume greeted us upon entry even before Mrs. Reddig did. I did not care for its heavy musk, but I could tell that it was expensive. Graeme's mother was petite and thin and seemed to be dripping with make-up and jewelry. She was one of those women who wore rings on all of her fingers, and when you looked into her eyes what drew your focus was her mascara. I could picture her wearing pearls to the gym.

She shook my hand with a loose, anemic grip. "Hi, nice to meet you," she said with exerted enthusiasm. I discerned that she was assessing me in those two seconds, and I felt a compelling urge to show her the labels on the inside of my clothing and assure her that I was not quite the Pennsylvania hillbilly that she had probably imagined.

"Well, Molly and I are taking off to go meet up with Gabe and Pete Ellis and some of the guys," Graeme said, kissing his mother on the cheek.

"So soon? You just got here, Graeme," his mother complained, looking after him wistfully.

"You'll have me all day tomorrow, Mom," he promised, smiling.

"Just be careful, tonight," Mr. Reddig said, not glancing up from the magazine he was poring over at the table. "The police have been out in droves lately, and they sometimes set up a checkpoint on Highlawn."

We said our good-byes and jumped back into Graeme's SUV, heading a couple miles across town to his buddy's home. On the way, Graeme pointed out his old elementary school, a diner that was a favorite hang-out and where we'd probably end up later, and a few other nostalgia-invoking structures.

We drove into another development that made Graeme's neighborhood look positively modest, and parked in front of one of the largest estates I'd ever seen.

"His parents are vacationing in Mexico, so he has the house to himself," Graeme explained as we approached the massive double doors.

Graeme's friends were okay, but they were like all his friends at Durst. They dressed the same, acted the same, spoke the same. I could picture them living the same party lifestyle well into their thirties, finally settling down only after the linings of their stomachs could no longer handle so much abuse. I tried to get into the giddy spirit of the atmosphere, but for whatever reason, I was feeling lonely. I longed for a conversation with depth.

The following day we were lethargic and slothful, as the sleet pelting the windows discouraged us from going outside. We had a late lunch courtesy of Mrs. Reddig, who spent the meal criticizing her own cooking. She remarked that the potatoes were too cold and the meat too dry and the carrots overcooked, at which everyone fervently disagreed and insisted that the said offending dishes were just perfect.

The day wore on with the sound of football in the background, and while I wouldn't have minded watching the game, I joined Graeme's mother in the formal living room with a book that I had brought. As the shadows lengthened, snow flurries began to spiral down outside. The house was indeed cozy, and I only wished that we could have lit a fire in the splendid stone fireplace while I was sitting next to it, thereby completing the ambiance of the room.

As evening fell, Graeme asked if I wanted to go for a ride. We were overdue for a hanky-panky session, I figured, and I readily agreed. The snow was coming down steadily now in large, wet flakes. The SUV sailed through it easily enough, although we were one of the few vehicles out on the roads.

We drove down different roads until the houses thinned out a bit. Graeme assured me that there was a lover's lane type offshoot near one of the old stone farmhouses that sat on the edge of town. I didn't ask him how he knew this.

On my right we were coming up on a cemetery hedged in by a low stone wall. Graeme suddenly slowed down and pulled through its massive, wrought-iron entrance.

"Want to see something cool?" he asked me. If he meant in the cemetery, I wasn't sure. Graveyards creeped me out.

He shut off the car just inside the entrance and we got out. I shivered from both the cold and from our solemn surrounds, which were appropriately back-dropped by a slate gray sky.

I looked around in wonder. The cemetery was comprised of all kinds of crypts, mausoleums, and other massive monuments bedecked with winged cherubs and other sculpted angels. I felt as though I were walking onto the set of a movie, having never seen such a cemetery as this.

"This is where you go after kicking the bucket if you were really, really rich," Graeme explained. "People who were important in state and federal government are buried here, and art patrons and philanthropists and socialites."

I looked around curiously at the bleak surrounds, which seemed particularly eerie underneath the muting blanket of snow. My sneakers crunched in the inch or two of white powder, making the only audible sound.

I read the names where they were yet detectable under the falling flakes. "Whitehall" and "Wolcott" and "Weston" – they certainly had a monopoly on the *w*'s. Graeme had left my side and was weaving in and out between the different crypts. I kept close to the main road that ran through the middle, feeling as if at any moment some sort of gremlin or other-worldly creature might pop out from behind one of these monumental stones.

Finally, Graeme returned and clasped my hand. I breathed a sigh of relief, then remembered that in all the horror films the monsters always went after the guy and girl when they were together and feeling safe.

"Let's just sit here for a moment," Graeme said quietly, brushing off a bench that was bolted to a slab of cement near the main road. "It's so peaceful." I was secretly anxious to leave, but didn't want to ruin his graveside experience.

We sat for there several moments in silence, watching the snow swirl down from the austere sky, which now appeared to be a muted pink as dusk settled in. It was the same color that high school girls always seemed to choose for their tacky class rings.

As I surveyed the imposing tombs, I felt a growing melancholy settle over me like a thin blanket. I couldn't help but wonder about the souls whose decaying bodies slept in those crypts. How had they lived their lives, and where were they now? Had even a few of them not been so clouded by their riches that they were able to glimpse the Son of God before it was too late and put their trust in him? Had they finally traded in the wealth of this brief life for glories and treasures untold? Or had they come to the end and realized one minute too late that it had all been folly? That their mansions and millions were vanity, and were they now writhing in torment, with endless remorse punctuating their torture? I shivered again, and Graeme drew his arm around me tighter.

Yes, it seemed like the ultimate irony, having such a colossal grave marker. You were gone from this world forever, yet there was still some lingering attempt to impress. Like pride and ego would still have their say. Yet what did any of it matter, considering where you were now?

Graeme's arm slid off my shoulder and he turned to me suddenly, taking my right hand in his. He looked deep in my eyes, clasping my hand with his other. My hands were already turning a mottled red from the cold, and the sudden warmth was wonderful. I waited, gazing back at him expectantly.

"I love you," he said.

I studied the blue of his iris, unsure how to react. The discomfort I felt at that moment far surpassed any lingering creepiness I had from sitting in a cemetery. Alarmed and feeling very ill-prepared, I thought rapidly. I tried to think what some girl in a movie would do in this situation. I drew a breath finally. Leaning over, I pressed my lips to his in the best impassioned kiss I could muster. I faintly pictured a director off-stage complimenting me and encouraging me on my convincing style. A kiss was a great way to buy time.

We sat in huddled silence for a few moments more. To my relief, Graeme didn't say anything else. My rear end was numb and seemingly frozen to my jeans, and I was ready to leave.

Moments later we left the cemetery, but my discomfort did not ebb. I could picture this "I love you" business becoming regular fare, and frankly, I had not thought through what to do about it. I was fond of Graeme; certainly I did not love him, and just as certainly I could lie to him. Nevertheless, I didn't want to tell those words to anyone other than the one they were meant for, and to say them to Graeme would only cheapen the experience when that day – hopefully – arrived.

*****

I woke up in the guest room of Graeme's house that night, hair plastered to my forehead in sweat, staring wide-eyed into the darkness, struggling to calm my breathing. I had had a nightmare in which I was walking alone through an empty house. The house had possessed a terrifying feeling to it, and I had been warned by someone not to go in it. As I walked from room to room, a nameless horror had gripped me. Opening a set of double doors, I had come into a room in which, on the far side of it, the floor opened upon a great gulf, and flames of fire rose up from within the pit. As I had stood staring into the chasm, shrieks rose up to my ears. I had shuddered uncontrollably, stricken, before mercifully waking up.

Chapter 22 – Stepping Out

I suppose that it was safe to assume that I had not exactly hit it off with Graeme's mother. Not that I didn't like her, or could say for sure that she didn't like me, but there definitely didn't appear to be much of an instant connection between us. At first I thought it was because she moved in different circles than I did – or at least aspired to – but as I spent more time around her I realized that we simply had different interests, and the things that were important to her were not those things esteemed by me. Our age difference might have been a factor, but I didn't think it was prominent in why our personalities didn't mesh. If she had lived near us in Pennsylvania, she would not be someone with whom my own mother would ever be close friends. She was the kind of person, who, if ever taken out of her upper middle class suburbia environs, you couldn't picture surviving the shock.

Beyond our holding little in common, Mrs. Reddig emanated the distinct vibe that she did not regard my relationship with her son with any degree of seriousness. Something in the way she addressed the two of us when we were together, and the way she spoke to me individually, gave the impression that in her opinion, this relationship was nothing more than a middle school romance. It was hard to blame her for feeling that way, as I myself viewed the relationship with similar casualness. However, her open projection of such a view I couldn't help but find somewhat insulting.

Beyond that, it was a little embarrassing the way she fussed around Graeme like a mother hen. Worrying about things like his eating habits at college and whether his professors were overloading him in the homework department. Fine for a ten year-old, perhaps, but for an adult who'd already been away for some time at school, it seemed superfluous. He had brought home an enormous pile of laundry and when I peered into his room Friday morning I saw that she had washed and folded it all in neat little stacks. My mother certainly wouldn't have done that for me so long as I was capable and had as much time on my hands as we did for our break. There were other things, too, that

I couldn't help but find annoying. The way she spoke to him – babbled, I would have described it – and the way she tattooed him with a lipstick kiss every time he walked out the door irked me.

So when Mrs. Reddig asked me if I wanted to go with her to her aerobics class on Saturday morning, I had enthusiastically responded to her attempt to reach out, even though I had never done an aerobics class in my life outside of eighth grade phys. ed., and had positively no desire to do so again. All I had ever known of aerobics classes was whippet-thin instructors who had '80s hairdos and their middle-aged patrons in velour sweat suits, the latter having no hope of ever resembling their instructor. But since Mrs. Reddig had graciously extended her hand, I wanted to reciprocate the gesture. After all, it was only an hour of my life.

I had been spared much interaction with her Friday because Graeme took me into downtown Hartford to look around. We had later gone to a shopping mall, where I had learned the difference between the malls in *my* area and his. It wasn't just the high end stores. It was the way the people who shopped there dressed.

"Oh, they wear their mink coats in July," Graeme assured me, as I gaped at the ladies walking through the automatic doors, nearly every single one of them flashing gigantic diamonds and real furs.

"No way," I replied. *"Why?"*

"Because they have them and they want everyone else to know," he answered.

It was only a five-minute drive in Mrs. Reddig's Lexus to her gym, so we didn't have much time to generate conversation.

We entered the pristine fitness club and Mrs. Reddig registered me at the desk, and then detoured to the side into one of the largest aerobics room I had ever seen. It was lined with rubber balls and jump ropes and stacks of dumbbells, and the floors had the appearance as though they had just been buffed. I chose a step and followed Mrs. Reddig, hauling it towards the back of the room.

I listened politely as my boyfriend's mother chatted with some of the other members about a sale that was happening that weekend at some retail establishment, and observed detachedly as they compared fingernails. She did not introduce me, so I was spared having to make small talk myself.

Our instructor arrived moments later in yoga pants and a sleeveless nylon top. She was petite and pretty and had a long, perfectly smooth ponytail. She did not look as though she thought it was still 1988.

"Welcome, everyone!" she cried cheerfully as we moved into organized regiments with our step blocks. "I see we have a few newcomers here," she said, eyeing me with an overzealous grin. "I'm Patti, for those of you who don't know me."

She spells "Patti" with an "i," no doubt, I thought to myself as I stood placidly behind my step.

"Get – ready – to – step!" Patti shrieked, high-stepping her way over to the stereo. An explosion of sound energized the room. I felt fearful.

I had done step aerobics one year under force during gym class, but couldn't remember much about it and had no memory of the terminology. I studied Patti's legs, which seemed to be a blur, trying carefully to imitate her rapid movements.

"Tap it over!" she called out, looking right at me. Half the room followed her gaze and saw that I was the straggler. "Right foot on the *other side* of the step!"

I writhed. If her chipper eyeballs weren't boring holes into me I wouldn't be nearly so flustered.

"Step turn! Tap it over! Back! Pivot!" Patti barked at us like some lip-glossed drill sergeant.

Every time I finally got into the rhythm of the new step, Perky Patti would change up the routine on me, and I'd be left floundering on my step like some drunken soft-shoe shuffler. Not only that, I was getting tired already! I looked around at the synchronized older women hopping up and down around me. So much for my previous smugness. These aging Hausfraus were kicking my butt!

The mirrors and all the ample bodies spinning in them reminded me of some weird circus dream sequence from *The Twilight Zone*. It all started feeling a little surreal. I wasn't even paying attention any more. I was so lost.

Suddenly - *bam!* Before I even knew what had happened to me, I was face to face with the floor, noticing dust bunnies for the first time on the laminate surface. I heard the music suddenly stop.

"Are you alright?" someone was asking me.

Stiffly, I pulled myself up off the floor. "I'm fine," I said. I was in a jungle of varicose veined legs and beleaguered spandex. Twenty pairs of eyes were staring at me. With effort I smiled gallantly. "I must have added an extra step."

"I think you missed one!" Patti said helpfully, her bubbly voice having lost none of its pep. I wanted to string her up by her ponytail. "Should I go get the first aid kit? Do you need an ice pack?"

"No, I'm fine." I stood up gingerly. "I think I'll just sit back here along the wall and – stretch – for the rest of the class."

Graeme's mother came over, the picture of concern, and then suggested we leave. I assured her all was well and that I wouldn't hear of her missing out on the rest of her class. No doubt she was secretly relieved that she hadn't introduced me to her pals, as I would forever be known in Connecticut as "timber!" or "crash" or some similar moniker. I could picture the women asking for Saturdays to come "So...how is that girl doing? You know, the one who fell flat on her face during step? How do you know her again?"

My ears were flaming hot as I made my way back into partial obscurity next to the weight rack. I thought if there were such a place as purgatory, it would consist of Patti's chipper voice shouting out aerobic commands over techno music, while countless synchronized, rotund women in sweats spun around in endless mirrored images.

****

By Saturday afternoon, with the memory of my disastrous step routine fresh, and the suspended comfort of being someone else's houseguest beginning to wear upon me, I was ready to go home. In my boredom I had stumbled upon a couple of Mr. Reddig's Ken Follett novels, and after seeking out the steamy passages, I'd read them a couple times and returned the books to their places on the shelves. I sighed, figuring that to be the highlight of the trip. We were scheduled to leave the next morning, and I was looking forward to the return. It seemed like my stay at Graeme's had consisted mostly of us driving around, seeking out a secluded public place to fool around in private, and sneaking alcohol in the evenings, broken up by a little New England sightseeing here and there.

Graeme's mother was going shopping for the afternoon and, mercifully, I did not receive an invitation to come along. I figured she probably didn't trust me in a mall after I proved to be such a failure at the gym – maybe feared I might knock over a display or something.

Mr. Reddig popped his head into the den, where Graeme and I were watching some Clint Eastwood movie, and announced that he was going to the hardware store to pick up some part to a power tool. As soon as his car was out of sight, we sprinted frantically upstairs to Graeme's room.

We had left the door partly cracked in order to listen for anyone entering the house unexpectedly, but I guess we were so intensely involved in our own activities that we missed the light tread of footsteps outside in the hallway. Suddenly, a creak on the steps to the attic startled us both like gunshot. In unison, we snapped up to a sitting position on the bed, listened in deathly quiet, and turned as if cued – stricken – to stare at one another.

Graeme adjusted his rumpled clothing, threw on the shirt that had been discarded next to the bed, and tip-toed over to the door and peered out. Slowly, he opened the door and glanced into the hallway. He cocked his head for a moment, listening. Then I heard it, too. A pattern of footsteps above us, coming from the third floor.

Graeme sighed, quietly closing his bedroom door as I scurried to assemble myself. "It's Marcella," he asserted. "She totally heard us, and probably saw us, too."

"Is she going to say anything to your parents?" I squeaked, remembering how religious Graeme had said she was.

Graeme shrugged. The gesture opened up a sinkhole in my stomach. "I don't know," he said dully.

Terrific, I thought, feeling the blood which had drained so instantly from my face suddenly return in a rush. I wanted to pack up all my belongings and scuttle out of town that very hour.

We headed back downstairs and sat in tense silence in the den, trying to turn our focus to a movie on television. Graeme seemed calmer after a while, but I couldn't relax. I had a feeling akin to awaiting judgment for a crime of the worst kind.

Presently Graeme's dad came home and disappeared into his shop in the garage, and a couple hours later his mom pirouetted into the hallway, closing the door behind her while wrangling a mass of shopping bags. When she disappeared upstairs, I feared the worst. We hadn't seen Marcella since the incident, and I wondered if she would take the opportunity now to tell Graeme's mother about the illicit scene she'd witnessed.

We sat down for a late dinner which I had offered to help make. As I shredded lettuce for a salad, I had tried to read Mrs. Reddig's every expression and movement for signs that she had been tipped off about our bedroom treachery. Was it just me or was she cooler than usual towards me?

When Marcella joined us at the table I couldn't meet her gaze. The heat was already rushing up my neck and face and ears, and as soon as I choked my dinner down, I asked to be excused so I could run upstairs and pack. I couldn't remember the last time I'd felt so ashamed. I waited all that evening for Graeme to come in and tell me that we'd been found out, but he informed me that his parents had made no mention of the incident.

The next morning I was spared another encounter with Marcella, as I knew she was off at church, according to Graeme's father. Shortly before eleven, we bid his parents a quick good-bye, and headed – mercifully – back to Pennsylvania.

Chapter 23 – Close Encounters

Caitlyn returned from break firmly committed to her boyfriend, Dave. She had confided to me and Anise her unwavering love for him, avowing after five weeks spent at home with him again in their familiar surrounds that he was indeed the only guy for her. To my amazement, she adhered to this affirmation for nearly two weeks before I came back to our room one evening to find Alex Healy, one of Graeme's friends from Theta Chi, packed into her bunk with her – anchovy-style – watching a movie.

Anise had told me that her Christmas had been painful.

"My dad joined us even though apparently, he got an apartment already," she had reported. "Everyone was together, eating around the table like nothing had happened. But you could have cut the tension in the air with the carving knife. So we just ate ham and mashed potatoes and talked about nothing and acted as though everything was perfectly normal. It was awful." She laughed, a frightening sound, with a sharp undertone of pain in lieu of its usual mirth. "I actually couldn't wait to get away from there and back to school, can you believe that? And I don't even like this place!"

Since we'd been back the campus was abuzz with two primary news stories: an associate professor from China had been arrested during a trip he'd made over there to conduct research and had been imprisoned on charges of espionage; and, campus security was teaming up with local police to identify the perpetrators involved in the theft of the historic statue from atop of Old Main. A fraternity was the primary suspect, perhaps the same culprits who had once run an ad in the local newspaper, listing the college president's car for sale.

Word of the Chinese professor's imprisonment impacted me. While I hadn't known him, I had seen him several times around campus – a slight, bookish man with glasses too large for his face. Even though I'd never spoken to him nor had him teach a class, there was a timidity about him that was evident in all his mannerisms and the way he walked. He was the kind of person you wanted to pat on the back and reassure that everything was going to be alright, and maybe even keep as a pet. I found myself thinking about him at random times of the day, wondering how he was being treated by his captors and if he was scared to death. I knew that imprisonment in China meant something entirely different than it did here – it might very well contain torture, starvation, and other forms of abuse. *You inbred communists,* I had thought to myself, just as much to the faculty and staff of the campus I was attending. *This is what your values inevitably lead to when they're carried out – they always go further than the kind of society your ideologues had envisioned.*

The Germans had a saying and it sprang now to mind – "*So fängt es immer ein.*" It always begins the same way.

The local press was all over the story, and there was even word of the governor of the state getting involved. I endeavored to pray for him, but when I actually stopped and tried to focus on a heartfelt prayer, it felt hollow and forced, as uneasy as any other conversation might have been with someone with whom I was on questionable terms.

Occasionally I would run into Jen or some of the others from the Christian fellowship. The campus was too small to avoid it. We'd exchange mumbled "hellos" and ask how the other was doing, and reply with opaque responses which always seemed to incorporate the word "busy." For someone who hated small talk anyway, this chance encounter when I had been so noticeably absent from the group was always particularly painful.

The end of the first semester brought other changes to the campus as well. Several acquaintances hadn't come back. Anise found out that Luke's father had suffered a heart attack and that Luke wasn't coming back for the semester.

Adam, famous for swallowing the quarter, had transferred to a community college close to home. Unbeknownst to me, Adam had suffered from clinical depression, and having never felt as though he fit in at Durst hadn't helped his illness.

One girl in our dorm had been expelled for plagiarism on a final; Caitlyn had shared that and some other gossip with me and Anise over lunch.

"So, apparently Jamie Madeira went home for fall break and her dad took one look at her and bought her a treadmill for her dorm," Caitlyn said, her voice lowered dramatically.

Jamie was a very pretty blond girl in our freshman class, someone who I had taken notice of shortly after move-in day, pondering wistfully what advantages I would have if I had Hollywood good looks like her. Her petite frame had doubled in size since move-in day, and while she still moved in the elite popular circle of Durst's beautiful (and more importantly, wealthy) she clearly had lost some of her iconoclastic power thanks to the extra pounds. Her apparent nickname, which I'd heard snickered among the guys several times, was "tank."

"How can a treadmill fit in her dorm?" Anise wanted to know.

"She's in a suite, so I guess it's in the common area," Caitlyn replied.

"That's embarrassing," Anise replied.

The idea of a parent buying an expensive piece of exercise equipment for his child was foreign to me, especially when there was brand new, top-of-the-line cardio and weight machines that our tuition was paying for, located only a stone's throw away from the dorms.

"Wouldn't that hurt your feelings?" Caitlyn asked me and Anise.

"Yes," I replied, trying to imagine what Jamie's father had actually said to her. I wondered if he was worried about her health…or if he was worried about her image.

"Oh!" Caitlyn's eyes grew huge and she dropped her sandwich on her plate with a *thud,* as though she had just thought of something that would change the course of mankind. I followed her stare to another freshman, a girl by the name of Karyn, whom I knew only from seeing her from a distance in physics. "Guess what?" Caitlyn continued. "You know Tad's girlfriend?"

"Yeah," Anise answered. Tad had eventually realized his efforts to pursue my lovely friend were futile and had moved on to other prospects.

"Well, Chris told me that she just recently got on the pill."

"Uh-huh," Anise said, biting into a breadstick.

"Well...I guess you have to wait through at least one full cycle to make sure the pill's effective," Caitlyn continued. "And...I guess they were impatient and didn't wait long enough."

"She's pregnant?" Anise whispered, shooting a glance in Karyn's direction.

"She *was* pregnant," Caitlyn said ominously. "They had originally planned to go to her house together over break so that he could meet her family. Instead, they told everyone that they were taking a "road trip" and they went to get her an abortion."

I lowered my eyes from Caitlyn and stared into my soup.

"So, apparently Karyn's taking the whole thing kind of hard. I don't know what Tad thinks about it all."

"Did they both agree to it?" Anise wanted to know.

"As far as I know," Caitlyn said. "Neither of them wanted to be freshmen in college and parents." She took another bite of her sandwich. "So, now they just have to live with it."

"Oh, wow, that sucks," Anise said, tossing the remainder of her breadstick in her salad dish and wiping her fingers with a napkin. She stared wordlessly across the cafeteria at the subject at hand.

I barely knew Karyn, and I didn't like Tad all that much, but Caitlyn's news made me feel all heavy and tight inside.

My eyes followed Karyn as she walked around the island in the cafeteria, filling a glass of juice. I wondered what she was feeling right at that moment. I also wondered who among her friends and family – if anyone – she trusted enough to tell what she and Tad had done.

Truth be told, the idea of getting pregnant scared me more than any venereal disease out there. I didn't even want to *think* about such a nightmare.

*****

A chill, listless February melted into a mundane March. The gray, limestone buildings seemed sullen against the backdrop of even grayer winter skies. The vindictive wind showed up now nearly every day, whipping through the campus and making the walks to class that much longer.

Word of an earthquake in India had seized the headlines, footage of weeping women and the rubble of houses dominating television screens in the HUB. The Christian Fellowship spearheaded efforts for donations, teaming up with an international relief organization to deliver aid.

"All creation groans for and suffers the pains of childbirth together until now." The verse sprang unbidden in my mind as I grimly watched the coverage.

My time was consumed more than ever with Graeme. Hardly a day went by when I wasn't with him, usually hanging out in his room for hours at a time, often spending the night. He had even surprised me once by buying me a toothbrush, combs, and a contact case just for use in his room.

With Graeme wanting so much of my time, and dorm life monopolizing the rest, I had to make a decision to make the library my home-away-from-home, allotting myself Graeme only as a "reward" after I had covered so much homework.

It wasn't easy, particularly in respect to physics, which I had passed with a lackluster C+ and now was taking the second part in order to fulfill my science requirement. Had this kind of science come naturally to me, it wouldn't have been so bad, but I felt as though there were a mental barrier which not only prevented me from understanding some basic principles of physics, but which psychologically had the effect of demoralizing me before I even began to read. It astounded my thinking to know that there were people out there who actually enjoyed this stuff, let alone were good at it.

Nevertheless, I diligently began retracing the ground from the first days of class, some of the most basic ideas only now seeping in as I re-read the material for a second and even third time. Of course, there were several chapters I had missed due to the goings-on the nights before. No wonder I fell so far behind so quickly. If only I'd grasped the material at the time it was being taught! Why couldn't I just "get" it the first time around like others? As I sat in the loud open silence of the library, I thought how the snowball effect of building on one concept and then moving to the next had had a massive head-start on me. Discouraged, my mind would quickly begin to wander. I pictured myself as a little cartoon character, running down a slope of snow, a snowball accumulating in mass behind me, slowly overtaking me.

Chapter 24 – Mirror, Mirror

Sex dominated both my waking and sleeping moments. I couldn't seem to stop thinking about it. I had reasoned that if Hank were to ditch his girlfriend, ask me out, and we were to begin dating, we still wouldn't get married at least until after the last semester of college were over for both of us. That was a whole three-and-a-half years away! I wondered if it were possible to combust from abstaining so long when one was sure that one's entire body was composed only of nerves and hormones.

The flip side to this unpalatable prospect was the realization that if I *were* involved with Hank, I knew I could somehow manage to wait for that long. Hank was just…different. The thought of a relationship with him – talking for hours with him, exchanging thoughts with that amazing mind, the simple pleasures of taking a walk or going to a diner or sitting outside with him on a deliciously warm August night – was in itself so sublime that I knew I would be content with that indefinitely. In fact, deep in my heart, I truly believed that if for some reason, we *couldn't* be physically intimate, and I could only ever wake up next to him and get to see him lying there in bed next to me every morning, that that would be enough to make me happy for the rest of my days. Of course, it wouldn't be ideal.

*****

The end of freshman year loomed three weeks away, and I couldn't believe that after that, I'd be home for three months. I had a standing offer to work at my old job at Shady Oaks during that time, but other than that, I really wasn't looking forward to the return home.

Shady Oaks was a retirement home split into residential and retirement living. I had worked in their dining facilities during junior and senior year of high school and the summers in between, and had befriended several of the elderly residents who came there for meals. They would be glad to see me, and I them.

All of them, except the sour-faced Gladys Hauger, of course, who seemed to think that any and all staff at Shady Oaks showed up strictly for the purpose of submitting themselves to her verbal abuse. I recalled vividly my first day there when I had failed to make her coffee just right, half decaf and half regular with no sugar and two creams. She had decried me as an imbecile in front of the other 100+ residents, most of whom either ignored her or couldn't hear her. I was advised by another worker not to take it personally, because she treated everyone in such a manner.

The perpetually bad thing about working in a nursing home environment was coming in with the knowledge that there might be an empty chair at the place of a resident whom you knew and loved. Then you would hear the story whispered from one staff person to another. "Yes, he looked perfectly fine after he left dinner last night, but when they went in to check on him in his room this morning…"

Graeme wanted me to come up again for another visit during the extended summer break, but after the housekeeper incident, not to mention my vaudevillian show on the step at his mother's uppity gym, I was in no hurry to return. He was already planning to make a couple trips to see me on the weekends, but introducing him to my old friends from high school and youth group seemed unlikely. I worried that he'd find my hometown terribly dull, and perhaps start regarding me differently, too, as he saw me for the first time in my native habitat.

The thought of returning home after a year away at college painted an image in my mind of some mechanical doll that had been released into the world and finally come alive – had discovered it actually was human – and then was forced to return to its box after the revolutionary discovery. I was dreading going back. It wasn't that my old town was so terrible. But I was not the same person who had lived there, and not the individual whom everyone would expect me to be.

Beyond the prospect of living with my parents again and facing separation from my friends and the college atmosphere I'd come to love, I was also uncomfortable with the idea of having to face my church family on any given Sunday. Once I had opened my Bible recently to look up a scripture reference for Tad, who had had a question involving his religion class. To my amazement, verses of the Bible which I had known and read over and over all my life suddenly looked foreign to me. More than that, it was almost as though they didn't make sense, and I felt something akin to scoffing rise up in me as I glanced over previously warmly familiar words. It suddenly made sense to me in that instance how non-believers viewed the Bible, and why the words didn't resonate meaning to them. The realization, I suppose, should have left me unnerved, but instead, I accepted it coolly and then stuffed it out of sight as I had learned to do with all the other little checks that I used to sense in my spirit. I had long ago discovered that if I ignored the little voice long enough, it grew fainter and fainter.

*****

Jon, who had shared another German class with me into the second semester, had been absent for the third day in a row. It was amazing the difference in the quality of the air when his feet were not present. I was sorry that he wasn't around, though. I wanted to talk with him about the upcoming dance that the fraternity was hosting. I had just received my official invitation in my mailbox earlier that day, the Greek letters embossed on the front stirring excitement in me already.

Graeme had mentioned the event to me already, and I was thrilled at the prospect of a formal. Any occasion to dress up in a gown, get my hair coiffed, and drink alcohol – all in the same evening – was a merry prospect. Best of all, Caitlyn and Anise had been invited as well by two of the brothers. We had promised to help each other with dress shopping, and to hunt costume jewelry and accessories.

"I couldn't care less about Nathan," Anise had confided, upon receiving the invitation. "I'm just happy we'll get to hang out together."

"You mean 'Nathaniel,'" I had corrected her, referring to the guy who had invited her.

"Whatever. I'll call him 'Nate' if I can't remember."

"Graeme's going to fall flat on his butt when he sees you," she had assured me. "We'll find something so hot that they'll have to wire his jaw shut for the evening, it'll be all the way down on the floor."

*****

The dreaded physics exam was at last finished. Most of the questions on it had looked familiar to me from what I had studied, and I hoped that the answers I gave were what they wanted. I had done my best, I reasoned. Well, maybe my second-best.

I still had two term papers to write, but the worst was behind me and the formal was ahead of me, only three days away.

Caitlyn, Anise and I had gone shopping the afternoon following my physics exam for our dresses and accessories. I had my prom dress waiting as a back-up if I didn't find anything, but had had an idea of a lilac-colored gown accessorized with white elbow gloves for the gala. Caitlyn just wanted to find a "little black dress." To me, however, a formal should be just that – all decked out, because there were so few occasions any more for which to dress lavishly.

The envisioned gown became a reality after hitting our fourth store (and after discovering prior to that that halter necklines gave my shoulders an unflattering and formidable linebacker look). For some women there is a gasp that escapes us when they discover the perfect dress, and as soon as I saw myself in the floor-length gown with its jeweled embellishments, I knew lightning had struck.

"Roll out the red carpet!" Anise said appreciatively when I had emerged from the dressing room. "You look like you belong in Hollywood."

"Nice threads, Moll," Caitlyn approved. "That's a great style for you."

I *felt* elegant alright, and dreamily pictured Graeme glimpsing me in the gown for the first time. The price tag would cost me three full weeks' worth of dining room wages, but I didn't care. I looked *good*.

Anise found a canary yellow cocktail dress that set off her clear, olive-colored skin tones beautifully. Caitlyn was torn between three black dresses that looked nearly identical to me, and at last settled on one of them that looked exactly like one that was in her closet and that I'd seen her wear on one of her first dates with the long-past Ryan. No matter, she would steal the show in whatever she wore.

The three of us emerged from our shopping spree clutching our various treasures and happily exhausted. We had, however, one more stop to make.

"All set for the big transformation?" Caitlyn asked me.

I nodded uncertainly.

"There's no turning back after this," Anise warned. "Once you start coloring your hair, you won't be able to stop."

She and Caitlyn had persuaded me to get my hair cut and highlighted for the big event. I had been talking about it for weeks, more as a distant idea than a reality, and the two of them were holding me to my word.

My hair was full of natural highlights – strawberry and gold and corn silk – but I was going to get it lightened and professionally cut. I had been kind of excited leading up the big event – when we were only talking about it – but now that the day had finally arrived, I was frightened. As Caitlyn, Anise, and I drove in Anise's car to the salon, my trepidation grew. I felt like Mary, Queen of Scots, on her way to her beheading, accompanied by her entourage.

At the salon, Anise pored over several books and magazine pages after the stylist administered my foils, helping me decide on a cut. Caitlyn meanwhile flirted with a gay guy who worked there, their duo of giggles filling the small space.

Selecting the right hairstyle was tough. On the models, every haircut looked fantastic. I wanted to be careful to choose something that didn't leave me with a gaping forehead or added another inch to my face.

Anise convinced me finally to go with a basic trim and to get some bangs. I was scared to turn my long locks into bangs around my face, but she was persuasive and said that now was the best time to go for it. Bangs would look great with my up-do for the formal, and if I truly hated them, I had the entire summer break to let them grow out, safely away from the scrutiny of the college.

The scissors moved quickly and deftly and I gazed at portions of my hair now lying on the floor at my feet. As the stylist moved around me, chatting the entire time, I hoped that she was paying attention to what she was doing and that she wouldn't suddenly sneeze in the middle of a snip.

At last, she was finished, and as she blow-dried my hair, I was startled at the difference in my appearance. The highlights restored me to a sunny blond closer to that of my childhood color, and the bangs gave me a softer, sexy look.

"You're like a different person," Anise commented incredulously. "It looks fantastic."

Caitlyn pulled herself away from her newfound effeminate flirtation and agreed with Anise's assessment.

I was secretly pleased with the new look, and instantly regretted having waited so many years to do something with my hair. I wondered what Hank would have thought of my upgraded appearance.

"Wow, I wouldn't even recognize you from the girl I met back in August," Caitlyn said.

It was true. I did look different, and not just because of an hour spent on my hair. It occurred to me that I looked older – years older – than I did eight short months ago. I studied myself carefully in the mirror. It was something about my eyes.

*****

My new hairstyle was a mini-sensation. Graeme loved it.

"Good golly Miss Molly!" he remarked, ready to attack me as soon as he saw me for the first time.

He wasn't the only one apparently who noticed. I drew a lot of stares the first few times I walked across campus with my new 'do. I felt exuberant, tossing my head as I walked, undulating with self-confidence. All I needed was an excuse to smile flirtatiously over my shoulder and they could cast me in a shampoo commercial.

And was it my imagination, or was Professor Holz suddenly bantering with me and chatting a lot more than usual after our final ethics class?

The woman at the salon had given me some pointers on how to style my hair, and I had bought a new ceramic iron with my now dwindling dining room wages. Anise was going to help me with an up-do for the formal, and I couldn't wait to step into my new gown.

*****

That evening Graeme and I instant messaged one another while I was supposed to be working on a paper.

"Wish you were here with me instead of working on that paper," he wrote.

"I know. Gotta do it."

"Wish I were kissing your sweet lips right this minute."

"Me, too."

"and then your neck…"

I closed my eyes and decided to change the subject before I completely lost my resolve to work on the paper.

"Missed Jon again in class today," I wrote. *"Is he sick?"*

"You didn't hear the news?"

"No. What news?" I waited anxiously. Graeme didn't write anything further for several minutes.

"What news?" I repeated.

"Sorry, someone just came to my room to borrow something. What were we talking about?"

"Jon," I wrote immediately.

"Oh. Yeah. Jon's parents came to pick him up this weekend. He had tens of thousands of $$ in gambling debt and ended up

having to sell his car to help pay for it. He was going to flunk this semester anyhow."

Stunned, I sat back in my chair.

"You there?"

"I'm in shock."

"Yeah, it sucks....so when do you think you'll be finished there?"

I wrote Graeme a flippant response, my mind fixated on Jon's unfortunate and sudden disappearance. Although we weren't good friends, I felt sorry for him that he'd gotten into so much trouble, and even worse for his parents. What humiliation! I wondered what would become of him, and if his parents were the kind that would be compassionate towards him and forgive him, and help him with his addiction to gambling.

*****

The campus seemed quieter the rest of that week, almost as if for the first time since we'd arrived, students were actually studying. Graeme was bogged down in papers himself and so I was particularly looking forward to spending some time with him at the formal that weekend. It was now only two days away.

I fell asleep that night with dreams of dancing and romancing swirling around me. Hours later, I woke up in a sweat from a nightmare that had seemed so intensely real that I was terrified to fall back to sleep for fear of dreaming it again. I dreamed that it was late at night and I was driving, and ahead of me in another car Caitlyn and Anise were passengers with a third person, an unknown driver. As their car slowed to a halt, it suddenly went up in flames before my very eyes. Horrified, I realized that my friends had been killed. As I sat there, watching helplessly, the driver of their car stepped out of the wreckage, unharmed. It was a man – a slight man whom I glimpsed had a pasty-gray complexion and black hair cropped so short that it looked almost to be painted to his skull. He approached my car and lowered his head to eye-level with me through the window. His eyes were translucent and I recoiled at the sight of him.

"Shouldn't you have been riding with me, too?" he asked, grinning eerily.

Chapter 25 – Intelligence Report

Anise and I both slept late that Saturday before setting out to spend the rest of the day getting ready for the formal. Caitlyn was joining us later, after she finished taking a history exam that had been rescheduled for noon that day. We were going to do each other's hair as well as administer manicures and pedicures.

As we filed, buffed, and painted our nails, we prattled about everything from music to men – mostly men. I felt lighter and brighter than I had in a long time. The evening awaited me, dreamy and fantastic. I loved dressing up and having an excuse to do so, and I couldn't wait to dance, to drink, and to spend the whole crazy night with my closest friends. Most of all, I was looking forward to Graeme's dazzled expression as he glimpsed me in my garb for the first time, proudly escorting me into the ballroom.

My last term paper and the pending return to my parents' house were put out of my mind. There would be time to think about all that later.

There was something else on my mind, though.

"You're the only one I can tell this to," I confided to Anise, letting out a sigh. I examined my cuticles, feeling hot blood stealing up my neck. "I've been thinking about going all the way with Graeme."

"Really?" her tone was breathless shock. I glanced at her, then quickly looked away. I couldn't read her faint smile, but she seemed pleased. Perhaps she was glad not to be the only "experienced" one among us. Perhaps she felt that we'd finally be on an equal plane at last, I wasn't sure.

"I think about it all the time," I confessed. "I can't *stop* thinking about it." I sighed. "And I'm so insanely sick of fighting the feelings I have all the time...stopping short right in the middle of it." I scrutinized the stitching on Anise's comforter, running my forefinger over it. "It's so frustrating. *Not* to mention, the pressure I sense from Graeme."

"Why, has he been pressuring you?" Anise's brow furrowed.

"N-no, nothing like that," I said hurriedly. "I just know everything that *I'm* feeling he's sensing, too. It doesn't make things any easier."

Anise nodded knowingly. "It's only natural. We're creatures of passion and hormones. We're *supposed* to be doing this at this stage in our lives. And, if you feel you're ready, then I say 'go for it.'"

Secretly, I thought that it wasn't a matter at all of feeling ready. In reality, it was hard to believe that I was even *contemplating* doing what I was now thinking. It was a feeling of being constantly compelled and propelled towards something, so that over time, it seemed ever more inevitable. But I couldn't explain to Anise the jumble of thoughts and emotions that pulled me in all different directions over the subject. Kendra would not have understood, either. She would have been properly horrified, and would probably have urged me to a nunnery. Well, perhaps that was a slight exaggeration. But she couldn't possibly have understood or sympathized with my dilemma, with how far away I was from the girl she knew in high school. The aloneness of my massive unshared burdened overwhelmed me. If only there were someone out there who understood what I was struggling with, who understood my terrible quandary. Someone who would listen and truly hear me, and who could counsel me without condemning me.

Anise continued on the subject, offering me advice on protection from pregnancy and other bits of knowledge that she wouldn't suppose I'd know. We chatted at length, with me occasionally interrupting to ask questions like some student to her tutor.

It was nearly two o' clock and I was famished. Anise called in a large pepperoni pizza, shoving a container of wax into the microwave as she did so. As soon as she ordered the pizza, she called Caitlyn on her cell phone. "Where are you, hussy?" … "Well, we're waiting for you, get your sexy butt up here" …. "Yeah, she's here." …"What's going on?" …"Alright, well hurry up…we're gettin' pizza. What do you want on it?...Okay…Ciao."

Caitlyn walked in the door five minutes later. She dropped her books on her bed, and to my surprise, said nothing about the glamorous appearance of either one of us. She stood there gazing at me, a funny expression on her face. I wasn't sure, but it seemed as though she were troubled, yet there was a hint of triumph in her eyes.

"I just found out some news," she announced.

I stopped what I was doing, a hairpin poised over my head, and turned to look at her. Something in the tone of her voice sent a shiver through me. Anise ripped a line of wax from beneath her eyebrow and grimaced. She disposed of it and gingerly touched the tender, reddened skin above her eye. "What is it?" she asked, looking at Caitlyn in the mirror.

"This morning while I was waiting in line to get a bagel I overheard a couple guys from Theta Chi talking about some things that went on over at the house last night," Caitlyn began. "Apparently, they had quite a party."

"Oh, really?" Anise asked. She turned to me. "I'm kind of surprised that we weren't invited. Graeme goes to most of them, doesn't he?"

"He had a paper that was due today and told me he'd be at the lab, pulling an all-nighter," I answered.

Caitlyn drew a deep breath and turned to me. "Actually," she said slowly. "That's what I was going to tell you. There *was* no paper."

I stared back at her, my mind struggling to interpret the meaning of her words. She opened her mouth to speak again, and as she did so, a sinking feeling settled over me, pulling me towards the earth, working its way down my body until it settled into a hard, knuckled ball in the pit of my stomach.

"That's just what he told you."

"What do you mean?" I asked, clearing my throat so that my voice could get out.

"Apparently, this particular party was for brothers only – as well as associate members," Caitlyn continued. "They hired..." she trailed off for a moment. "They hired...*live entertainment.*"

As Caitlyn proceeded to tell me the details that she had gleaned I felt the ball in my stomach loosening and spreading into a feeling of queasiness. According to her source, Caitlyn relayed that there had been two females paid to perform for the guys, and as she explained a summary of the night's events as delivered by Alex, I felt the strength slowly seeping out of my muscles. I sank to the bed, not wanting to hear another word, but powerless to do anything but sit there and listen.

"How is that stuff even *legal?*" Anise cried at one point, recoiling in horror after one particularly gruesome detail Caitlyn recounted. "That's prostitution!"

I listened with a kind of deathly calm, my mind suddenly barren of any single thought. I grappled for any substantial thought on which to seize and cling to for the sake of sanity. My mind flashed back to the time when I had bungee-jumped during a family vacation to the Great Smoky Mountains. On that first free fall, there had been a total absence of any thought, almost as though my brain had decided of its own accord to shut down rather than try to process what was happening at that very moment – specifically, that I was hurling towards the earth at 65 miles per hour.

Presently, I heard Caitlyn saying my name. I turned to look at her blankly. "Are you okay?" she asked.

I nodded, still trying to sustain a thought.

"Wait a second," I said, shaking my head as I struggled to clear my mind from the bomb that had exploded in it. "How do you know for sure that Graeme was there?"

"I saw Alex Healy just now on the way back from taking my final, and pried it out of him. He admitted that what I'd heard was true. At first he kind of denied that Graeme was there, but I could tell he was lying. Graeme said that under no circumstances were you to find out. He knew you wouldn't be happy." She looked at me with a kind of condescending pity. "But you're my friend and I had to tell you. I'm really sorry. I'm so sickened by it myself I'm not sure I want to go now." She turned to Anise. "Your date was *not* there, by the way."

Anise clasped my hand and stared intently into my face as I studied the design in the throw rug on the floor, unwilling to meet her gaze. I had never cared for the color of it since Caitlyn had first introduced to our dorm room, but had not wanted to hurt her feelings. Now, I suddenly resented its zany pattern of ostentatious colors with a senseless hostility.

"Are you okay?" Anise asked me, the deep concern in her voice dislodging some of my shock and replacing it with an element of self-pity. I nodded wordlessly, still gazing at the despised rug beneath my manicured toes.

There was a knock at the door. As Caitlyn went over to answer it, Anise began muttering curses and violence-laden threats of physical dismemberment projected at Graeme. I knew somewhere in the back of my mind that such remonstrations were her way of expressing her fierce solidarity with me, along with the utter helplessness she no doubt felt in being able to do nothing to alter the unhappy situation.

"Pizza's here!" a male voice cried out cheerily from the doorway. Anise and I lifted up our eyes to glimpse a good-looking guy in a maroon polo shirt holding a folded white box. He grinned flirtatiously, eyes passing over each one of us as if he'd hit some sort of estrogen jackpot.

Caitlyn turned to me and Anise, but before she could say anything, Anise jumped up from her place beside me on the bunk and grabbed her change purse off the cheap, laminate bureau.

"You- you *men*," she muttered at the poor pizza boy, thrusting a handful of bills in his direction and wresting the pizza from him as he stared at her in bewilderment. "Keep the change," she growled, before slamming the door shut.

Anise dropped the box of pizza down on the desk with a thud. The warm smell of cheese and spices served only to aggravate my stomach even more.

Anise came to sit by me on the bed again. Caitlyn took a seat across from me on her own well-frequented bunk. "So what are you going to do?" Anise asked, her voice now gentle, the fury driven out of it like a passing thunderstorm.

I was silent for a moment. "Well, I *won't* be forced to take any step aerobics classes in Connecticut any time soon at least," I managed to joke.

Anise smiled and Caitlyn laughed. "Are you alright?" she asked.

A myriad of feelings was passing through me like a parade. My astonishment at Caitlyn's story had quickly dissolved into the impotent, sickly sensation of betrayal (which had to be the worst feeling in the world – rejection, but with a knife in the back), to disgust, and finally – rage. I was furious at Graeme for what he'd done and even more so for lying to me about it, and absolutely wrathful that he had deliberately conspired with others to cover up his actions. Had he been standing there in front of me, I was sure I would have thrown a punch at him. Of course, Anise would have beaten me to it, with more deadly results.

I caught a glimpse of myself in Caitlyn's full-length mirror that we'd hung on the back of our door on move-in day. It was actually a comical sight: the costly gown, the showy accessories, and the upswept hair that had taken Anise so long to do…all at odds with my utterly downcast expression. I was a scorned Cinderella, unhappy not because the ball was over, but because she had discovered before it had even begun that her prince was actually a toad.

As my anger flared over the thought of the money I'd spent on the superfluous dress and the energy I'd expended on looking so much forward to the ill-fated event and the time wasted preparing for it all, I realized that there was someone with whom I was even more angry than Graeme – myself. How could I have given so much of myself to him? All the wasted days, yes, but even worse, I had traded an element of my very soul for him. How could I have been so foolish?

I had traded peace of mind and singleness of purpose for the right to do whatever I pleased, with grossly unsatisfying results. The obvious truth which I had suppressed was now glaring at me right in the face: Graeme was nothing more than a novelty, a poor distraction from all the things that really mattered to me, a cheap consolation prize.

This realization should have made the present moment a lot more bearable, but I still felt horribly insulted, betrayed. Not to mention the tremendous disappointment that was flooding over me at the realization that I would *not* be stopping the show that night in my scarlet gown, *femme fatale* style. My much-anticipated evening had been derailed to the gutter.

"I'm fine," I finally said, trying to sound brave. I rose to my feet, brushing myself off even though the shimmering gown was spotless. Caitlyn and Anise were watching me intently as though I might be suicidal. "Would you unzip me?" I asked Anise. "No need for these right now."

"Aren't you going to talk to Graeme first?" Caitlyn questioned.

"About what?" I replied dryly. "Whether he preferred the blond over the brunette? No, I am not going to waste another moment of my time with him." I removed the glittery rhinestone necklace from around my neck. I paused as I crushed them onto the top of the dresser, staring at nothing. "I've been a fool."

"I'm so sorry this happened," Anise murmured as she helped me out of my superfluous attire.

In truth, I felt sorry for myself. To be treated so unjustly and so insufferably, and on the eve of what was to be such an important evening. It was horrendous. A sudden, venomous hatred for men everywhere instantly shot through me like an arrow. Animalistic, carnal cheats!

"I'm ditching my date and staying with you tonight," Anise affirmed staunchly.

"Me, too, Moll," Caitlyn piped up, a bit uncertainly, I thought.

"No way," I said to Anise. "Your date wasn't a part of this – whether intentionally or by chance – and he doesn't deserve to suffer for Graeme's stupidity." I pulled out a bobby pin with trembling fingers. My rage was returning. There was such a range of emotions surging through me that I wondered if people ever *could* spontaneously combust.

I wanted to shame Graeme, just as he had done to me. My mind schemed ways to intensify his humiliation. He would be coming to the dorm to pick me up at five that evening, and I imagined his face when he rang and rang the buzzer to my room and there was no reply. I pictured him trying to call the room and then enlisting the help of others, before finally realizing – or being informed – that I was not to appear that night. I could picture the indignation all over his face before he went on a cursing spree, then had to decide whether to forfeit the evening entirely or arrive solo, either way to the knowledge and scandal that would precede him through the gossip channels. Or perhaps Anise would be here when he arrived, and she would say, "This is your date for tonight" and hand him a porno magazine instead.

I gave up the salacious fantasy with a sigh, realizing that to indulge in such a thing would be to degrade myself as well, and waste even more of myself on him. Besides, there was a good chance that Anise's and Caitlyn's dates would accompany him, as they were coming around the same time. To do such a thing would place the duty and discomfort of an explanation on my friends, and I would not do that.

Beneath the cesspool of emotion, however, relief, like a tiny bud nearly covered by damp, rotting leaves, was revealing itself. Beyond the present deluge of whirling, teeming thoughts, the realization that I would at last be free – or unencumbered to choose freedom – was like a tiny beam of light penetrating the thick blackness. Hardly significant, perhaps, but there.

"Could I borrow your car?" I asked Anise. "I just want to get off campus for a little while and collect my thoughts."

"Of course," Anise agreed. "But are you sure you don't want me to come with you?"

"Thanks, but I'm fine," I said. "At least, I will be."

While Anise rummaged through her handbag for her keys, I gathered myself together and breathed deeply, feeling very much like a boxer stepping into the ring. I picked up the telephone receiver, my forefinger hesitating for a moment over the buttons. Exhaling, I dialed Graeme's extension, hearing my pulse pounding as his line rang.

"Hello?" The once familiar and welcome sound of his voice sounded foreign.

"Graeme? It's me."

"Hey, you," Graeme said enthusiastically. "All ready for tonight's big events?"

"Why? They can't be as exciting for you as *last* night's 'big events.'" I bit back the reply and hesitated. Confrontation was not my forte, and already I felt my resolve waning.

"Molly? You there?"

An image suddenly flashed in my mind of what Caitlyn had reiterated had transpired before Graeme's willing eyes last night, and anger charged through me like voltage on an electric fence.

"I won't be able to go with you to the formal tonight," I stated crisply.

"What? Why? What's wrong? Are you sick?"

"In a way, yes I am. And in fact," I continued, ignoring his pretense of confusion, "I won't be going *anywhere* with you from here on out."

"Molly, what in *hell's* going on?" Graeme's voice reached a feverish crescendo.

"I think you have a rough idea," I replied calmly, the passion in his voice offsetting my own. "Think back to recent events...as in – oh – the last twenty-four hours."

Graeme grew immediately silent, probably unsure of how to parry the remark.

"There are only two things I ask," I continued. "That you won't try to call me or come over or in any other way try to get in touch with me, and that you'll return my Guinness t-shirt to me through student mail." It was my favorite shirt, and I really wanted it back.

His silence was all the confirmation I needed. A wave of fresh fury washed over me.

"Yeah, I found out. I hope it was worth it," I said gravely, and quickly hung up.

*****

I drove through miles of rolling pastures, past unconcerned cows whisking their tails in the late afternoon sun, and fields of dandelions. Ordinarily, I would have enjoyed the scenery, but today, my eyes barely noticed it. I was lost in thought.

It seemed like I should have had this wonderful, overwhelming sense of liberty. Instead, I actually felt very much lost – anxious even – and more restless than before. It seemed as though my world had collapsed inward on itself, and although the world I was in might not have been the greatest, it was a familiar one. Now that it was no longer there, I felt scared, panicky. Had it been anything less than what had happened, I would have considered swallowing my pride and making amends with Graeme. Not because I cared for him so much, but because somehow I had gotten on this path that had led me to where I now was, and I found myself in a wilderness – alone. With him there I had not sensed the solitude and the stark desperation of my habitat. Now that I was by myself, I realized that I was far from home in an unknown land, and I had no clear means of how to get back to the place where I once had been.

Once in German class Frau Bund had explained to us that when the Allies liberated the concentration camps after World War Two, they were stunned to find that the captives did not bound out of their barracks and into freedom, rejoicing. Instead, they had to be led by the hand – slowly, cautiously – into sunlight and freedom. The reason for this was that the prisoners had grown so accustomed to their conditions – to the filth and the stench and the lice – that the prospect of open surrounds was overwhelming to them. Despite living in the most detestable conditions imaginable, they were comfortable. They had grown to feel secure in their chains, and freedom felt foreign and overwhelming.

Chapter 26 – Leaving Las Vegas

The days that followed were a kind of hollow, blended blur of motion and emotion. I had dreaded the end of the school year and my subsequent return home so much, and now it seemed like the few remaining days were an eternity that would never come to an end.

In addition to my topsy-turvy state of mind, I was now a gossip target and felt like a social pariah among many of the guys I'd come to know through Graeme. Every time I crossed paths with one of them, interaction was slightly awkward and strained. They had been my cronies, my fellow partiers, and now that loose connection was frayed. The campus was too small to avoid seeing anyone for long, and I felt trepidation now whenever I ventured out of the dorm. It struck me as ironic that now the atmosphere was as charged when running into them as it was with members of the Christian fellowship.

Details of the missed formal were relayed to me through Anise and Caitlyn, both of whom had attended the evening's festivities. Graeme, of course, had been forced to show up alone, and had done so with at least the manifestation of having a good time. The reason behind his stag appearance was quickly and widely known. Rumors and scandal were, after all, the only things that traveled faster than light.

While I had expected and even dreaded Graeme's pursuit to gain me back, I had not anticipated that he would instead fall just as silent as I. Funny thing human nature. I had been bracing myself to resist any temptation to mend the relationship that had become such a staple in my life, even dreading it. Yet now that I didn't have to fight the anticipated battle, I felt slighted, further rejected that he didn't even care enough to try.

Anise theorized that I had wounded his ego in front of his buddies and for that reason he was reeling from the damage.

"Kind of a cardinal relationship sin when it comes to men," she offered. "He'll be back."

I truly didn't want him back but I didn't want to be ignored. Every day at school was a burden, yet the prospect of going home for the summer was gloomy. I felt trapped in my new way of life but didn't know how to go back to the way things were before college. I no longer knew who I was, or simply how to *be*.

The worst was seeing Taylar's evil smirk each time I encountered her in the hallway or somewhere else on the campus. Triumphant and gloating, she was delighted to see the two of us estranged. I knew easily that she was the type of girl who would never have given a second thought to the goings-on of the Theta Chi party, and would have attributed it to "that's what guys do."

There were many such girls, to my surprise, who didn't seem to mind at all that guys looked at porn or went to strip clubs or generally objectified and degraded women. Such females thought it was mainstream and normal and that girls like me were the ones who were extreme, and thereby gave the men who did such things not only a free pass to continue such behavior, but to find fault with females such as ourselves who had a little more self-respect. The great irony, I was learning, was that such guys labeled us women who disdained these antics as being "insecure."

In my miserably jumbled mentality, I poured everything that I had into my remaining two finals, seizing upon the term papers as something stable upon which to fix my energy and thoughts. When I turned in my last paper four days after the ill-fated fraternity formal, I was confident that I had given forth my best effort ever.

After I slipped the final paper – a six-page thesis on German Expressionism – into Frau Bund's mailbox, I slowly walked back to the dorm in a kind of melancholy. All around the campus was quiet, the only activity being a handful of students walking here and there, or a vehicle being loaded with suitcases and posters and sometimes beer bottle collections. Existence was winding down at last at Durst, and both faculty and students were preparing for three months of the other life that lay outside its campus.

As I ambled along, I looked over the limestone buildings once more with sudden fondness. There was and would always be a soft spot in my heart for this place. It was my first experience away from home for an extended amount of time, and good or bad, it was now a solid piece of my personal history. I did wish that I could go back to life as I'd known it before college, but I was likewise glad I was not the same, wide-eyed and naïve little person who had arrived.

Returning to my hometown, I didn't know what to expect. I had outgrown the person who everyone back there had come to know, and felt as though I would be returning to them a stranger, yet they would anticipate and expect the same things from me. The notion was wearisome.

With resolve, I began to pack my clothes and books and personal items back in the room. I was to leave the next morning – my parents were coming to pick me up. Anise, Caitlyn, and I were planning to have our own celebratory party in the room that night, complete with adult beverages that had been secured for us by one of Caitlyn's 21 year-old admirers. I was really going to miss Anise, especially since she had plans to spend most of the summer in Italy with extended family who lived over there. I wouldn't see her until we returned next year.

As I packed my things and pondered my suddenly mundane life, there was a knock at the door. I opened it to find Graeme standing there, holding a bag.

"Can I come in?" he asked.

I was caught off guard at the sight of him. Mutely, I nodded and stepped back to allow him in.

"I brought over your shirt and a couple other things that you'd left in my room," he said, handing me the bag he'd been holding. I glanced at his hands as he held out the plastic sack. Why had it never occurred to me before that they were girly? Pale and feminine, I thought. I glanced in the bag, not really seeing the contents, but giving my eyes somewhere else to look.

"Molly," he said, almost plaintively. "I screwed up. I am the biggest jackass in the world."

Yes, you are, I thought. I said nothing.

He studied me. "Please let's not throw away a whole year because I was stupid. Please, can't we try again? Start over? I can't even tell you how sorry I am, how much I've hated myself the last few days."

We finally have something in common, what a shame, I thought dryly. Still, I said nothing. I felt somewhere inside a piece of me melting, wanting to take the bait simply for the sake of returning to what was familiar. Even though it meant being in a bad place, at least I would know *where* I was.

I shifted from one foot to the other, uncertain of what to say. I hadn't planned on getting into a discussion with him – I knew it was pointless – but I wanted desperately to hold onto a thread of keeping something that had grown so comfortable alive, even though it wasn't healthy.

"Molly, I *love* you."

"Is that what you call it?" I replied, finally finding my voice, the part of me that was beginning to melt immediately freezing solid again. The irony of his words abruptly struck me, and I continued with sudden vim. "Lying to someone, betraying them with your actions? *Love?*"

"Molly-"

"If so, then it's fitting that you told me that you loved me for the first time in a cemetery." I narrowed my eyes with sudden anger. "I gave you my affection and my time and I even told you that I loved you, too. I wish I hadn't, wish I could take it all back. But I can't. All I can do is move forward, and ensure that that's *all* you'll ever get from me."

He swallowed. "Molly, there must be some way to make this up to you. These last few days have been hell without you. I can't stand it." He truly looked as though he might cry, which did nothing other than to repulse me even further.

"Please leave," I said tersely. "I have to get ready to go."

"I'm going to do everything to prove to you that I've changed," he continued, ignoring my request. "I'm not going to give up on us."

"Good-bye, Graeme," I said, slowly shutting the door. As it closed on his face, I could hear audible sobs in the hall.

"Oh, how ghastly," I whispered, embarrassed by the commotion. "Real men know *when* to cry."

*****

I said my good-byes to Caitlyn, Anise, and many of the other girls in the dorm the next morning. Anise stopped by to bid me a final farewell on her way to her exam. I had slept late and woke up feeling groggy and achy, my body's way of informing me that it had received too much alcohol the night before.

My parents arrived at eleven. I was glad to see them, even though I was reluctant to return to life under their roof. As I dully walked down the steps of the dorm, lugging my boxes and crates and suitcases into the back of their SUV, it seemed as this first year of college must somehow have been a dream. It didn't seem possible that so much had happened in the course of nine months. I climbed into the backseat feeling hollow. I turned to gaze one last time at the campus, feeling much like Lot's wife leaving Sodom.

Chapter 27 – Home Again

So I returned to my home town and to my former life, with things much the way they had been and as I had known them prior to my year away. The only thing that was changed was me. The lens through which I looked at everything in life was altered. My perspective had changed, and therefore what I held to be true – and how I responded to things – had also altered.

The residents at Shady Oaks who still were in possession of their faculties seemed glad to see me. I was happy to be reunited with my handful of "favorites" – the Heplers, Mrs. Jacoby, and the inseparable friends, Mr. Titus and Mr. Stewart, who always were found sitting together, saying little, but smiling as though life couldn't possibly get any better. There were a few more empty seats since last I'd been there, an ever-present reminder of our own mortality. Gladys was of course in stellar health, and acknowledged my presence on my first day back with a *"humph."*

"I remember you," she had said sulkily.

"And I remember *you,"* I had replied cheerfully.

Service at the sole fast food restaurant was still slow, and the transvestite who never failed to be working there whenever I went through the drive-thru, day or night, still creeped me out with his dirty fingernails every time he leaned through the window and handed me my bag. Nevertheless, it was strangely comforting to see him again.

Mrs. Eldridge across the street faithfully talked my ear off whenever she saw me outside, reminiscing about the days of her youth and all the men she could have had if she hadn't married Mr. Eldridge. Then I'd eventually be rescued when her stalwart old husband would open the front door and call her to lunch or dinner, which he prepared for the two of them every day.

I deliberately avoided passing by Hank's house, wondering with dread if I'd eventually run into him when he was with *her*. I hadn't spoken to him or heard anything about him since that fateful phone call back in the fall. Since we had not moved in the same social circles, there was little fear of me having to hear anything through his old high school friends.

Graeme called me once but I made short work of him over the telephone. A gut-wrenching, emotion-drenched letter came a few days later, and I had balled it up in the trash. The thought of him now simply annoyed me. I secretly wondered how I could have been so foolish about this guy? What if – what if I had acted on those impulses I'd shared with Anise that weekend of the formal? I shuddered, thinking about what a narrow escape it had been.

So the days filed by, each looking very much like the one before. I took on full-time hours at work, and spent my free time saturating my consciousness with fiction. I was constantly in the library, always seeking out new literature. I steadfastly avoided any novels that might contain erotica, not wishing to be reminded that that particular world was now cut off to me, and seemed like it might be forever.

I attended church with the rest of my family occasionally, not feeling much of anything when I went there, hearing the words from the pulpit and mouthing the words on the projector, but impotent to apply them to myself.

Once, I had run into Kendra's mother at the supermarket, and had been informed that Kendra was taking two summer classes, and would be home the first week of July. If it hadn't been for that encounter, I probably would not have known. Our contact had cooled considerably since the first semester, and I traced back our last e-mail to March. She had written me, and I had neglected to respond.

The most alarming discovery to me was that, desperate as I was to "go back" to my former way of life before I'd so badly transgressed at college, it wasn't as simple as I had imagined. I regretted my sins, but somehow I didn't – couldn't – *feel* sorry for them. I was frightened about my standing with God and a couple times said aloud, "Lord, please forgive me." The words were forced, hollow. Perhaps it was because I was more afraid of dying – of passing out of this life unforgiven – than I was truly remorseful over all the things I had done. I didn't feel as though He had heard. Even if He had, I didn't sense within my soul that I had truly repented – nor that I had been forgiven. Once, I went so far as to dwell on the most heinous of my iniquities and tried to force myself to cry. Nothing came out. It was like having the dry heaves.

To complicate my deadened spiritual condition, my thoughts seemed to have a life of their own when I was awake, and even though I wasn't involved with anyone physically any more, I couldn't stop entertaining images of the acts themselves. If I hadn't been living at home, I would have surely rented a dirty movie to watch. I would later come to understand that one of the terrible things about getting bogged down in a particular sin is that afterwards, even after repentance and forgiveness, one is susceptible to that sin again. Kind of like having cancer. Even when it's in remission, you need to be forever on the lookout for its reappearance.

The nightmares that had become my staple in the dorm continued. One night, I dreamt that I was in a prison cell, with a concrete floor. A handful of strangers shared the cell with me. The whole place was dark and dank. In my dream, terrorists had been pursuing us, and now we were waiting for them to execute us.

I woke up from this dream, like so many others, drenched in sweat, the sheets and pillowcases damp beneath me. Staring at the blue shadows on my walls, I prayed. "God, please, *please* take me back. Deliver me from this life I've managed to make a mess of for myself. Please, God! Save me from myself."

*****

On a humid, overcast day towards the end of July, two things of consequence occurred. At the mall, I ran into Hank's best friend from high school, and Kendra called me to see about getting together.

I had just walked by a kiosk where they sold cheap pin-up art – everything from cutsie puppies and kittens looking plaintively off-camera to barely dressed young women in seductive poses – when I heard my name called.

I turned and saw Danny Clevenger, Hank's best friend, standing there. He was smiling at what must have been a surprised look on my face.

"Molly, how ya doin'?" he asked me.

"Danny!" I grinned, trying to recover and appear at ease.

"How was your first year of school?"

"Amazing!" I replied enthusiastically. I hated it when people used the word "amazing." Phonies! But no need for Danny to think it was anything less than that, or that I hadn't left high school entirely behind me.

We chatted for a few minutes about everything except that which was most important to me, and then I turned to go.

"Have you seen Hank lately?" Danny asked me suddenly.

My heart stopped.

"No, I haven't," I replied, wagering that the calmness I feigned could win me an Emmy.

Danny gave me a long look, and then added cryptically, "He broke up with his girlfriend."

"Oh, really?" I responded nonchalantly, feeling the color drain from my face and hoping wildly that he didn't notice.

He smiled. "I'll see you later, Molly."

The rest of the day, I replayed Danny's words in my head, searching for meaning behind his smile and wondering why he had mentioned such a thing to me. Did he have a reason for telling me this bit of news? Could Hank be pining for *me?* Then I second-guessed myself and surmised that it was just as likely that Danny was being a jerky guy and simply playing with my emotions. Perhaps he was wondering if he'd catch me squirming when he mentioned Hank's name, and maybe he got some kind of sadistic pleasure in doing so. The thoughts ran in circles around my head until – by the time I reached home my temples were throbbing.

I congratulated myself, however, for having taken the time to style my hair, apply make-up, and attire myself in one of my more flattering outfits before I'd left the house. Perhaps Danny had taken notice and would relay something about my new appearance back to Hank. "Yeah, that Molly sure was looking good," I pictured him saying, as Hank listened with renewed interest.

It was after dinner that evening – a dinner in which my father complained that I was acting all withdrawn again – that the phone rang and my sister announced that it was for me. It was Kendra.

"Hey!" I said with overwrought enthusiasm. I immediately felt on guard.

"Molly, it's so good to hear your voice," Kendra murmured. I knew that she meant it. Kendra was always, always genuine, which now only accentuated the fact that I felt like such a counterfeit. "I was wondering if we could get together soon. I was hoping to see you."

I was nervous about the prospect of seeing Kendra, scared to death that her discerning heart would read the blackness and bleakness of my own. However, I verbally agreed that it would be great to see her again, and found myself making plans to get together that following evening at a local coffee shop in the neighboring town.

After the usual pleasantries had been exchanged, and we had spoken at length about Kendra's own romantic encounters and anecdotes at college, she finally took advantage of a slightly uneasy pause to ask me abruptly – boldly – what my relationship with the Lord looked like.

I stared back at her unwavering gaze, then down into my cup of hot chocolate as if some wisdom might be found in its murky depths. "Well, you know. I've had the usual first-year peccadilloes," I wanted to reply lightly, downplaying the question. "Went a little off the beaten path, learned some hard lessons. But, that's all behind me now. Me and the Lord are an item again."

Tempted as I was to deflect her observations, make excuses and tell her that I was really just fine, I didn't this time. Kendra was a Spirit-filled woman. What if the Lord struck me down for lying to her, just like He did Ananias and Sapphira when they lied to Peter? What did I have to lose except face? Might there also be extraordinary relief in finally sharing this burden I'd been bearing alone for so long?

"Not so good," I said quietly, after an extended pause. I had no desire to provide her with any of the details of my past year, but figured I could at least tell her the truth. "I've been living the prodigal's life." I traced the rim of my mug with my thumb. "I want to get back – really, I do. But I'm a long way off. And...I don't even really know *how* to get back."

Kendra listened with compassion in her eyes. Finally, she said, "It's a long road. But it's a good road."

She then offered to pray for me. It made me uncomfortable, but I acquiesced. Again, I had that uneasy feeling that refusing prayer might warrant God hurling a lightening bolt at me, leaving only a smoke ring right there in the café where I had formerly been sitting.

"You're in the position of the rich young ruler," Kendra said, after we'd opened our eyes and I was determinedly stirring my cocoa with a coffee straw. "You have a choice to make between what it is that is most important to you in life – your own will, or His."

As I drove home, her words reverberated loudly, drowning out thoughts of the cryptic encounter with Danny from the day before. I felt more uncomfortable than ever, anxious even, because I knew she was right even though I felt so powerless to change my situation. "Faithful are the wounds of a friend," I thought wryly.

Chapter 28 – An Encounter with Truth

Three nights after my reunion with Kendra, I awoke around three in the morning and found it impossible to go back to sleep. This time, there was no nightmare. Rather, I woke up suddenly – fully awake – as though someone had called my name. I lay in bed for over an hour, turning from side to side and anxiously watching the minutes creeping by, knowing that I had to get up in just a few hours to go to work. Earlier that evening, I had just finished the last book that I'd taken from the library, and so I didn't have anything left to read.

I headed out to the living room and switched on the television, hoping to find some late night reruns that might bring on fatigue. Flipping through the channels, there was almost nothing that wasn't either too loud or too annoying or too repetitive with infomercials, and I finally gave up after another twenty minutes of feeling wide awake.

Finally, I switched on the computer in the office den, bathing the darkened room instantly in a haze of blue light. Surfing the internet, I began reading the latest celebrity fashion reviews, relishing the scathing wit of the critic, who with some choice, scorching phrases could level Hollywood *haute couture* and the celebs who sported it into nothing more than the ridiculous.

My aimless web surfing took me from one fluff site to another, until finally I grew weary of the mindlessness of my activity. I was about to shut off the computer when I noticed an advertisement in the bottom corner of the page for meeting local Christian singles.

Out of curiosity, I clicked on the link. When the site asked for a credit card to sign me up for a trial membership, I lost interest. I wondered if there was a free religious dating site that I could browse out of curiosity. The concept struck me funny – a Christian meat market, I thought. I speculated whether there'd be any hot guys listed on there, or only homely Lonelies who couldn't get a date anywhere else. Depressing as the thought was, I wanted to see if I was correct.

Typing some phrases into a search engine, I scrolled down through the links that appeared. There were so many I hardly knew where to start. While I was perusing them I noticed a link entitled "Life Without Marriage."+ Curious, the title peaked my interest over the other links, and I clicked on it.

The link brought up an article on 1 Corinthians 7, and I read with interest its author's commentary on that scripture, and about what Paul was expressing in regards to the benefits of both matrimony and singlehood.

At the bottom of the page, there were several more links to other articles by the same author, and I was so drawn into his keen thoughts and the depth of his writing that I clicked on another one of his works.

This link brought up what was a commentary on the prior chapter, I Corinthians 6. Fascinated, I read the background the author provided on the city of Corinth. On the little hill that rises behind the ancient city, there was built a temple to Aphrodite, and every evening the priests and priestesses -- male and female prostitutes -- would come down from the temple into the streets to ply their trade. It was known throughout the length and breadth of the ancient world as a city of great and widespread immorality. It was the sensuality capital of the world, what Americans might equate as a kind of ancient Las Vegas.

The author went on to dissect the scripture, pointing out that the Corinthian church was plagued with the same problems that the church today faces.

I was familiar with verses 18-20 at the end of the passage, about the body being a temple of the Lord, but I had never really concentrated on the passage preceding them:

[15]Do you not know that your bodies are members of Christ himself?

Shall I then take the members of Christ and unite them with a prostitute?

Never! [16]Do you not know that he who unites himself with a prostitute is

one with her in body? For it is said, "The two will become one flesh."[b]

[17]But he who unites himself with the Lord is one with him in spirit.

The commentator went on to say that the members of the Corinthian church thought that they could separate the spirit from the flesh, with one not affecting the other, and therefore many of them were engaging in the same sexual immorality that was rampant in their community. But Paul was quick to point out to them in his letter that the spirit and the body were inextricably linked, and that the body itself is a member of Christ himself. Therefore, to fornicate with these temple prostitutes was the same as to make Christ come down and be joined with a prostitute. What a despicable thought!

As I read this, it suddenly hit me – full force – that everything that I had done with Graeme had come at the expense of Christ. I felt immediately flushed, sick with myself at the very idea. It dawned on me at that moment that I was breathing heavily – panting, even – and that my fingers felt clammy.

Silently, I slipped out the front door of the house and began walking around the neighborhood in the quiet calm of the cool of the night. I didn't see the houses or trees or yards as I walked by, but rather my mind was all around what I had just read. I was aware of the deepest shame I'd ever felt, and yet something else was going on inside my soul at the same time. It was as though suddenly, I was able to *feel* again – to be tender enough to have genuine emotions. That hadn't happened in so long, I was wondering if I'd ever really be capable of such sensations again. It was as though I had slowly been turning into stone over time, and now, something had cracked me.

I knew, then, that God still loved me. He hadn't taken his Holy Spirit from me, because I could sense His presence right there. I also knew that I wanted Him more than ever.

Under a willow tree on the edge of a property that had been up for sale all summer, the owners already vacated, I knelt in the grass and cried and cried and cried. As images flashed through my mind of not only my depravity, but of all those times that I had willfully turned away from the reproving love of my Lord, the tears came even harder. To any passersby, I must have been quite a sight, weeping away in my pajamas and bare feet in the dead of a July night. I didn't care. I knew that at last, I was coming home.

*****

From that night forward, change began to seep into my life. It was a process to be sure – a sort of melting away of myself. The more my own self ebbed, the more room that there was for Him. As the days went by, I realized that I would not – could not – return to the same person that I had been before I'd left for school. My experiences and misdeeds and encounters had left me altered, scarred. They were now forever part of my being, just as we are all part of the people, places, and poisons we've imbibed.

I began reading my Bible regularly, and found that not only did the words make sense to me again, they were charged. Certain scriptures seemed to leap off the pages, and I began to see meaning in them that I'd previously missed.

Psalm 119:45 became my go-to verse: "I will walk about in freedom, for I have sought out your precepts." It dawned on me that in my desire for liberty outside the realm of my faith, I'd instead walked into bondage. Freedom was indeed found in Christ's law of perfect love.

If there was a positive aspect that I could take away from all that had happened at college, it was that any pride I had unknowingly harbored based on my own merits of living a decent life was forever gone. Whereas all my years growing up I had subconsciously been thankful that I wasn't like the "wicked," described throughout the Bible passages I had read, now I knew that these very scriptures pertained *especially* to me. I had no sufficiency, no case to plead on my own deeds any more. Without the shadow of a doubt, I needed to rely solely on His grace, for it was by *His* righteousness I was held, not by my own.

Perhaps because of this new conviction, the grace meant even more to me. Now when I sang the words of the songs at church, I meant each word with all of my heart. Likewise, the scriptures that I would read resonated even deeper. She whom much has been forgiven, loves much.

*****

One evening in the middle of August, after coming home late from a long day at work, there was a message waiting for me. Hank had called.

After taking about twenty minutes of pacing to rid myself of restless energy and nerves, I dialed his number with slightly unsteady hands, resenting myself for being such an emotional pansy.

"Hello?" The sound of his warmly familiar voice on the other end reduced my insides to syrup.

"Hello, Hank," I said. Nothing else came to mind to say.

"Molly," he replied. I detected beneath the unflappable equanimity a note of enthusiasm in his voice. "Hang on a second," he said, "Gotta turn down this music." I heard some thumps in the background, and then the sound of him picking up the receiver again.

"Wondered if you wanted to go for some gravy fries at the Jupiter Diner?" he asked.

"Tonight?" I replied.

"Yup."

I considered it dolefully. Badly as I wanted to go – to see him again after nearly a year, I had planned on going to Wednesday evening service that night with Kendra at another church. She and I had gone several times to this particular mid-week worship time since my "road to Damascus" encounter, as I had dubbed it. Oh, of all the evenings he could have asked!

"I'm afraid I can't go tonight," I said finally, slowly. "I have something else going on."

"Gotcha," Hank said lightly. "Well, it was just a thought. Another time then."

"Would Friday night work?" I ventured.

"Friday I'm going with my mom after work to the driving range. Later would work swell," he suggested glibly. "I'll come a-calling around eight…if that works for you."

I was starting to be able to read between his goofiness enough to know that when he tried to sound nerdy, it was a sure indication that he was trying to hide his feelings as well.

The End

Additional copies of this book are available at your local bookstore or at

Evangel Publishing House
2000 Evangel Way
Nappanee, IN 46550
574-773-3164

For a complete list of EPH titles, please visit

www.evangelpublishing.com